Contents

Acknowledgements

The author would like to thank the following for all their help and encouragement with the book: Dr. Ross McKibben, Martin Collier, Rosemary Rees, Alison Smith, and my guinea-pigs in L6hB2: Anthony, Freddie F, Jonathan, Marcus, James, Tallie, Toby, Sam, Fred H, Henry, Hamish, Lucas, George and Cecily

The author and publisher would like to thank the following individuals and organisations for permission to reproduce the following material:

Photographs

p. vi (top and bottom): Rex Features/ITV; p. 2: Reproduced by kind permission of Private Eye magazine: Ken Pyne; p. 11: Getty Images/Hulton Archive; p. 19: Express Syndication; p. 26 (top): Moviestore Collection Ltd: Ealing Studios; p. 26 (bottom): Ronald Grant Archive; p. 31 (top): Getty Images/ Hulton Archive; p. 31 (bottom): Alamy Images/Pictorial Press; p. 35: D. C. Thomson Co., Ltd; p. 36: Getty Images/Hulton Archive; p. 41: Mirrorpix; p. 44: Getty Images/Hulton Archive; p. 49 (left): Getty Images/Keystone; p. 49 (right): Alamy Images/Trinity Mirror/Mirrorpix; p. 53: Getty Images/ Popperfoto; p. 68: Rex Features/Nilss Jorgensen; p. 79: Getty Images/Central Press; p. 80: Ronald Grant Archive; p. 85: Rex Features/Today; p. 94: Rex Features/ABC Inc/Everett; p. 98: Copyright © News Group Newspapers Ltd; p. 101: Copyright © News Group Newspapers Ltd; p. 106: John Frost Historical Newspapers/Independent News & Media PLC; p. 112: iStockphoto/Giovanni Meroni; p. 117 (left): Rex Features; p. 117 (right); p. 136 (left): Solo Syndication/ Associated Newspapers Ltd; p. 136 (right): Steve Bell 1993/ All Rights Reserved; p. 143 (top): Mirrorpix; p. 143 (bottom): Copyright © News Group Newspapers Ltd; p. 150 (left): Getty Images/Hulton Archive; p. 150 (right): Rex Features/Sipa Press; p. 151 (top): Mirrorpix; p. 151 (bottom): Mirrorpix; p. 157: BBC Photo Library; p. 164 (top): Heritage Images/ Land of Lost Content; p. 164 (bottom): Shutterstock/USTIN; p. 171: Irish Studies Centre

Written sources

p. 2: Extract from Media Watch website is used by kind permission of Media Watch; p. 2: *Mass Media and Society into the 21st Century* © Lyn Gorman and David McLean. Used by kind permission of Blackwell Publishing; p. 4: *Walking in the Shade: Volume Two of My Autobiography, 1949–62* by Doris Lessing. Published by Flamingo © 1997. Used by permission of HarperCollins Publishers Ltd; p. 14: *Austerity Britain 1945–51* by David Kynaston © 2007. Used by kind permission of Bloomsbury Books; p. 16: *The Uses of Literacy* by Richard Hoggart © 1957. Published by Chatto and Windus. Used by permission of Random House UK; p. 17: *Few Eggs and No Oranges* by Vere Hodgson © 1950. Published by Persephone Books. Used by permission; p. 20: *BBC Variety Programmes Policy Guide for Writers and Producers*, published by the BBC in 1948. Used by permission of the BBC; p. 21: A recollection of radio in the fifties by 'Greasy, posted on Greasy Spoon Café Website. Used by permission of Greasy Spoon; p. 24: *The Finest Years: British Cinema of the 1940s* by Charles Drazin © 2007. Published by I. B. Tauris. Used by permission of the publisher; p. 25: *Classes and Cultures: England 1918–1951* by Ross McKibbin © 1998. Published by Oxford University Press. Used by permission of Oxford University Press; p. 25: *British Cinema of the 1950's: The Decline of Deference* by Sue Harper and Vincent Porter © 2003. Published by Oxford University Press. Used by permission of Oxford University Press; p. 28: *Austerity Britain 1945–51* by David Kynaston © 2007. Used by kind permission of Bloomsbury Books; p. 33: *Never Had It So Good* by Dominic Sandbrook © 2005. Published by Abacus. Used by permission of Little Brown Book Group Limited; p. 34: Letter to *Daily Mail*, October 1949. Used by permission of the *Daily Mail* and Solo Syndication; p. 40: *Britain 1914–2000* by Derrick Murphy. Published by Collins Educational. Used by permission of Collins Educational; p. 43: *Never Had It So Good* by Dominic Sandbrook © 2005. Published by Abacus. Used by permission of Little Brown Book Group Limited; p. 43: 'Yeah, Yeah, Yeah', published in the *Daily Mirror* on 6 November 1963. Used by permission of the *Daily Mirror*; p. 45: 'Beatlemania', published in the *News of the World* on 17 November 1963. Used by permission of *News of the World* and NI Syndication; p. 45: *White Heat: A History of Britain in the Swinging Sixties* by Dominic Sandbrook © 2006. Published by Abacus. Used by permission of Little Brown Book Group Limited; p. 45: An interview with John Lennon, published in the *Evening Standard* on 4 March 1966. Used by permission of the *Evening Standard* and Solo Syndication; p. 45: *Revolution in the Head: The Beatles' Records and the Sixties* by Ian MacDonald © 1994 © 2008. Published by Vintage. Used by permission of Random House UK; p. 50: *White Heat: A History of Britain in the Swinging Sixties* by Dominic Sandbrook © 2006. Published by Abacus. Used by permission of Little Brown Book Group Limited; p. 51: *The Labour Case* by Roy Jenkins © 1959. Published by Penguin Books; p. 52: *Britain 1914–2000* by Derrick Murphy. Published by Collins Educational. Used by permission of Collins Educational; p. 54: Interview with Mary Quant © Guardian News & Media Ltd. 1967. Used by permission of *The Guardian*; p. 54: An article by Prudence Glynn, published in *The Times* on 16 September 1966. Used by permission of *The Times* and NI Syndication; p. 57: *Manifesto* of Clean-Up TV by Mary Whitehouse and Nora Buckland. Used by kind permission of Media Watch UK; p. 58: Office for National Statistics. Crown Copyright; p. 60: Table showing the circulation of British National Newspapers in thousands of copies from 1939 to 1999. Compiled by the Audit Bureau of Circulations Ltd. Used by permission of ABC;

Edexcel GCE History

Mass[...]nd Social Change in Bri[...]

Stuart [...]

Series ed[...]

Unit 2[...]

A P[...]

Published by Pearson Education Limited, a company incorporated in England and Wales, having its registered office at Edinburgh Gate, Harlow, Essex, CM20 2JE. Registered company number: 872828

www.pearsonschoolsandfecolleges.co.uk

Edexcel is a registered trademark of Edexcel Limited

First published 2010

14
10 9 8 7 6 5

British Library Cataloguing in Publication Data
A catalogue record for this book is available from the British Library

ISBN 978 1 846 90506 3

Edited by Tracy Hall
Typeset by Florence Production Ltd, Stoodleigh, Devon
Original illustrations © Pearson Education 2010
Illustrated by Florence Production Ltd, Stoodleigh, Devon
Picture research by Zooid Pictures
Cover photo/illustration © Getty Images/Hulton Archive
Printed in the UK by CPI

Dedication
This book is for my parents with love.

Websites
There are links to relevant websites in this book. In order to ensure that the links are up to date, that the links work, and that the sites are not inadvertently linked to sites that could be considered offensive, we have made the links available on the Heinemann website at www.pearsonhotlinks.co.uk. When you access the site, the express code is 5063P.

p. 62: Review of *Darling* by Ewan Davidson. Used by permission of the British Film Institute; p. 71: Interview with Cleo Sylvestre in *Black in the British Frame* by Stephen Bourne © 2005. Published by Continuum. Used by permission; p. 74: From an episode of *Coronation Street*, broadcast in 1976. Used by kind permission of the producers of *Coronation Street*; p. 77: 'Punk Rock: Artifice or Authenticity by Stuart Borthwick in *Popular Music Genres: An Introduction*. Published by the Edinburgh University Press. Used by permission of Edinburgh University Press; p. 77: *History of Modern Britain* by Andrew Marr © 2009. Published by Pan Mcmillan. Used by permission of Pan Macmillan; p. 81: *The Report of the Committee On Obscenity and Film Censorship*. Used by permission of Cambridge University Press; p. 81: *Crisis? What Crisis? Britain in the 1970s* by Alwyn Turner © 2008. Published by Aurum. Used by kind permission; p. 82: *The People's Peace: British History Since 1945* by Kenneth Morgan © 1999. Published by Oxford University Press. Used by permission of David Higham Associates; p. 88: *Television Drama: Realism Modernism and British Culture* by John Caughie © 2000. Published by Oxford University Press. Used by permission of Oxford University Press; p. 90: Professor Julian Petley's discussion on documentary film making held in Birmingham in January 2004. Used by kind permission of Julian Petley, professor of Screen Media and Journalism at Brunel University; p. 92: *Good Times, Bad Times* by Harold Evans © 1983. Reprinted by kind permission of Sir Harold Evans; p.93: From *The New York Times*, © 1987 *The New York Times*. All rights reserved. Used by permission and protected by the Copyright Laws of the United States. The printing, copying, redistribution, or retransmission of the material without express written permission is prohibited; p. 93: *Flat Earth News* by Nick Davies © 2008. Published by Vintage. Used by permission of Random House UK; p. 95: *Before the Oil Ran Out: Britain, 1977–86* by Ian Jack © 1988. Used by permission of HarperCollins Publishers Ltd; p. 96: Professor Norman Stone, 'Through a Lens Darkly', published in *The Sunday Times* on 10 January 1988. Used by permission of *The Sunday Times* and NI Syndication; p. 96: 'The Last New Wave: Modernism in the British Films of the Thatcher Era' by Peter Wollen, © 2006 in *Fires Were Started: British Cinema and Thatcherism*. Published by Wallflower Press. Used by permission; p. 102: Interview with Patrick Bishop. Used by kind permission of Patrick Bishop; p. 102: Julian Barnes, 'The worst reported war since the Crimean', published in *The Guardian* on 25 February 2002. Used by permission of the author and United Agents; p. 102: *Media and Society into the 21st Century* © Lyn Gorman and David McLean. Used by kind permission of Blackwell Publishing; p. 105: Nicholas Hellen and Jonathan Carr-Brown, 'Barons of BBC Relish Chance of a Sexed-Up Row', published in *The Times* on 29 June 2003. Used by permission of *The Times* and NI Syndication; p. 105: *Flat Earth News* by Nick Davies © 2008. Published by Vintage. Used by permission of Random House UK; p. 107: Barry Shelby and Sarah Coleman, Suicide and Suspicions over War in Iraq', posted on the Worldpress website on 13 August 2003. Used by permission of All Media Inc; p. 118: 'Jeremy's Happy Slap Ordeal', published in *The Sun* on 7 December 2007. Used by permission of *The Sun* and NI Syndication; p. 119: Daniel Martin, 'Children who use mobile phones are "five times more likely to develop brain tumours"', published in the *Daily Mail* on 23 September 2008. Used by permission of the *Daily Mail* and Solo Syndication; p. 121: Office for National Statistics. Crown Copyright; p. 126: From a letter to the author, written in December 2009 by Daniel Bennett. Used by permission of Daniel Bennett; p. 128: Tara Brabazon, 'The Isolation of the iPod People' published in *The Times Higher Education Supplement* on 3 April 2008. Used by permission of *The Times Higher Education*; p. 129: From the Website of the Pirate Party, used by kind permission of the Pirate Party. www.pirateparty.org.uk; p. 129: From an article in the *Daily Mail* by Tom Utterly, published on 28 August 2009. Used by permission of the *Daily Mail* and Solo Syndication; p. 129: 'The hidden dangers of illegal downloading', part of the International Federation of the Phonographic Industry's *Digital Music Report*, published in 2008. Used by kind permission from IFPU London; p. 131: Dr Aric Sigman, 'Well Connected?: The Biological Implications of "Social Networking"', published in *Biologist* on 1 February 2009. Used by kind permission of the Society of Biology; p. 132: Nicole Martin, 'Record Number of Homes Have Broadband' published in *The Daily Telegraph* on 26 August 2008. Used by permission of *The Daily Telegraph*; p. 132: Information from 21st Century Challenges website. Used by kind permission of Martha Lane Fox; p. 138: *Grand Inquisitor: Memoirs* by Sir Robin Day © 1990. Reprinted by kind permission of The Estate of Sir Robin Day; p. 142: BBC news report on the birth of Prince William 21 June 1982. Used by permission of the BBC; p. 147: Tara Conian, 'Channel 4 backs Dispatches in police row' published in *The Guardian* 10 May 2007. © Guardian News & Media Ltd. 2007. Used by permission of *The Guardian*; p. 152: *Diana: Closely Guarded Secret* by Ken Wharf © 2003. Published by Michael O'Mara Books. Used by permission of Michael O'Mara Books; p. 153: David Matthewman, diary entry for 31 August 1997. Used with kind permission of David Matthewman; p. 153: John Edward, 'I never knew there were so many flowers in the whole world', published in the *Daily Mail* on 2 September 1997. Used by permission of the *Daily Mail* and Solo Syndication; p. 158: Monica Dickens, 'Women are born to Love', published in *Woman's Own* magazine on 21 January 1961. Used by permission of IPC Media; p. 162: Office for National Statistics. Crown Copyright; p. 163: *White Heat: A History of Britain in the Swinging Sixties* by Dominic Sandbrook © 2006. Published by Abacus. Used by permission of Little Brown Book Group Limited; p. 166: Crown copyright; p. 168: Peter Tatchell, 'Ads – A gay-free zone', published in *Campaign* magazine on 30 January 1998. © Peter Tatchell. Used by kind permission of the author; p. 169: Office for National Statistics. Crown Copyright; p. 172: Letter from the West Indies High Commission to the Secretary of State for the Colonies. Crown Copyright; p. 174: Milton Shulman, published in the *Evening Standard* 21 February, 1968. Used by permission of the *Evening Standard* and Solo Syndication; p. 174: *Crisis? What Crisis? Britain in the 1970s* by Alwyn Turner © 2008. Published by Aurum. Used by kind permission; p. 188: History of Punk by A.S. Van Dorston. Used by kind permission of Anthony S. Van Dorston, Fast 'n' Bulbous, www.fastnbulbous.com; p. 189: Interview with Cleo Sylvestre in *Black in the British Frame* by Stephen Bourne © 2005. Published by Continuum. Used by permission; p. 190: S. Malik, 'Race and Ethnicity', in A. Briggs and P. Colbey (eds) The Media: An Introduction, published by Longman © 2002. Used by permission of Pearson Education; p. 190: Dr. Gavin Schaffer, 'Till Death Do Us Part', a conference paper delivered at the University of Portsmouth in July 2008. Used by kind permission of Dr. Gavin Schaffer.

Every effort has been made to contact copyright holders of material reproduced in this book. Any omissions will be rectified in subsequent printings if notice is given to the publishers.

CHIPS
+ PEAS
£ 3·25
RICE

Introduction

The photographs on the opposite page are of the same man: the actor William Roache MBE. Born in 1932, William originally wanted to be a doctor. However, like all young men who left school between 1949 and 1960, William was conscripted into the Army for 2 years of National Service. Many hated life in the Army, but William decided to stay on for a further 5 years, rising to the rank of Captain. Only later did he turn to a career in drama. William has had a long and varied career as an actor, done lots of charity work, had two wives and has four grown-up children. He is most famous for playing the character Ken Barlow in the television soap opera *Coronation Street*.

Ken Barlow is the only character from the original episode, screened on 9 December 1960, who is still in the show. In 1960, Ken was an ambitious History and English student at Manchester University, frustrated by the differences between his modern, intellectual views and those of his more traditional, working-class family. Ken often rowed with his parents and dreamed of leaving his home town of Weatherfield. However, when his mother was run over by a bus in 1961, he finally made the decision to get a local job to support his father. Since then he has had a range of jobs in Weatherfield: teacher, journalist, taxi driver, warehouse manager, and has most recently worked in a café. His first wife was electrocuted by a hairdryer, his second committed suicide. His third wife, Deidre, having divorced Ken, was wrongly imprisoned for fraud, but was released and later remarried Ken. In Britain, almost as many people watched Ken's marriages to Deidre in 1981 and 2005 as watched Prince Charles' marriages to Princess Diana and Camilla Parker Bowles. Although he has been married for much of the time, Ken has also had 27 girlfriends. He has three biological children, but it is his adopted daughter Tracy who has caused him the most trouble – she was sentenced to life in prison in 2007 for murdering her boyfriend. Despite all of this, Ken is known as one of the duller characters who has lived on *Coronation Street*!

For Ken since 1960, and for British society since 1945, a good deal has changed, from the way people live and work, to the way they think about particular issues. Mass media have played a part in these social changes, but the extent of their contribution is not at all clear.

Questions

This book is about mass media, popular culture and social change in Britain since 1945. It is a huge, diverse field of investigation and there are many ways in which this book could have been introduced.

1 Why start with Ken Barlow? Try to think of at least two ways in which Ken usefully opens a debate about mass media, popular culture and social change in Britain since 1945.
2 What problems are there in starting a discussion of this topic with Ken Barlow as the focus?
3 How would you have introduced this book? (You might want to return to this question at the end of the course!)
4 Pick two of the dates from the timeline which you think might have had the greatest impact on popular culture and British society. Explain why you think these changes could have been more significant than the others.

The timeline below gives a brief overview of the key changes in mass media since 1945:

1946	Re-launch of television broadcasting by the BBC after the Second World War (radio broadcasts had run since 1922 and throughout the War)
1948	First sale of LP (long play) and EP (extended play) records
1950	First sale of EP playing jukeboxes
1953	Huge sales of televisions to watch the coronation of Elizabeth II
1955	Launch of ITV
1957	Transistor radios become widely available
1964	Launch of BBC2
1967	Launch of BBC Radio 1
1972	Sound Broadcasting Act allows the growth of independent radio stations
1978	VHS cassettes and video recorders go on sale in Britain
1982	Launch of satellite television in Britain
	Launch of Channel 4
1983	First mobile phones become available. Mass usage only begins in the mid-1990s
1983	CDs and CD players begin to sell in large numbers
1984	Cable and Broadcasting Act allows television channels and other services to be provided to homes by cable
1990	Broadcasting Act decreases regulation of mass media
1993	The World Wide Web and web browsers make the Internet user-friendly
1998	Mass sales of DVDs and DVD players begin in Britain
2001	First sale of Apple iPod. Over 200 million were sold by 2008

UNIT

1 Mass media: moulder or mirror of popular culture?

What is this unit about?

This unit seeks to clarify what is meant by the key terms in the title of this book: mass media, popular culture and social change. As you go through the unit you will be encouraged to discuss the meaning of these terms and to explore issues raised by a number of sources that relate to these terms.

Key questions

- What is mass media?
- What is popular culture?
- What is society: how can it change?
- How are media, popular culture and social change linked?

Timeline

1439 Johannes Gutenburg invents the first mechanical printing press

1476 William Caxton brings the printing press to England

1621 Nathaniel Butter prints the first newspaper in English called *Corante*

1702 The *Daily Courant* becomes the first daily newspaper in England

1895 A number of European and American inventors begin to show short, silent films to public audiences

1896 Guglielmo Marconi patents the radio in Britain. His invention is based on the work of a range of scientists since 1885

1922 The British Broadcasting Company makes its first radio broadcast. The company is dissolved and replaced by the British Broadcasting Corporation in 1927

1927 British Broadcasting Corporation (BBC) is established by a Royal Charter. The success of the American film *The Jazz Singer* ensures that films with sound are the future for cinema

1929 The BBC makes its first television broadcast. Television broadcasts are suspended after the outbreak of the Second World War in September 1939

Source A

1.1 'How TV changed Britain', a cartoon by Ken Pyne published in *Private Eye*, June 2004

SKILLS BUILDER

1 What does this cartoon suggest about the impact of television on modern British society?
2 Is it realistic that television could have had such a large impact?

What is mass media?

This book is about the impact that mass media have had on popular culture, and on British society, since 1945. Opinions are strongly divided about the scale and nature of this impact. Sources B and C are two examples of the wide spectrum of views on the matter.

Source B

Many people recognise that television has a global impact on moral, ethical, social and political issues as well as the power to influence our society for good or ill. Gone are the days when broadcasters can realistically say that they simply reflect society as it is. More and more society reflects the false attitudes and behaviour portrayed by some parts of the media.

From the Mediawatch-uk website, the website of the group of the same name who campaign for decency and accountability in the media

Source C

Mass media, and especially the visual media, have, from the very beginning, been the object of criticism from moral reformers, alarmed by what they assumed to be the harmful influence on youth of sex and violence in movies and television programmes. Insofar as these critics assumed the power of media to create values and alter behaviour independent of other factors, they greatly exaggerated the media's role.

From L. Gorman and D. McLean, *Media and Society into the 21st Century*, published in 2009

This is a history, as opposed to a media studies, textbook. It will not deal with theories of media in great depth. However, in order to engage with the arguments hinted at in Sources B and C, we need to understand the nature of mass media. There are two main ways in which historians may consider the impact of mass media on society:

- the impact of mass media as technology
- the impact of mass media in terms of their content.

What is mass media: content or technology?

In his 1964 book, *Understanding Media: the Extensions of Man*, the Canadian academic Marshall McLuhan argued that 'the medium is the message'. In order to understand what he meant by this, and decide how far we agree with him, we first need to know what a medium is.

A medium is something through which information is brought to the senses, or through which we can affect something remotely. The most abundant example of a medium is air – air molecules carry sound information to our ears and our own speech to others. For thousands of years, humans have created their own artificial **media** to send and receive information. However, before the 15th century, there was no medium capable of bringing a lot of information to a mass audience. Writing was developed at least 4500 years ago, but the technology used to reproduce information in text, such as carving on clay tablets, writing on papyrus or vellum (calfskin), was far too expensive and time consuming to be done on a large scale. The first *mass* medium was the printed word, perfected in Europe by Johannes Gutenburg (1398–1468), a German goldsmith and printer. After 1439, his printing presses produced thousands of copies of books and pamphlets. William Caxton (1422–92) introduced the printing press to England in 1476, publishing Chaucer's *Canterbury Tales* that year. As books became cheaper, they became available to a much wider audience, although one still limited by general illiteracy.

The rise of the printing press led to the rise of 'the press' itself: newspapers were printed in Britain from the 17th century onwards. However, it was not until after 1880, with the rise of mass literacy through compulsory education, that the press may be thought of as a truly *mass* medium.

After the 1890s, it became possible to talk of mass *media*. The development of radio technology meant it became possible to **broadcast** sound information to a mass audience. At about the same time, film technology was developed. In the first decades of the 20th century huge crowds could now see (though until 1927 not hear) drama and news films in cinemas across the country. Television cannot really be considered a *mass* medium in Britain until after the Second World War: moving pictures were not broadcast to televisions in British homes until 1929 and before 1939, the BBC only broadcast television signals to around 12,500 television sets in London. Television broadcasts were suspended during the Second World War and not resumed until June 1946.

SKILLS BUILDER

1 In what ways do Sources B and C disagree?

2 Which viewpoint do you find more convincing? Explain and discuss your answers.

Definitions

Media

The plural of medium.

Broadcasting

The term originally described the way farmers used to scatter their seeds. In 1909, an American radio technician coined the term to mean transmissions that were meant for many different radio receivers, as opposed to 'narrowcasting' for just one receiver, like a ship's radio.

Question

McLuhan argued that the growth of 'print culture' changed the way people thought and contributed strongly to social change. How could the rise of books and newspapers do this?

McLuhan argued that it was not so much the news or entertainment *content* of these sound and image broadcasts, but the *medium itself* that changed how people thought and how society was organised. Source D, one woman's memory of the arrival of television, is an example of what McLuhan meant.

Questions

1 How does Source D state that the television set affected the average British family?

2 McLuhan argued that whereas 'print culture' encouraged individualisation, electronic culture has led to a return of an oral and visual culture.

a) How could the rise of radio, cinema and television do this?

b) How persuasive do you find McLuhan's argument?

Source D

Before, when the men came back from work, the tea was already on the table, a fire was roaring, the radio emitted words or music softly in a corner, they washed and sat down at their places, with the woman, the child . . . They all talked . . . And then . . . television had arrived and sat like a toad in the corner of the kitchen. Soon the big kitchen table had been pushed along the wall, chairs were installed in a semi-circle and, on their chair arms, the swivelling supper trays. It was the end of an exuberant verbal culture.

From Doris Lessing, *Walking in the Shade*, published in 1997

SKILLS BUILDER

Perhaps the most important example of the 'medium as the message' is the Internet, now widely available on home computers and mobile devices. Unit 7 explores in depth how the 'new media' are changing the way that people think and live, but Source E could form the basis of a preliminary discussion about this issue.

Source E

A key finding of the study is that the more hours people use the Internet, the less time they spend with real human beings. This is an early trend that, as a society, we really need to monitor carefully.

From Norman Nie and Lutz Erbring, *Internet and Society: A Preliminary Report*, published in 2000

SKILLS BUILDER

Think of ways in which the media might be owned or controlled. For each scenario, consider the benefits and drawbacks for society.

Who should own and control the mass media?

The author of Source B represents many who disagree with McLuhan's views. They argue that the content of mass media, and who decides what that content should be, is of vital importance when looking at the impact of mass media on society. Given the potential influence of printed and broadcast information, it is no surprise that many people have argued, and sometimes struggled over, who should control mass media and decide what they should ideally be used for.

At one end of the spectrum, there have been those who ideally see mass media as a **fourth Estate**, a champion for the masses and a key safeguard of liberty and democracy. At the other end, many modern critics argue that mass media cannot be an independent check or balance on powerful financial and political interests in society because they are a part of those interests. Private companies, funded by advertising, have dominated the mass media in America from the outset. Although government loosely regulates what is allowed to be broadcast, many would argue that the media firms have a vested interest in a close relationship with the government: governments enjoy good media coverage while media firms benefit from favourable taxes and legislation. Governments have directly controlled mass media in dictatorships such as Nazi Germany and Soviet Russia. There are still examples of this type of political control today: the Chinese government controls China Central TV, known aptly as the CCTV network! However, the situation in Britain, and in other countries that have modelled their media regulations on Britain, is more complicated.

Radio and televisual technology both emerged in Britain as the result of private research and entrepreneurship. However, the government thought that the new broadcast technologies were too important to be left in the hands of businessmen. Politicians also feared that the total government control of the new technologies would promote dictatorship. A clever compromise was arrived at: in 1927, the British Broadcasting Corporation was founded not by an Act of Parliament but by a Royal Charter. The BBC's output would be controlled by an independent **quango**, the Board of Governors (replaced by the BBC Trust in 2007), and only occasionally by parliamentary legislation. The BBC would be funded, not directly from tax revenue, but from the licence fee, a charge on the ownership of TV sets. Thus, the BBC would be free from both direct governmental control and the demands of advertisers who preferred cheap, tacky shows that appealed to a mass audience, like those being produced in America. In Source F, Lord Reith, the first Director General of the BBC, explained how he saw the Corporation's role as a **public service broadcaster**.

Source F

So the responsibility at the outset was conceived to carry into the greatest number of homes everything that was best in every department of human knowledge, endeavour and achievement; and to avoid whatever was or might be hurtful. In the earliest years accused of setting out to give the public not what it wanted but what the BBC thought it should have, the answer was that few knew what they wanted, fewer what they needed. In any event it was better to overestimate than underestimate. If another policy had been adopted – that of the lowest common denominator – what then?

From Lord Reith, *Into the Wind*, published in 1949

Definitions

Fourth Estate

The term was popularised by writer and MP Thomas Carlyle (1800–59) to mean the press as a balance to the other three powers: clergy and nobility in the House of Lords and the House of Commons.

Quango

From quasi non-governmental organisation, an administrative body outside the government, but whose members are appointed by the government.

Public service broadcaster

A radio or television company run to serve the public interest rather than for profit.

SKILLS BUILDER

1 What kinds of programmes do you think Lord Reith would have favoured?

2 On what grounds do you think some contemporaries would have criticised Lord Reith and his choice of media content?

Definitions

Monopoly
The position of having no competition in a given trade or market.

Independent television and radio
Broadcasting by private companies who aim to make profits by maximising advertising revenue. While their programmes aim to attract the largest possible audience, the content has been regulated by quangos.

Dominant elites
People who hold a great deal of power over society because of their wealth, their position in important organisations, or a combination of both.

'Elite' music, art, literature
Artistic works that are thought to require a good deal of education and sophistication to enjoy and appreciate.

The BBC was established as a **monopoly** public service broadcaster in Britain. As such, it has attracted criticism from many sides over the years. Firstly, from those who wanted the public to 'get what it wanted'. **Independent** television (ITV), funded by advertising, was launched in 1955, and radio in 1972 (although 'pirate radio' had transmitted into Britain from outside the country since the 1930s). Secondly, from those who worry that since 1955, the BBC has gradually abandoned their public service ethos, and competed for ratings with commercial television by 'dumbing down' its programming. Thirdly, there are those who worry that the BBC has not been truly independent of the government. All of these criticisms are explored later in the book.

Question

The diagram below summarises the possible spectrum of mass media/content control. Where on the line would you place the British media today? Explain your answer.

←	→
Content generated and broadcast by individuals in the interests of freedom of expression and information, e.g. the press as fourth Estate, or more recently blogging.	Content generated and broadcast by **dominant elites**: political elites in the interests of their own power (e.g. China), commercial elites in the interests of profit (e.g. America).

Popular culture: what is 'culture'? What is 'popular'?

SKILLS BUILDER

There are several ways in which popular culture may be defined. Before you read on, consider how you might define both 'popular' and 'culture'. These are difficult terms to define, so try to be as precise as you can. Good luck!

Culture

There are three definitions of culture that are most commonly used. Culture can be taken to mean 'high culture' – someone may be said to be 'cultured' if they have good taste and a thorough knowledge of **'elite' music, art, literature**. However, this is clearly not what is meant in the sense of popular culture. Culture can also mean all forms of artistic output in society: books, music, drama and so on; it is possible to imagine a 'popular' form of this culture. However, more broadly, culture could be taken to mean a shared set of values, attitudes and ways of doing things among a people, or a group within society. A study of this culture would go beyond art, and could include anything from holidays to religion and sport. In practice, both the second and third forms of culture may be considered when looking at popular culture:

- culture in terms of artistic products (confusingly, all usually referred to as 'texts')
- culture in terms of a way of life (usually called 'lived culture').

To a large degree, the worlds of 'elite' and popular culture have remained quite separate since 1945, with different trends almost wholly independent of one another. Some important exceptions include the way in which the 'New Movement' of literature and poetry in the 1950s fed into film making, and the role of universities and arts colleges in producing some of the most popular comedians and rock stars since the 1960s. Throughout the book you will encounter more specific examples of the ways in which elite and popular culture are linked.

SKILLS BUILDER

1 From the following list of words and phrases, decide whether you would classify them under the heading of 'texts' or 'lived culture'. Are there any words which are harder to place than others? If so, why?
Christmas celebrations, *Coronation Street*, punk fashion, *The Beano*, rock and roll, gangs, gardening, FA Cup final on television, family life, *The Sound of Music*, the TV show *Big Brother*, women at work, ready meals

2 Now that we have a clearer idea of what we mean by culture, look back at the range of definitions you came up with for 'popular'. See how many you came up with that agree with the definitions below.

'Popular' most simply refers to large numbers, as in popularity:

- Some have defined popular culture in terms of numbers of sales, for example of books, CDs, DVDs. However, at what level of popularity does something suddenly make it *popular* culture? What about widely sold 'elite' culture, such as classic novels? Can these be considered as part of popular culture?
- Others have defined 'popular' in terms of the numbers produced. In this sense, popular culture is seen as that which is mass produced and designed for quick consumption rather than lasting importance. This 'mass culture' is designed to maximise profits by giving the consumers what they want: cheap, flashy, sexy entertainment.

'Popular' can also mean 'of the common people' as opposed to 'of the elite':

- Some have therefore taken 'popular' to mean inferior because ordinary people are less highly educated than the elites, their cultural products fail to meet the quality or 'difficulty' of 'high' culture. But what about the examples of 'high' culture that become popular, such as the famous opera arias sung by Pavarotti? What about examples of popular culture that over time become thought of as 'high' culture, such as the works of Charles Dickens?
- Alternatively, some have seen the culture of the people as a genuine, authentic type of culture, as opposed to the synthetic, industrially produced 'mass culture'. However, who are 'the people'? Does this refer to a particular class of people, or a group of people who are somehow against 'mass culture'? What about the examples of 'authentic' culture that became mass produced, such as rock and roll?

Questions

1 Is it possible to belong to more than one culture? Explain your answer.

2 How far do you think 'elite' culture and popular culture influence one another? Can you think of any examples?

Although this range of definitions could be confusing, they do allow us to think much more clearly about what popular culture has been in Britain since 1945 and about the ways in which popular culture has changed in that time.

SKILLS BUILDER

Draw a diagram, with a design of your choice, such as an ideas map or spider diagram, that in your view best represents the structure of British society today.

Think about the different types of group that exist and how they are connected to one another: is there a hierarchy and if so, is it as simple as the old feudal system you might have drawn as an 11-year old?

Once you have drawn your version of society, compare it with a neighbour and discuss any differences.

What is society? How can it change?

The word 'society' comes from the Latin *societas* meaning 'friendly association with others'. This sounds very much like one of our earlier definitions for culture: 'a shared set of values, attitudes and ways of doing things among a people'. There is a close relationship between culture and society; it is useful to think of a brain when considering this relationship. Just as a brain is a huge bundle of interconnected nerves that produces our thoughts and actions, so society is the structure of people in a group that generates culture.

We need to consider the large groups of people, such as class, that you may have identified in your diagram. However, we also need to look at the smallest units of society, the individual and the family, to see how changes at this level affect the construction of society as a whole. It is surely easier to consider the influence of mass media and popular culture on the perception and self-perception of individual men, women and children, than on larger groups such as 'the working class' or 'minorities'. As historians, we need to make generalisations in order to make sense of the huge amount of information available to us, but when we talk of 'teenagers' in Unit 3 or 'women' in Unit 9, remember that these are groups made up of a great range of individuals for whom the general conclusions might not necessarily apply.

Mass media, popular culture and social change: how are they linked?

Historians continue to argue about the extent to which mass media and popular culture have changed British society since 1945. Some historians would argue that mass media and popular culture have played a crucial role in changing the way British people live and think. Others have argued that factors such as increased affluence, changes in the law, education and employment, have had a far greater impact on British society and that popular culture and mass media merely reflect such changes.

SKILLS BUILDER

Copy and complete the diagram below by joining the boxes with arrows that show your initial thoughts on the relationship between mass media, popular culture and British Society. Label each arrow with an explanation of the connection.

Mass media	British society	Popular culture

Unit summary

What have you learned in this unit?

Mass media can refer to the technology used to convey information to a wide audience, or to the information content itself. Both the technology and the information can affect the nature of popular culture and the nature of society. Mass media technologies that have greatly affected British society since 1945 include the press, radio, cinema, television and the Internet.

Popular culture can refer to 'texts' (not just books) that are 'inferior' or made and sold in large quantities, or to widespread 'lived' activities such as Butlin's holidays or football matches.

Social change refers to the ways in which the attitudes and behaviour of the individuals who make up British society have altered since 1945. The question remains the extent to which British society has changed, and the degree to which mass media and popular culture have brought this about.

What skills have you used in this unit?

You have formed hypotheses about the nature of mass media, popular culture and social change. You have used a range of new terms to analyse the content of a range of sources. You have developed ideas to defend a position in discussion.

RESEARCH TOPIC

In pairs or small groups choose one of the following three countries:

- China
- Great Britain
- USA.

Carry out research in your library or on the Internet to find out in more depth which individuals or organisations have the most influence over mass media in your chosen country. Consider the impact of media control on popular culture and society. Feed your research back to the class using a poster or PowerPoint presentation.

SKILLS BUILDER

Have an initial class debate on the topic, 'This class believes mass media and popular culture to have reflected more than caused social change in Britain since 1945'.

UNIT

2 How austere was 'Austerity Britain' 1945–54?

What is this unit about?

This unit explores the nature of British society in the 9 years that followed the end of the Second World War. Once you have seen what life was like for British people at this time, you will be able to gauge how far Britain has experienced social change since 1945. In particular, this unit considers the impact on British society of the most important mass media of the time: newspapers, **radio** and cinema.

Key questions

- What were the key features of British society 1945–54?
- What were the key features of British popular culture 1945–54?
- How far did mass media affect British attitudes 1945–54?

Definition

Radio

From the Latin *radius*; just as a radius of a circle goes out from the centre, so radio waves are sent out in all directions from their point of origin. 'Radio' was the American name for the 'wireless'; its usage was popularised in Britain by the Second World War.

Timeline

Year	Date	Event
1945	**8 May**	Victory in Europe Day. Victory in Japan follows on 15 August 1945
	July	General Election: Clement Atlee (Labour) replaces Winston Churchill (Conservative) as Prime Minister
		BBC Light Programme replaces wartime Forces' Programme
1946	**June**	Television licences introduced and BBC television broadcasts resume
		Bread rationed for the first time since 1918. It is not de-rationed until July 1948
	September	BBC Home Service and Third Programme are launched
	November	National Health Service Act. The NHS is launched in July 1948
1947	**August**	League football restarts after wartime suspension
	November	Potatoes are rationed this month under the Potato Control Scheme
1948		Co-operative Wholesale Society opens the first supermarket in Britain
	22 June	The ship *Empire Windrush* docks at Tilbury, London with 492 West Indian males and one stowaway woman
	July	Olympic Games held in London
1949	**March**	End of clothes rationing

		National Service Act: all males who reach the age of 18 between 1949 and 1960 must spend 18 months (later 2 years) as conscripts in the Army
1950	**February**	General Election: Atlee returns with a majority of five seats
1951	**May–September**	The Festival of Britain is held in London
	October	General Election: Churchill is Prime Minister of a Conservative government
1952	**February**	First television detector vans launched to find the estimated 150,000 unlicensed television sets in Britain
		Abandonment of wartime identity cards
	6 February	Death of King George VI. His daughter Elizabeth is proclaimed Queen
	November	*New Musical Express (NME)* magazine publishes the first UK singles chart
1953	**April**	Ian Fleming publishes first James Bond novel, *Casino Royale*
	2 June	Coronation of Queen Elizabeth II
1954	**4 July**	End of food rationing

Source A

2.1 A photograph of a street in Newcastle, taken by Bert Hardy in 1950

SKILLS BUILDER

Before we can judge how far British society has changed since 1945, we need to gain an idea of what Britain was like in the years that immediately followed the Second World War. Photographs are an important source of evidence; the historian David Kynaston chose this photograph to be on the front cover of his book *Austerity Britain 1945–51*.

1 What does this photograph suggest about life in Britain in 1950?

2 How useful is this photograph to an historian who wants to find out about British society and popular culture between 1945 and 1954?

What were the key features of British society 1945–54?

The common view of Britain during these years is as follows:

- The British emerged from the war with great **austerity**, bound together by strong moral values, close-knit communities and a strong sense of duty and **deference**. They lacked luxuries, made do with what they had and, despite the tough conditions, people were happier and healthier than they are today. Mass media from the time, newspapers, radio and cinema, reflected the austerity of the British people, and reinforced their values.
- The austerity of British people's lives in these years stands in stark contrast to the 'permissive society' that developed in the 1960s; all of a sudden the British became more relaxed in their attitudes towards authority, sex, drugs and censorship. The British contentment with simple living gave way to rampant **consumerism**. Newspapers became full of photos of models such as Twiggy (see page 53), while radio blared out the latest pop hits and cinema undermined authority with its new, hard-edged films about working-class life.

Kynaston reflected these commonly held views when he called his book on British society between 1945 and 1951 *Austerity Britain*. We now need to explore how far this stereotyped view of Britain 1945–54 is accurate; in particular we need to consider:

- the structure of British society
- British attitudes towards class, authority, women, family, minorities and consumerism
- the key features of British popular culture.

Definitions

Austerity

Strong self-discipline and moral strictness, with simple living and a lack of luxury.

Deference

Respect for social superiors.

Consumerism

Preoccupation with consumer goods and their acquisition.

Quantifiable

Things that can be counted or measured with a good degree of accuracy.

Question

Apart from photographs, how can historians try to find out what life was really like for British people between 1945 and 1954?

The structure of British society

It is fairly straightforward to research **quantifiable** things about societies in the past. This can include the size of the population, where people lived or what jobs or possessions they had. Much of our evidence comes from the Census, a survey of the population carried out by the government every 10 years. Unfortunately, the 1941 Census was cancelled due to the war. Nevertheless, it is possible to put together a good overview of British society in the years after the Second World War using the 1951 Census.

The 1951 Census recorded 50.3 million people living in Britain. Missing from this survey were the 250,000 Britons killed in battle and 60,000 civilians killed by German bombing. Then, as now, far more people lived in England than in Scotland, Wales or Northern Ireland: around 84 per cent of the UK population lived in England. Around 80 per cent of Britons lived in urban areas, with 40 per cent living in the densely populated areas of Greater London, the West Midlands, Merseyside, south-east Lancashire, the West Riding of Yorkshire, Tyneside and Clydeside. These urban areas suffered most from German bombing: many town and city centres, including London, Coventry, Portsmouth, Plymouth, as well as 750,000 homes, had been seriously damaged. It was many years before all evidence of this destruction had been cleared.

In 1951, the poorest people were still crowded into older, inadequate houses in city centres; seven million of these homes did not have a hot water supply. Ten per cent of homes did not have electricity and a quarter lacked an indoor toilet. Over a third of homes did not have a fixed bath; most people in such homes bathed once a week in an iron tub in front of a coal fire. People who lived in such houses could not afford to pay the bus or tram fare to work from the newer houses on the outskirts of town and had to live in city centres close to their place of work. In 1951, Britain was still predominately an industrial, manufacturing nation; around 60 per cent of the workforce was employed in manual labour. Women usually only worked until they got married (see pages 158–61 for more). People whose jobs ranged from unskilled labourers to skilled mechanics would generally think of themselves as 'working class'.

The general health of the British people was in many ways better in 1951 than today. They had a less fatty and sugary diet (especially when sweets were rationed between 1942 and 1953), and did more physical work and exercise. Despite this, Britain had a lower life expectancy than today. The launch of the National Health Service in 1948 helped to make a range of medical services available to far more people, helping the sick to recover and the elderly to live longer. Britain had, on average, a younger population in 1951 than today: the mini '**baby boom**' that immediately followed the end of the war, meant that there were far more teenagers in the 1960s than in the 1940s. The population was far more racially **homogenous** in 1951 than today, with only a few small black, South Asian and Chinese communities living in London and western port cities such as Liverpool and Cardiff. Legally, any citizen of a British colony or dominion (one quarter of the world's population) was allowed to enter and settle in Britain without a visa between 1948 and 1962. However, mass immigration from the West Indies, Pakistan and India did not really begin until the British government advertised in those countries for workers to fill a labour shortage in 1948. Most West Indians settled in a few boroughs in London and in Birmingham, while most Pakistanis and Indians settled in the industrial towns of south-east Lancashire. Their numbers were still small in 1951, but rose rapidly in the 1950s and 1960s.

British people are far wealthier today than they were in 1951: average wages have grown faster than the price of an average basket of goods, and there is a far wider range of products available in today's shops. The British had survived the war without bread rationing, but in 1946 even this basic staple joined a range of food and other products that could only be purchased with ration coupons. In 1946, roughly a quarter of all consumer expenditure was controlled by rationing; this rose to 30 per cent in 1948, before being cut back to around 12 per cent in 1949. Although rationing was not totally abandoned until 1954, the majority of people in 1951 felt better off than their parents' generation had been. Source B gives a short, selective summary of the more tangible differences between Britain in 1945 and Britain today.

Definitions

Baby boom

A rapid increase in the rate of birth, common after the end of a war as husbands return home. The children born during this period are referred to as 'baby boomers'.

Homogenous

All of the same kind.

Source B

Britain in 1945. No supermarkets, no motorways, no teabags, no sliced bread, no frozen food, no flavoured crisps, no lager, no microwaves, no dishwashers, no **Formica**, no vinyl, no CDs, no computers, no mobiles, no duvets, no Pill, no trainers, no hoodies, no Starbucks. Four Indian restaurants. Shops on every corner, pubs on every corner, cinemas in every high street, red telephone boxes, Lyons Corner Houses, trams, trolley-buses, steam trains . . . No laundrettes, no automatic washing machines, wash day every Monday, clothes boiled in a tub, scrubbed on the draining board, rinsed in the sink, put through a mangle, hung out to dry. Central heating rare, chilblains common. Abortion illegal, homosexual relationships illegal, suicide illegal, capital punishment legal. White faces everywhere . . . A **wireless** in the home, *Housewives' Choice* or ***ITMA*** on the air, televisions almost unknown, no programmes to watch, the family eating together . . . Suits and hats, dresses and hats . . . no leisurewear, no 'teenagers' . . . Meat rationed, butter rationed, lard rationed, margarine rationed, sugar rationed, tea rationed, cheese rationed, jam rationed, eggs rationed, sweets rationed, soap rationed, clothes rationed. Make do and mend.

From David Kynaston, *Austerity Britain 1945–51*, published in 2007

Definitions

Formica

The brand name of a heat-resistant plastic work surface common in many kitchens.

Wireless

Just as today we talk of 'wireless broadband' when we refer to an Internet connection without a cable connection, so British people referred to radio as 'wireless', short for wireless telegraphy: the information was sent without a wire.

ITMA

It's That Man Again, a popular comedy show.

Intangible

Something that can't be touched or measured precisely.

SKILLS BUILDER

1 What does Source B tell us about the family, consumerism, class, gender roles and the position of ethnic minorities in Britain in 1945?

2 What does Source B *not* tell us about British society in 1945? What more can you add from the information in the main text on pages 12 and 13?

3 How far does Source B support the view that British society was austere in the years immediately after the Second World War?

British attitudes towards class, authority, women, family, minorities and consumerism

It is fairly straightforward to find out what people bought and how they lived in 1945, but how are we to try and find out those more **intangible** things about British society? What did people think about? What were their attitudes to family, marriage and sex, to figures of authority, to minorities, to work, leisure and entertainment? It is difficult to see into people's hearts and minds, but a range of evidence exists that allows historians to make some reasonable generalisations. Important sources of information include:

- Mass Observation – This was a project launched in 1937 that recorded the thoughts, observations and conversations of a representative sample of Britons. Around 500 volunteers were asked to keep a diary about their everyday lives. It was turned into a consumer survey in the early 1950s, but reverted to its social research function in the 1980s.
- Polls – There are a number of companies that specialise in finding out information on all kinds of topics. They are usually employed by large firms and political parties. Major polling companies include Gallup (1935–), AGB (1962–), MORI (1969–), YouGov (2000–).

- Academic research – Research into sociology and anthropology began long before the Second World War, and blossomed with the expansion of universities after 1963. Such research provides invaluable insights into contemporary society for historians.
- Government papers – Civil servants carry out a lot of research on behalf of politicians to help them prepare for debates on bills put before the House of Commons.
- BBC audience research – From 1939, the BBC had a Listener Research Department. In 1950, it was renamed the BBC Audience Research Department to include television audiences.
- Mass media – There are lots of films, recordings of radio and television programmes and collections of newspapers and magazines that give historians a good idea about people's tastes.

The main text and sources below give some information about British views between 1945 and 1954. You should look ahead to the pages listed below for more information on attitudes towards a particular issue.

Class (see page 179 for more)

Class is a confusing, and sometimes unhelpful concept for historians to use when they look at societies in the past. Before 1900, most Britons would have classified themselves in terms of where they lived, their religious views, or perhaps a vague notion of 'working class' or 'middle class'. It was not until the rise of large, powerful trade unions, and the '**progressive**' response of the Liberal Party and later the Labour Party, that many people began to think of themselves as belonging to a particular nationwide class. It was only after 1918 that all men over the age of 21 had the vote (women aged 21–30 had to wait until 1928). With some interesting exceptions, most working-class people voted for the Labour Party, while most of the middle and upper classes voted for the Conservative Party. Class identity was formed from many variables: where you lived and worked, your leisure pursuits, dress and accent (or 'lived culture'). However, General Elections (at least one every 5 years), and the way newspapers reported political stories, reinforced class identities. Source C gives an indication of what class people felt they belonged to in 1948.

Source C

When a representative sample of the British public was polled in 1948 there was little hesitation over opting for appropriate class labels, even if there was an evident tendency for some manual workers to put themselves in the middle class: asked, without prompting, to allocate themselves to a social class, 2 per cent said 'upper', 6 per cent said 'upper-middle', 28 per cent said 'middle', 13 per cent said 'lower-middle', 46 per cent said 'working', and only 5 per cent recorded 'no reply'.

From Arthur Marwick, *British Society Since 1945*, published in 2003

Definition

Progressive

Politicians or their policies that sought to advance the living and working conditions of the working classes.

Questions

1. If 60 per cent of the workforce did manual work, why do you think only 46 per cent of those polled in 1948 said that they were working class?
2. Of which class are you a member? Explain your answer.
3. Do you think class is an important part of people's identity today?

Authority (see page 180 for more)

It is difficult to generalise about attitudes to figures of authority because of the range of different types of authority. At one extreme, the royal family was hugely popular (see pages 141–45 for more), while policemen were also widely respected (see *The Blue Lamp* on page 25). However, a 1947 Mass Observation report into religious attitudes, revealed that the British were already becoming a largely secular, 'de-churched' population: while 70 per cent believed in God, only 17 per cent of the population went to church every week. This suggests a general lack of deference towards religious leaders. Lastly, while some politicians were greatly respected, not least wartime Prime Minister Winston Churchill, the general attitude towards politicians as a whole is that they were untrustworthy and self-seeking.

Women and family (see page 179 for more)

While many younger women worked in the years after 1945, there was a clear expectation that they would stop work when they got married to fulfil their duties as a housewife while the husband earned the family income. As Source D suggests, in some areas this resulted in separate, well-defined roles and lives for husbands and wives. However, a number of reports, such as the 1949 Royal Commission on Population, suggested that 'the wife's role as a companion to her husband as well as a producer of children', was already the norm; this suggests greater equality of roles within marriage. Divorce was much more difficult to gain before legislation was passed in 1969 to make it easier. Due to wartime strains on relationships, divorce rates rose from 6000 to 60,000 between 1939 and 1947; however, divorce rates fell in the 1950s and 1960s and the nuclear family of husband, wife and children remained the norm. Source E sheds further light on the role of British women during these years.

Source D

. . . wives talked 'over the washing-line, at the corner-shop, visiting relatives at a moderate distance occasionally, and perhaps now and again going with her husband to his pub or club. He has his pub or club, his work, his football matches. The friends at either or all of these places may well not know what the inside of their house is like, may never have "stepped across the threshold"'.

From Richard Hoggart, *The Uses of Literacy*, published in 1957

Source E

We were back early. I made up the fire and soon had tea ready. Toasted fruit bread – I put raisins and a little honey in one of my little loaves when I baked . . . I did not feel I cared whether I had any food or not, and what I had soon satisfied me. I could have giggled wildly at my husband's attitude, barely speaking when spoken to . . . I cannot believe at one time I worried and worried and let [his moods] drive me into a nervous breakdown. Now any breakdown would not be mine. I feel often I look at a rather tiresome stranger . . . I sat and embroidered my cushion cover, feeling tonight I'd be well to start my blouses this week and then I'd have a bit of useful sewing on the go.

From Barrow housewife Nella Last's diary entry for Mass Observation on 3 March 1946

Sex (see pages 179–80 for more)

Co-habitation without marriage, sex before marriage and homosexuality were all taboo in the years 1945–54. This is not to say that these things never happened, merely it was not as acceptable to discuss or practise them openly as it became in later twentieth century Britain. Source F is a summary of the key findings of one survey into people's sexual attitudes in the early 1950s.

Source F

I should like to emphasise that half the married population of England, men and women alike, state that they have had no relationship, either before or after marriage, with any person other than their spouse, and that the numbers are even greater in the working classes. My personal impression is that this is a very close approximation to the truth.

From Geoffrey Gorer, *Exploring English Character*, published in 1955. Gorer was a social **anthropologist** who based his conclusions on 11,000 questionnaires on people's sex lives and attitudes towards relationships

Racial minorities (see page 180 for more)

The small number of racial minorities in Britain before 1954 and the concentration of these people in a few cities meant that few Britons had any direct contact with other ethnic groups. In cities such as London and Birmingham, which received immigrants from West India, attitudes ranged from fear and contempt to curiosity and tolerance. Although a work of fiction, Andrea Levy's *Small Island* is based on wide research and is a good guide to race relations in post-war Britian.

Definition

Anthropologist

Someone who studies how people behave and creates theories to explain this.

Consumerism (see pages 178–79 for more)

Although many items of food remained rationed until 1954, spending on food remained around a third of total household expenditure, a similar figure to that of 1914. After clothing, fuel, transport and necessary services, this did not leave much money for spending on luxuries. Diaries such as those of Nella Last reveal that people mended and re-used clothing and household items far more than they did in the late twentieth century. While Nella greatly enjoyed new items such as a car and a refrigerator, and looked forward to more affluent times ahead, it is clear that she was not obsessed with material goods. Historians generally accept that this was a common outlook of British people between 1945 and 1954. Sources G and H are examples of the British outlook in the post-war years.

Source G

Now we could hardly believe it but last week we had eggs off the ration. An absolutely remarkable and unheard-of event. What this means to us only an English housewife can understand. We have been fobbed off with dried eggs and egg powder and lately not even that. And at last actually we could beat up two eggs and put them in a cake for the first time in 10 years.

From the diary of Vere Hodgson, a welfare worker from London, written in March 1950

Source H

A working man is a great realist. He sees life as it is – as a constant struggle with its ups and downs. He is little influenced by books or literature, and is more genuine and natural than people from other classes. If you ask working men about their views on life, in a large majority of cases you will get the answer: 'Life is what you make of it', 'I take life as it comes' or 'I try to make the best of it'.

From Ferdinand Zweig, *Labour, Life and Poverty*, published in 1948. Zweig was a Polish-born economist who spent 7 months interviewing around 350 working-class Londoners about their spending habits

SKILLS BUILDER

1 What can we learn from Sources F, G and H about the attitudes of British people in the years after the Second World War?

2 How far do the sources support the idea that the British held 'austere' attitudes in these years?

3 Which of these sources do you think offers the most valuable insights into the way British people thought during these years? Explain your answer.

What were the key features of British popular culture 1945–54? How far did mass media affect British attitudes 1945–54?

British popular culture (texts) was dominated by newspapers, radio and cinema. In order to determine how far these forms of mass media affected British popular culture and attitudes, we first need to find out who controlled them and what kinds of material they produced. Keep in mind the key question: did mass media reflect, or *mirror*, existing attitudes, or did they help shape, or *mould*, new attitudes?

Newspapers

At the start of the century, there were many independent, regional newspapers that were often closely linked with a political party. However, the first quarter of the century saw the rise of 'press barons', such as Lords Northcliffe, Rothermere and Beaverbrook, who built up large chains of newspapers. They often used their newspapers to support their political views, but as businessmen, they increasingly put profits before politics. Their quality titles such as *The Times* or *The Daily Telegraph*, what we would refer to today as 'the **broadsheets**', attracted elite, wealthier readers, and the barons were able to charge large fees to luxury goods firms who wished to advertise to a select audience in these newspapers. For 'the **tabloids**', such as the *Daily Mirror*, it was total sales alone that dictated how much companies would pay for advertising space. A circulation war led to the gradual downgrading of political coverage and the rise of 'human interest' stories that had a more general appeal. Source I is an example of a front page from 1951, while Source J gives information about newspaper readerships in the late 1940s.

Definitions

Broadsheet

A newspaper printed on large sheets of paper.

Tabloid

Tabloid originally referred to tablets made from compressed medicine powder. To begin with, the 'tabloid press' referred not to the shape of the newspaper, but to the compressed nature of the news. Most modern tabloids, such as the *Daily Mail* or *Daily Express*, were in fact printed in a broadsheet format until the 1970s.

Source I

DAILY EXPRESS

THIRD EDITION

No. 16,046 FRIDAY NOVEMBER 23 1951 CONTROLLING SHAREHOLDER LORD BEAVERBROOK Weather: Cloudy Price 1½d

CHARGE 'Fake call' allegation over passport | PAY Miners' talks go on 9 hours | BRIBERY Footballer says: I was offered £200 | HOME GUARD Full strength force for danger area

WIFE IN MYSTERY TRIP

'London let her go to Moscow'

AFTER BAN BY AUSTRALIA

Express Staff Reporter: Canberra, Thursday

MRS JESSIE STREET, wife of the Lieutenant-Governor and Chief Justice of New South Wales, got a United Kingdom passport to travel behind the Iron Curtain after a telephone trick was played on the British Passport Office in London.

No Iron Curtain visits, said Australia...

NOT BACK

PROBE STARTS

MRS STREET

Power cuts UN

HOME GUARD IN 'DANGER' AREA

Express Political Correspondent

125,000 needed

Special training

Head squashes 'anti-strike' suspicions

Red uranium

How nice, How nice to be in the Navy

(UNO STYLE)

Two only

Tried again

'MAN CALLED ON ME IN THE DARK'

SOCCER BRIBE ATTEMPT No. 2

Player tells of £200 offer

Express Staff Reporter

A SECOND football club has reported an attempt to bribe one of its players to make his team lose a match, and a bookmaker said last night: "A big betting syndicate is at work."

'EASY MONEY'

£6,000 BETS

CENTRE-HALF WILLIE TELFER

MOSSADEG TO EAST: 'LINE UP'

NEW ATTACKS

"THE COMMODORE"

Army train races to flood area

TWO MEN BATTLE IN SNAKE PIT

Express Staff Reporter: Sydney, Thursday

A MAN jumped into a pit of poisonous snakes at a Sydney exhibition today and fought an attendant who followed and tried to stop him fondling a huge tiger snake, one of Australia's deadliest.

Police probe baby case

Big-hat man seen in taxi

Bite is fatal

New Bill sanctions £1,500 jobs

Mother or baby—no orders

School blackmail

£29,000 for Italy

'Peace' scooters

JUST BORING

POCKET CARTOON By OSBERT LANCASTER

Mine pay talk goes on 9 hours

By TREVOR EVANS

Guards peer escorts the Princess

Boy swallows his mouth-organ

In West camp for ever says Adenauer

From DENIS MARTIN: Paris, Thursday

3 a.m. LATEST

CHILD DIES IN COTTAGE FIRE

Manchester CEntral 2112 London · CEntral 8000

Mr Butler for Rome

More meat quickly —and certainly

The pig is the fastest breeder of high-quality meat that there is; and every scrap of him can be used.

One brood sow will multiply herself not less than sixteen times in a year!

To-day many pig houses lie empty and there is room for more pigs on every farm.

Yet money and labour and freedom cannot be found for expansion of this home production.

Yet this very home production of food is surely part of our defence programme and it would cost but a small portion of our spending to give ourselves more meat—in the store-house and on the plate.

Press then for the expansion of the pig industry, for more pigs on every farm; for remember food is an armament.

This isn't politics, it's plain commonsense.

Issued by

MARSH & BAXTER LTD

in the interests of National nutrition

The head is 20—and a fanatic

WIDE WIDE WORLD

PAGE TWO, COL. THREE

2.2 The front page of the *Daily Express*, printed on 23 November 1951

Source J

A Mass Observation study in the summer of 1947, carried out among almost a thousand Tottenham residents, revealed that almost half the sample said they never read books at all, but only one in ten went without reading a daily paper (the *Daily Mirror*, the *News Chronicle*, the *Daily Herald* and the *Daily Express* being the most popular), and a mere one in 20 did not read a Sunday newspaper (with three out of five favouring the *News of the World*). Non-readers of books, a group far more working class than middle class in composition, were asked to explain their lack of interest:

'None of them subjects is interesting to me. All I like is gangster stories, though there's precious chance of reading here. Three rooms we got and three kids knocking around. No convenience, no nothing except water. I'm glad to get out the house I can tell you.'

A summary of extracts from a Mass Observation report in 1947

SKILLS BUILDER

1 Which of these two sources do you find the more useful for finding out about newspapers and their influence in these years?

2 How far do these sources, and the information in the main text on page 18, suggest that newspapers moulded or mirrored British attitudes before 1954?

Radio

There were some key differences between the press and radio (or wireless) during these years. Unlike the fierce competition for newspaper sales, the BBC had a monopoly on radio broadcasting in the UK until 1973. Given that by 1951, 90 per cent of British homes had a wireless receiver, the BBC had a potentially powerful means of influencing national culture. Without the pressure to sell advertising, Lord Reith and his successors at the head of the BBC were largely able to treat the 'audience as "public" not "market"': to try and improve cultural and educational standards, rather than attract as many listeners as possible. Source K gives an idea of the aims and preoccupations of those in charge of the BBC in 1948.

Questions

1 What do these strict guidelines tell us about the influence that BBC chiefs hoped they would have on British society?
2 Does it tell us anything about popular culture?
3 What does the fact that these banned words are now in a textbook tell us about social change in Britain?

Source K

Humour must be clean and untainted directly or by association with vulgarity and suggestiveness. Music hall . . . standards, are not suitable to broadcasting . . . There can be no compromise with doubtful material. It must be cut. There is an absolute ban on jokes about lavatories, effeminacy in men, immorality of any kind; on suggestive references to honeymoon couples, chambermaids, fig leaves, prostitution, ladies' underwear, e.g. winter draws on, animal habits, e.g. rabbits, lodgers, commercial travellers. Good taste and decency are the obvious governing considerations. The vulgar use of such words as 'basket' must also be avoided. Swearing has no place in light entertainment and all such words as God, Good God, My God, Blast, Hell, Damn, Bloody, Gorblimey, Ruddy etc, etc, should be deleted from scripts.

From *BBC Variety Programmes Policy Guide for Writers and Producers*, better known as 'The Green Book', published by the BBC in 1948

Definitions

Empire Day

From 1901 this was a celebration of the British Empire held on 24 May, Queen Victoria's birthday. In 1958 it was re-named Commonwealth Day; since 1977 it has been held on the second Monday in March.

Immediacy

The quality of something being immediate or direct.

Historians David Cardiff and Paddy Scannell have argued that the BBC 'functioned as an instrument of social control' that provided 'reassuring symbols of national community'. They argue that programmes such as the monarch's Christmas message (broadcast since 1932), anniversary programmes for New Year and **Empire Day**, acted as a 'social cement that reinforced the sense of belonging to our country'. Radio certainly had an impact on British culture. During the war, many radio programmes, such as *Workers' Playtime*, had been aimed at groups in factories to boost morale. After the war, radio programmes were targeted at listeners at home. In this way it promoted the domestication of leisure time. It also enhanced existing feelings of national identity through its ability to give **immediacy** to an event and to reach out to the most remote parts of the country. BBC radio news, read by 'the best of the ruling classes' (dressed in dinner jackets in the early days), was trusted far more than the press. Radio also broadened horizons: the working classes, rather than 'listening in' for a particular programme, usually had the radio on all the time, and sometimes listened to unexpected programmes. Source L is one recollection of listening to the radio in the 1950s.

It is possible to exaggerate the extent to which radio affected British culture. Firstly, Britons already had a strong sense of national identity before the rise of radio as a mass medium; this was partly forged by the First World War, but also by national newspapers, nationwide rail and postal connections, national football leagues and county cricket. Secondly, it became clear in the late 1940s that Lord Reith and his successors were not entirely able to 'give the public slightly better than it now thinks it likes'. Sir William Haley, the post-war Director General of the BBC, explained that he hoped to 'lead the listener from good to better by curiosity, liking, and a growth of understanding', from the Light Programme to the Home Service and finally the Third Programme. While the names of these stations might be unfamiliar, you might get a better idea of their intended audience when you learn of their more modern names: in 1967, the Light Programme was split into two stations, Radio 1 and Radio 2, while the Third Programme became Radio 3 and the Home Service became Radio 4. In fact, there was very little progression in tastes: the 'middlebrow' Home Service broadly catered for the middle classes with news, plays and lectures; the 'highbrow' Third Programme, with classical music and 'difficult' culture, appealed only to the most highly educated and attracted less than 2 per cent of all listeners. The Light Programme, with its mix of comedies, soaps such as *Mrs. Dale's Diary* and *The Archers*, variety shows and famous personalities, remained by far the most popular channel, with around two-thirds of the 11 million daily listeners. Many of the daytime shows were aimed at women (a reflection of the clearly divided roles for men and women), with the most popular ones including *Housewives' Choice* and *Woman's Hour*. Source M is a transcript from the first ever edition of *Woman's Hour*, presented by a man, Alan Ivimey.

Source L

The great days of the wireless were the fifties. Its main job was to lift up our hearts, and this was done with laughter. Lord Reith, who looked after our morals, was often hoodwinked by some of the comedians. 'Double Entendre' was the order of the day. For those who got away with it life was great, but for those who didn't, work dried up very quickly.

A recollection of radio in the 1950s by 'Greasy', a young boy at the time, posted on the *Greasy Spoon Café* website

Source M

Ivimey: Good afternoon. I have three ladies round the table to keep me in order today – Edith Saunders.

Saunders: Good afternoon.

Ivimey: Marion Cutler, who's been looking into the working of that splendid service to housewives and mothers begun during the war, the Home Help scheme.

Cutler: Good afternoon.

Ivimey: And Maguerite Patten, who wants to save some of those tea-time tragedies, when the lovely cake you've baked comes out with a hole in the middle instead of a nice brown bulge . . .

From *Woman's Hour*, broadcast on 7 October 1946

Question

What can we learn about popular culture in the years after 1945 from Source M? Can we learn anything about British society from it?

For children, there was *Listen With Mother*, which always began with the famous phrase, 'Are you sitting comfortably? Then I'll begin', *Children's Hour* and, for older children, *Dick Barton: Special Agent*, which gained audiences of over 15 million. On Sundays, when the Light Programme broadcast dreary shows dedicated to religious services and music, many of these listeners abandoned the BBC and tuned in to 'pirate radio' stations. Stations such as Radio Luxembourg and Radio Normandy had broadcast into Britain from beyond its shores since the 1930s; younger listeners especially liked the all-day popular music and famous disc jockeys, 'American gimmicks' that Reith feared so much.

Possibly the only 'Americanisation' of British culture that occurred as a result of radio in this period was the popularity of 'big band' swing music. Dance halls remained very popular and a number of American dance crazes hit the UK, such as the Swing Jive, the Lindy Hop and the Jitterbug. In general, however, the Light Programme was a conduit for the traditional variety acts that had entertained British crowds for decades. The most popular comedy programmes included Tommy Handley's *It's That Man Again (ITMA)* (1939–49), *Take It from Here* (1948–60), and *The Goon Show* (1951–60). Sources N and O are extracts from the scripts of *ITMA* and *The Goon Show* (you can use the Internet to research these shows).

Source N

Fred: Pray, silence for his nit-wit the Mayor!

Tom: Hello folks! I'm back in my Mayor's parlour – up to my usual parlour games. I introduced one or two of them to the council last week. We were going to play oranges and lemons, but as we were all over seven and one of us over the eight, we played carrots and turnips instead. What with the potatoes in my socks and the leeks in the roof, I can only describe the result as stupendous! And then we played 'Tiddley-Winks' with the lady councillors – they supplied the tiddley and I supplied the winks. After that –

Sydney: Boss, boss – you'll have to call the police!

Tom: I've called them every name I can think of –

Sydney: But boss – all them crooks you let out [of prison] last week is shooting up the town – they're all over the place.

Tom: They can't be worse than the crooks on the council!

From the script of *ITMA No.5*, broadcast in 1942

SKILLS BUILDER

1 How similar are the sources of humour in Sources N and O?

2 The comedy programmes in Sources N and O were hugely popular. Do they, and the information in the main text, suggest that radio mirrored or moulded British attitudes before 1954?

Source O

Hern: Yessirree, land of plenty and fun, the good ole USA, Uncle Sam's country, have a cigar . . . straight from the dollar country.

Captain Pureheart: You can't fool me. You're an American!

Hern: Er . . . Now, captain, what the Americans would like to know is, will the Crystal Palace make money?

Pureheart: Money? What's that?

Hern: Oh, just an old American word.

Pureheart: Well, I hope the Crystal Palace will help do away with our poverty.

Hern: Poverty? What's that?

Pureheart: Just an old English word. Now, gentlemen of the press, you've come here for a story.

Reporters: Yes, yes, yes.

Pureheart: Right. Now, once upon a time, there were three bears. A big bear, a little bear, and a teeny-weeny . . . [cuts to music link]

Narrator: And so the Crystal Palace project was started. Pureheart spent the first few weeks playing around with a model.

Pureheart: Yes. The frontage is very good, but these sides should curve a little more, and this bit here needs attention. There . . .

Model: Oooh! You artists are all the same.

Workman: [Gulps] Good. I say, captain, look! There's a man and woman wandering about the Palace!

Pureheart: What! I say, you two! Come over here. How dare you come poking around? It's all out of bounds! Who do you think you are? Your conduct is most un-British! You ought to be ashamed of yourselves! What have you to say, eh?

Queen Victoria: Young man, we are not amused. Come, Albert!

From Spike Milligan, *The Goon Show*, broadcast on 5 February 1952

Cinema

Just as popular radio programmes can tell us something about general likes and dislikes, so films can tell us something about the cultural values of audiences to which directors hoped to appeal. Some caution must be exercised when drawing such conclusions: cinema is a form of escapism, and what was acceptable on screen might not necessarily be acceptable in the real world. In addition, the British Board of Film Censors (BBFC) acted rather like the BBC's 'Green Book' as it prevented bad language, sex and subversive ideas from reaching British audiences. Cinema also attracted a predominantly working-class, and increasingly youthful, audience; what appealed to these viewers might not be to everyone's tastes. Lastly, it was only in the larger cities that cinema-goers would have a choice of films to watch: most high street cinemas in towns had just the one screen with one film showing at any one time. The first multiplex cinema in Britain (built in Milton Keynes) did not open until 1985.

Cinema had been one of the most popular forms of entertainment in the inter-war period. The introduction of 'talkies' in 1928 further increased the popularity of going to the pictures. While it remained highly popular immediately after the war, attendance figures had already slumped by 1954. Source P provides a number of possible reasons why this might have happened.

Source P

Annual admissions had already fallen from their immediate post-war peak of 1.6 billion to a more modest 1.4 billion in 1950. They fell still further during the 1950s, by almost two-thirds, to 515 million. The film trade blamed the arrival of television, and it was partly correct. But it was not only the arrival of television that kept people away from the cinema. By 1952, takings for other forms of entertainment, such as football, cricket and dog-racing were also down. Increased home ownership, the growth of Do-It-Yourself, the advent of central heating, the ready availability of refrigerators, clothes washers, and record players, all meant that, for many, real life started to become as enjoyable as that on the screen.

From Charles Drazin, *Cinema The Finest Years: British Cinema of the 1940s*, published in 2007

Question

What does Source P suggest the decline of cinema attendance tells us about British popular culture?

In addition to these problems, British cinema had always suffered from extremely strong American competition. In the 1940s, about 80 per cent of the films shown in Britain were American; only a **Quota** Act passed by the government in 1938 ensured that the number of British-made films was as high as 20 per cent. Even before the war, writers and journalists had noted youths dressing like gangsters and factory girls looking like actresses, using American slang such as 'oh yeah?' and 'sez you!'. One British film maker who tried to resist what he saw as an unhealthy Americanisation of British culture was the Methodist mill owner, J. Arthur Rank. He invested significant sums of his own fortune in the film industry and by the mid-1940s was responsible for over half of British film production. Even Rank struggled to compete with the Americans and the government had to set up the National Film Loan Finance Corporation to fund new British films after 1953. Source Q is one historian's conclusions about the impact of American films on British culture before 1954.

Definition

Quota

The share of a total allocated to or allowed by an individual or group.

Questions

1 What is meant by 'Americanisation'?
2 How Americanised are you?

American films had been far more popular than British films before the war, but improved production and acting, and the toning down of elite manners and accents, made British films more popular. In particular, the gentle, middle-class Ealing Studio comedies, such as *Kind Hearts and*

Source Q

By the 1950s the English had become very familiar with the United States as it appeared in American films. But they were not completely taken in, and there is little sign of the wholesale Americanisation that people so feared before and during the war. Nor is there much to suggest that American movies were socially subversive in practice. They were energetic etc, but theirs was a democracy of manner rather than content. In the end, their result was probably to increase the demand for a . . . glamour whose implication was, if anything, conservative rather than democratic.

From Ross McKibbin, *Classes and Cultures: England 1918–1951*, published in 1998

Coronets (1949), *Passport to Pimlico* (1949) and *The Lavender Hill Mob* (1951), appealed to British audiences. The other popular British film genre after the war was the 'spiv' film. The spiv was a young, dangerous man, usually dressed like a gangster, who profiteered from criminal activity. In *The Blue Lamp* (1950), and in previous films, such as *Waterloo Road* (1945), *They Made Me a Fugitive* (1947), *Brighton Rock* (1948) and *The Third Man* (1949), the spiv was an outsider, a villain who always got his comeuppance. *The Blue Lamp* was about a wise, kindly police constable called George Dixon, who is killed by a young 'spiv', Tom Riley. When Tom Riley is caught, the decent values of the community are affirmed. Source R is one example of historians' conclusions about important differences between *The Blue Lamp* and the most popular British film of 1961, *Saturday Night and Sunday Morning*.

Source R

The differences between *The Blue Lamp* and *Saturday Night and Sunday Morning* indicate the widespread change that took place in the attitudes of occasional cinema-goers during the 1950s. Whereas the first film reinforced and celebrated the established social order, the audiences for the second film gazed in awe-struck fashion as the young working-class Arthur Seaton boozed and bonked his way through his provincial weekend: 'All I'm out for is a good time. The rest is propaganda.' British cinema played a vital role in the culture and society of the 1950s. It responded, in an uneven and faltering way, to the great changes taking place not only in the social landscape but in the emotional one too.

From Sue Harper and Vincent Porter, *British Cinema of the 1950s: The Decline of Deference*, published in 2003

Sources S and T are the posters that advertised the two films. Look at the sources and then answer the questions that follow.

Source S

2.3 Poster for *The Blue Lamp*, released in January 1950

Source T

2.4 Poster for *Saturday Night and Sunday Morning*, released in November 1960

SKILLS BUILDER

1 How far do Sources S and T support the conclusions reached by the author of Source R?

2 Do you find Source R, or Sources S and T, more useful when researching popular culture and social change?

3 How far do Sources R, S and T, and the information in the main text, suggest that cinema moulded or mirrored British attitudes before 1954?

Unit summary

What have you learned in this unit?

Britain was gripped by the physical and psychological effects of the Second World War in the years after 1945; damaged towns and rationing contributed to a generally drab atmosphere. Compared to the years that followed 1954, British society was conservative. However, it is possible to exaggerate the universality of austere attitudes to hierarchy, sex and family life.

The most important mass media in the years after the Second World War were the radio, newspapers and cinema. Of all the media, radio was the most influential; the BBC attempted to use its near monopoly on this medium to promote civilised culture. However, the BBC did broadcast a good deal of popular music and comedy that passed on traditional variety culture to a mass audience.

What skills have you used in this unit?

You have analysed source content to find out information about British society and popular culture. You have evaluated these sources to decide how far their content gives useful or reliable information about the past. You have cross-referenced a range of sources to show the points on which they support or contradict each other.

SKILLS BUILDER

Work in a group and prepare answers to the questions below for discussion.

1 Read Source U. In what ways does it suggest that life and attitudes in Britain were 'austere' between 1945 and 1954?

2 Look at Sources A, I and S. How far do these pictorial sources support the picture of British society given in Source U?

3 Looking back over this unit, what would you identify as the most significant differences between British society 1945–54 and that of today?

4 Having looked at British society and examples of popular culture between 1945 and 1954, would you agree that mass media moulded more than it mirrored British attitudes?

Source U

Britain in 1945. A land of orderly queues, hat-doffing men walking on the outside, seats given up to the elderly, no swearing in front of children, censored books, censored films, censored plays, infinite repression of desires. Divorce almost an unthinkable social disgrace, marriage too often a lifetime sentence. Children in the street ticked off by strangers, children in the street kept an eye on by strangers, children at home rarely consulted, children stopped being children when they left school at 14 and got a job. A land of hierarchical assumptions, of accent and dress as giveaway to class, of Irish jokes and casually derogatory references to Jews and niggers . . . A sense of history, however **nugatory** the knowledge of that history. A land in which authority was respected? Or rather, accepted? Yes, perhaps the latter, co-existing with the necessary safety valve of copious grumbling. A land of domestic hobbies and domestic pets . . . A deeply conservative land.

From David Kynaston, *Austerity Britain 1945–51*, published in 2007

Definition

Nugatory

Worthless or trivial.

Exam tips

This is the sort of question you will find on your examination paper as an (a) question:

Study Sources K, L and O.

How far do Sources K and O support the opinion given in Source L that radio programmes undermined 'austere' British attitudes between 1945 and 1954?

Explain your answer, using the evidence of Sources K, L and O. (20)

Don't bring in lots of your own knowledge. All (a) questions focus on the analysis, cross-referencing and evaluation of source material. Your own knowledge won't be credited by the examiner, and you will waste valuable time writing it out.

- Do remember that the only own knowledge you should introduce will be to put the sources into context.
- Don't describe (or even re-write) the sources; the examiner will have a copy of the exam paper.
- When you come to plan and write your answer, don't base your paragraphs around each source: this will not allow you to cross-reference the sources and access the top marks. Instead, base your paragraphs on ways in which Sources K and O do support Source L, and ways in which they do not. You could use a table like the one below to help with the planning stage.

View in Source L	Points in Sources K and O that support this view	Points in Sources K and O that oppose this view	Reliability of points in Sources K and O?

RESEARCH TOPIC

Popular culture 1945–54: film and radio

Pick a film, or a radio programme listed in this unit, or in the list below, and carry out some further research about it. Go to www.pearsonhotlinks.co.uk to access links to useful websites. To access the site; enter the express code 5063P.

- What is it about?
- Who were the stars?
- Is it possible to learn anything about people's tastes or attitudes from the film or programme?

The list below details some of the most popular films in the years after 1945, and where they were made.

1945 *The Seventh Veil* (UK), *Brief Encounter* (UK), *The Lost Weekend* (US)

1946 *The Wicked Lady* (UK), *It's a Wonderful Life* (US), *Song of the South* (US), *A Matter of Life and Death* (UK)

1947 *Courtneys of Curzon Street* (UK), *Black Narcissus* (UK)

1948 *The Best Years of Our Lives* (US), *The Red Shoes* (UK), *Oliver Twist* (UK), *Hamlet* (UK)

1949 *The Third Man* (UK), *Kind Hearts and Coronets* (UK), *Passport to Pimlico* (UK)

1950 *The Blue Lamp* (UK), *Cinderella* (US)

1951 *Quo Vadis* (US), *The African Queen* (US), *The Lavender Hill Mob* (UK)

1952 *The Greatest Show on Earth* (US), *Singing in the Rain* (US)

1953 *From Here to Eternity* (US), *Genevieve* (UK)

1954 *White Christmas* (US), *The Belles of St Trinian's* (UK)

UNIT

3 Did rock and roll change British society 1955–69?

What is this unit about?

The key question in this unit is whether rock and roll inspired and drove important cultural changes in Britain in the 1950s and 1960s, or whether it was itself a product of more important underlying changes. In particular, the unit will assess whether rock and roll, and other new forms of popular culture, encouraged the growth of a separate 'youth culture'. While people remember The Beatles as icons of the 'Swinging Sixties', government legislation, increased affluence and the rise of television all had important effects on British society and popular culture.

Key questions

- How far did rock and roll shape youth culture?
- How far did rock and roll Americanise British culture 1955–69?
- How far did mass media promote rock and roll?
- What was the nature and significance of the impact of The Beatles on popular culture in Britain in the 1960s?

Timeline

1955	**5 April**	Churchill resigns. Anthony Eden becomes Prime Minister. Conservatives win the General Election in May
	13 July	Ruth Ellis is hanged. She is the last woman to be executed in Britain
1956	**8 May**	John Osborne's play *Look Back in Anger* is first performed
1958		Race riots take place in Nottingham and Notting Hill
	February	Campaign for Nuclear Disarmament launches
1959		Obscene Publications Act allows serious works of art to use 'obscene' words and images
	November	First section of the M1 motorway, between London and Birmingham, opens
1960		*Lady Chatterley's Lover* trial allows publication of this 'pornographic' novel
1961		Suicide Act means that suicide ceases to be a crime and those who fail to kill themselves will no longer be prosecuted
1962		Colour supplements first appear in Sunday newspapers
1962–63		The Beatles rise to fame with hits such as *Love Me Do* and *Please Please Me*

1965	Murder (Abolition of the Death Penalty) Act is passed
1966	England hosts and wins the football World Cup
1967	Abortion Act legalises abortion through the NHS
	Family Planning Act allows local health authorities to provide birth control devices. The contraceptive pill has been on sale since 1961
	Sexual Offences Act legalises homosexual acts between men over the age of 21, in private, in England and Wales (not in Scotland until 1980 or in Northern Ireland until 1982)
1968	Theatres Act abolishes censorship of plays on stage in the UK
1969	Divorce Act allows divorce to be granted after 2 years of separation if both parties want it, and after 5 years if one party wants it

Source A

3.1 A photograph of The Beatles taken on 6 February 1964

Source B

3.2 A photograph of The Beatles taken in June 1967

SKILLS BUILDER

1 How would you describe the images of the Beatles in Sources A and B?

2 What can we learn about changes in youth culture between 1964 and 1967 from the differences?

3 How far do you think pop stars affect youth culture today?

How far did rock and roll shape youth culture?

The invention of youth

In some cultures there is a clear distinction between childhood and adulthood, which usually involves come sort of event or ceremony to celebrate the 'coming of age'. In Britain, there are certainly children and adults, but, apart from in the Jewish tradition, it is not altogether clear at what age one becomes the other. It is still common to hear the phrase 'young man' or 'young lady', but it is now **axiomatic** to see 'teenagers' as a separate group, with their own tastes and experiences. This is a fairly recent development: the word 'teenage' was not coined until 1921, and 'teenager' only came into regular use in Britain after 1945. It is therefore necessary to look at the 'invention of youth'. A commonly held view is that the teenager was an invention of the 1950s, and of rock and roll music in particular. However, while rock and roll had a major impact on teenagers, it is clear that youth culture existed before the rock and roll era.

> **Definitions**
>
> **Axiomatic**
>
> Something that is self-evident or indisputably true.
>
> **Disposable income**
>
> Money left to spend after all essential expenditure and savings have been deducted from earnings.

There were a few long-term changes that gradually contributed to our modern concept of youth: the decline of child labour from the mid-nineteenth century, and the rise of compulsory education at the end of that century, contributed to the idea of a separate stage of life between childhood and adulthood with its own unique set of experiences.

> **Question**
>
> At what age are people thought of as adults in Britain today? Does it vary in different circumstances?

In the short term, the post-war 'baby boom' meant that the number of 15 to 19 year olds rose from 3,174,000 in 1951 to 4,282,000 in 1965. This increase in number alone contributed to greater conspicuousness of their activities.

The number of teenagers with a shared, separate identity to those both older and younger than them was also increased by government legislation.

- Firstly, the 1944 Education Act raised the school leaving age to 15. This led to the doubling of the number of pupils aged 15 or over in schools in England and Wales from 329,000 in 1955 to 785,000 in 1965. Rather than being assimilated as a 'young man or woman' into an older person's work-based culture, school offered older pupils a more flexible, alternative focus of identity.
- Secondly, the 1948 National Service Act meant that most boys who turned 18 before 1 September 1957 had to complete 18 months (later 2 years) of National Service. Only miners, farmers and those in the merchant navy were exempt; those who went to university could delay their National Service. Once their time in the armed forces was over, these men were still on the reserves list for four more years; they had to report for training at least three times in this period. Once their training was over, the conscripts could be sent anywhere they were needed. Many saw active combat duty in places like Malaya (now Malaysia) and Korea. Young men realised they could be sent to dangerous places on National Service and saw the 3 years between school and conscription as a 'limbo' period without any responsibilities.

Without the need to buy food or pay rent teenage workers had a good deal of **disposable income**. Whereas their parents might have had to go through a poorly paid apprentice period for a skilled job, the growth of production-line technology meant there was greater demand for flexible, unskilled labour. Teenagers benefited from the comparatively higher wages of this sort of work throughout the 1950s and 1960s. In his survey, *The Teenage Consumer* (1959), the sociologist Mark Abrams calculated that the five million teenagers in Britain earned 10 per cent of the national income and spent most of their money on entertainment and luxuries.

Source C

. . . British teenagers in 1959 spent 20 per cent on clothes and shoes; 17 per cent on drinks and cigarettes; 15 per cent on sweets, snacks and soft drinks in cafés; and the rest, just under half the total on entertainment of various kinds, from cinemas and dance halls to magazines and records. Many of these markets had come to depend on teenage spending. Teenagers bought over a third of all bicycles and motorbikes for example. Their purchases accounted for nearly a third of the markets for cosmetics, film admissions and public entertainments in general. And young people accounted for more than 40 per cent of the markets for records and record players . . . Teenagers looked for products that were 'highly charged emotionally'; that offered something different from what their parents liked, and that carried connotations of excitement and modernity.

From Dominic Sandbrook, *Never Had It So Good*, published in 2005

SKILLS BUILDER

1 What can we learn from Source C about youth culture at the end of the 1950s?

2 Does Source C suggest that youth culture was highly **commercialised** at this time?

The increased wealth of young people, together with a new sense of shared identity, led to some new leisure pursuits. In addition to the cinema and dance hall that were familiar to their parents, teenagers in the 1950s often went to the coffee bar or milk bar to 'hang out', 'see and be seen' and listen to music. The first coffee bars were opened by Italian immigrants in London in 1952; by 1957 there were over 1000 such bars across the country. Source D is one contemporary explanation of the attraction of coffee bars.

Definition

Commercialised
Exploiting an activity or product by turning it into something from which a profit can be derived.

Source D

I work just off Tottenham Court Road as a secretary, and then in the evenings I sometimes go and work in the coffee bar, everybody comes to meet their friends really, they get to know a lot of people, it's a very friendly sort of atmosphere much more than in a pub. You talk about music or the other people there.

From an interview with Miranda Kenny, a secretary from London. The interview was recorded in the late 1950s, but first broadcast on a Radio 2 programme called *Coffee Bar Kids* on 27 May 1995

The music was the key attraction on London's Compton Street. There were a number of coffee bars, such as the Two I's (run by two flamboyant Australian wrestlers) and Heaven and Hell, which became famous for their live rock and roll performances. In most coffee bars, especially in provincial towns and cities, the music was not provided by a live band, but by a **jukebox**. The jukebox was invented in America in 1927 and, as it gave listeners greater control over the music they heard in bars and cafés, quickly became popular. This was especially true in black communities as the radio stations, dominated by whites, refused to play their 'degenerate' music (what we know today as jazz, blues and rock and roll). The real breakthrough came in 1948, with the invention of the 7-inch extended-play (EP) **vinyl** record. EPs were far thinner than the old gramophone records, and smaller than the long-play (LP) records, so up to 500 of them could be loaded into a jukebox. By 1958 there were more than 7000 jukeboxes in Britain. As Source E reveals, even in smaller towns without a coffee or milk bar, the arrival of a jukebox in an ordinary café caused quite a stir.

Definitions

Jukebox

The word originally came from the 1930s black American slang word for dance – 'juke'.

Vinyl

A type of plastic used to make records. Grooves were etched into the plastic, which caused a needle to move and, when amplified, produce the desired sound.

Source E

It caused a sensation locally; there were editorials in the local paper. There were those for it and those against it. For those against it was pretty extreme: a jukebox now and Sodom and Gomorrah tomorrow! I remember going in [to the café] with my friends. There were old people having tea and buttered toast. There was a volume control at the back. We turned the volume to maximum, put in the thruppence and hit the button. There was a record called *Western Movies* which opened with a gunshot. The gunshot went off and the old people were dropping like flies!

From an interview with Paul Barratt in 1995. He had been a teenager in the 1950s in Penarth, Wales. First broadcast on *Coffee Bar Kids* on 27 May 1995

SKILLS BUILDER

1 Look back at Sources C, D and E. How far do the sources support one another about the nature of youth culture in the late 1950s?

2 Which of the three sources offers the best insight into the nature of youth culture at this time? Explain your answer.

3 How far do Sources C, D and E support the view that rock and roll 'invented youth culture'?

So far, we have seen that there were more teenagers in the 1950s than before the war, that they were wealthier, they spent their money on conspicuous or disposable items, or on things that gave them instant gratification, and that they liked to meet together in public. None of this sounds particularly threatening, or even divisive between the older and younger generation. How are we to explain, therefore, the sentiments expressed in Sources F and G about the perception of teenagers?

Source F

Teenagers are pampered with high wages, first-class working conditions and excellent facilities in education. Their outlook is centred in trashy books and films. The boys are hoodlums in embryo, defiant and uncouth, while the girls are brazen and unrefined. A rigorous period of military training might make men and women out of them, if they had the courage to face it.

From a letter written to the *Daily Mail* in October 1949

Source G

Nowadays in most papers and magazines it is emphasised that teenagers are very peculiar and that they should be treated with caution as though they were a peculiar sort of animal and not misunderstood, not upset, because their glands are changing, they're physically changing and mentally changing. I think it's emphasised too much. It is a difficult time of life, but I don't think we should be treated like some mysterious sort of specimen to be looked at from rather a long way away.

From an interview with an anonymous teenage girl on the Home Service programme *The Days of Our Years*, first broadcast on 8 February 1959

One last possible **enabling factor** for the rise of a distinct teenage popular culture was that teenagers were becoming sexually mature at a younger age due to improved diets after the end of rationing. The **Albermarle Report** (1960) noted that adolescents were taller, heavier and reached puberty at around 15, rather than 16 or 17 as in the decades before the war. Older contemporaries feared what they saw as the greater sexualisation of teenage girls, and the increased violence of teenage males. Sources H and I are examples of these 'worrying aspects' of youth culture in the 1950s (there is more information on media impact on sex and violence in Unit 9).

Source H

3.3 The front cover of *Jackie* magazine, published on 9 May 1964. *Jackie* regularly sold over a million copies each week in the 1960s

SKILLS BUILDER

1. What do Sources F and G suggest about the popular perception of young people by older generations? Use extracts from the sources to support your answer.
2. What are the strengths and weaknesses of these sources when using them to consider the rise of the '**generation gap**' in Britain?

Definitions

Enabling factor

A factor which allows later developments to occur; a necessary but not sufficient cause of something.

Albermarle Report

A report into the workings of the Youth Service in England and Wales; it was commissioned by the government, partly in response to growing concerns about a 'youth problem'.

Generation gap

Differences in opinions, tastes and behaviour between those of different generations.

Source I

CO·OPERATIVE

3.4 A photograph of a **Teddy Boy** in London, published as part of a *Picture Post* news story called 'The Truth about Teddy Boys' on 29 May 1954

Definition

Teddy Boy
Teddy, short for Edward, from the Edwardian style (i.e. during the reign of Edward VII 1901–10) of their long coats and drainpipe trousers.

Questions

1. How far does Source H justify fears of teenage 'sexualisation'?
2. What styles do you think influenced the Teddy Boy look in Source I?
3. Are there any similarities between this look and more modern youth styles?

While virtually no one noticed the long-term effects of diet on the behaviour of teenagers, everyone noticed the arrival of rock and roll. Soon, rock and roll was being blamed by many observers for the corruption of youth, for turning respectable, decent young people into delinquents. While it was perhaps understandable for contemporaries to make such a link, is it a fair conclusion for historians to make with the benefit of hindsight?

What was the impact of rock and roll on youth culture?

Rock music is so familiar to us today that it is difficult to recapture its initial impact on the British. The rise of rap music could be seen as a useful, modern analogy: loud, brash and sexually charged, it was exciting and appealing to the young; threatening and offensive to the old. Like rap, rock and roll was first devised and performed by black American musicians; the name itself came from black slang for sex. Again like rap, it did not truly become a part of mainstream youth and popular culture until it was popularised by white performers, with Elvis Presley as the 1950s equivalent of Eminem in the 1990s. Like the rap scene, rock and roll inspired styles of dress, speech and attitude that were seen as threatening to the values of decent society.

As far as most people in Britain were concerned, rock and roll began in March 1955 with the release of the film *Blackboard Jungle* at cinemas across the country. During the opening credits, a teacher arrives at the school gates and crosses the yard between groups of rude, hostile teenagers. All the while, Bill Haley's *Rock Around the Clock* is played loudly in the background. Source J is one historian's view of the importance of this moment of cinema history.

Blackboard Jungle was a huge hit largely because of the popularity of the music. Bill Haley and his band, the Comets, took advantage of the success of this film by starring in their own film in 1956: *Rock Around the Clock* had a fairly thin storyline about the discovery of a rock and roll band but the music, with songs such as *Shake, Rattle and Roll*, caused a great deal of excitement. During the screening of the film, more than 60 young men, mostly Teddy Boys, were charged with causing disturbances inside and outside cinemas. In some towns, police reported crowds of up to several hundred young people 'ranting and raving'. Blackburn went as far as to ban the film being screened on its cinemas! Source K gives some idea of the reaction of older people and the media to the release of the film.

Source J

In the two minutes and ten seconds it lasted on screen, this combination of image and song defined the cultural essence of rock and roll. It would be all about disorder, aggression and sex, a fantasy of human nature running wild to a savage beat.

From James Miller, *Flowers in the Dustbin: The Rise of Rock and Roll 1947–77*, published in 1999

Source K

Question: Should the film *Rock Around the Clock* be banned from our cinemas?

Jeremy Thorpe MP: This is a very serious historical question . . . What worries me is that a fourth rate film, with fifth rate music, can pierce through the thin shell of civilisation. Policemen's hats have been knocked off, people will be dancing in the streets, dustbins will be turned over, lampposts will be smashed, milk bottles will be strewn round, 2000 hooligans will be marching down the street. Faced with that, I don't think it unreasonable for the film to be banned.

[Lots of applause from the studio audience]

From *Any Questions?*, broadcast on the Light Programme on 13 September 1956

Questions

1 How far do you think films, or even a single film, can alter people's views and behaviour?

2 Does Source K suggest that older people in the 1950s were worried about the same aspects of young people's behaviour that worry older people today?

How far did rock and roll Americanise British youth culture?

Apart from the rebellion which rock and roll was seen to encourage in the young, contemporary critics such as Richard Hoggart feared what they saw as the Americanisation of British youth. In his 1957 book, *The Uses of Literacy*, Hoggart focused in particular on 'the juke box boys, with their drape suits, picture ties and American slouch . . . [spending all evenings in] harshly lighted milk bars . . . [putting] copper after copper into the mechanical record player'. He saw this as a 'thin and pallid' culture derived from brash American capitalism and consumerism. It is clearly true that American culture did have an impact on Britain after 1945: the British already knew a lot about American culture through their films; many Teddy boys chose to sport thick sideburns and wear neck-ties like the dangerous gambler figures in popular Westerns. The arrival of American GIs, in preparation for the assault on Nazi-held Europe, in many towns and cities across Britain between 1942 and 1945, further increased this knowledge. The long Teddy Boy coat was almost certainly an imitation of the loose, baggy 'zoot suit' worn by off-duty American GIs during the war and by West Indian immigrants after 1948. The look had emerged in London in 1952 and spread to other towns and cities in 1953; however, by 1956, when rock and roll really took off in Britain, the Teddy Boy style was already going out of fashion. The 'modern' or 'Mod' look that replaced it owed more to chic Italian tailoring than to the American styles still aped by the 'rockers' (see page 40). Hoggart also chose to focus on milk bars, while the Italian-inspired coffee bars became far more popular in the 1960s.

While the origins and first popular examples of rock and roll were American, the popularity of such music in the 1960s does not necessarily mean that British popular music had become totally Americanised. Many record companies had found British 'heartthrob' performers, such as Tommy Steele, Adam Faith and Cliff Richard, to imitate the young, lean and trendy Elvis, rather than the fat, middle-aged and balding Bill Haley. They led their artists to release safer, more respectable songs in a bid to appeal to the teenage girls who bought records and went to dance halls. By the early 1960s these once exuberant performers released a string of bland ballads (compare Cliff Richard's hit singles *Move It!* (1958) and *Summer Holiday* (1963) to get an idea!). Rock and roll had almost died out; many contemporary music journalists thought that 'trad jazz' would be the sound of the 1960s.

Things had looked so bleak for rock and roll that in 1962 one executive at Decca Records declared, 'Groups are out; four piece groups with guitars are practically finished'; with that opinion in mind, he turned down a little known band called The Beatles. As you will see from the enquiry at the end of this unit, it proved to be a rather costly error! While the music of the Rolling Stones was heavily based on American blues, The Beatles, The Kinks and many other pop/rock groups combined rock and roll with older, more traditional British music, such as **skiffle** (originally

Definition

Skiffle

A style of jazz or blues played on improvised instruments such as washboards and the tea chest bass.

American but developed into its own form in Britain) and music hall songs. Rather than one-way cultural traffic across the Atlantic, many of these bands gained huge success in American charts as part of the 'British Invasion' of 1964–65. Unit 4 discusses in more depth the growth of the 'Swinging Sixties' scene in Britain that became so popular in parts of America.

How far did mass media promote a new rock and roll culture?

Cinema

We have already seen that cinema was in the vanguard of rock and roll: not only did films such as *Blackboard Jungle* spread the new music and image, but cinemas were a focal point of the Teddy Boy violence that made the headlines. America turned out a huge number of '**teenpic**' films in the late 1950s and 1960s, with titles such as *Girls' Town* (1959), *Where the Boys Are* (1960), *Girls! Girls! Girls!* (1962) and *Beach Party* (1963), often released at the same time as the soundtrack on LP. There were a few British teenpics along these lines, such as *The Beat Girl* (1960), which starred Adam Faith and was the first film soundtrack to be released on LP in Britain, *Summer Holiday* (1963) with Cliff Richard and *A Hard Day's Night* (1964) with The Beatles. These films clearly cashed in on the existing success of their stars, rather than further promoting new rock and roll music. Many of the iconic films of the 1960s dealt not with cheerful exuberance of pop stars, but with the more violent and sexual behaviour of young, working-class people, that rock and roll, among other factors, was said to inspire (see Unit 4 for more on this).

Definition

Teenpic
Films about teenagers targeted at teenagers. Plots often revolve around problems with parents, school or relationships with the opposite sex.

Radio

Until the 1960s, BBC radio made few concessions to the popularity of rock and roll among younger listeners. The Board of Governors felt it was a waste of licence fee money to pay for 'needle time' (recording artists' copyright fees) while they had perfectly good orchestras and singers. This worked for classical music and 'big band' swing of the 1940s and 1950s, but could not successfully reproduce the latest hits of Elvis, Cliff, or Tommy Steele! The only programme dedicated to pop music, and hence increasingly rock and roll, was *Pick of the Pops*, launched in 1955. This was turned into a more familiar chart programme by DJ Alan 'Fluff' Freeman after 1961. As a result of this, a number of new pirate radio stations, such as Radio Caroline (1964–) and Radio London (1964–67), that specifically targeted younger listeners were launched. Radio London, or 'Big L' as it was known, exclusively played songs from the top 40 singles, or 'Fab 40' as the list was known. To gain a better idea about pirate radio stations, watch the 2009 film, *The Boat that Rocked*, which is clearly based on Radio Caroline. In August 1967, the Marine Broadcasting Offences Act banned pirate radio (although Radio Caroline ignored the ban). The BBC filled the gap for a pop radio station when it split the Light Programme into Radio 1 and Radio 2 – its first channel specifically dedicated to pop music and a younger audience.

From the start of the rock and roll era, commercial pirate radio did bring the latest musical trends to a national audience. There was a reciprocal relationship between the advertisers who sponsored shows, the record companies, and the DJs who all wanted to tap into the lucrative youth market. In doing so, they responded to a market that already existed, but, through the constant promotion of particular styles, helped to shape the popular forms of youth culture.

Television

Although television broadcasts had been resumed in June 1946, as the table below shows, sales of television licences did not really take off until the coronation of Elizabeth II, 7 years later.

Source L

Year	*1947*	*1955*	*1960*	*1965*	*1975*	*1985*
TV licences (thousands)	15	344	10,470	13,253	17,701	18,716

3.5 A table showing sales of television licences from 1947 to 1985. From Derrick Murphy (ed.) *Britain 1914–2000*, published in 2000

According to historian Bill Osgerby, the first popular music programmes on the BBC, such as *Hit Parade* (1952), 'were low-key in the youth appeal'. Even later programmes, such as *Six-Five Special* (1957) and *Jukebox Jury* (1959) 'made concessions to an adult audience through the inclusion of variety performers and dinner-jacketed compères'. However, *Six-Five Special* was clearly designed to appeal to a teenage audience, with presenter Pete Murray, who had been a DJ on Radio Luxembourg, opening the first show with the words, 'Welcome aboard the *Six-Five Special*. We've got almost a hundred cats jumping here, some real cool characters to give us the gas, go just get with it and have a ball.' It soon attracted audiences of up to 10 million and introduced many new pop acts to the nation. ITV responded with *Oh Boy!* (1958), which focused even more heavily on rock and roll, to the exclusion of skiffle, folk, jazz and blues which featured on the BBC programmes.

While television brought the sound and image of the rock and roll and pop stars into a large number of British households, it cannot be said to have originally pioneered or engineered youth culture: producers reacted to an existing teenage market and youth culture. Television did popularise later pop trends, such as the Mod or Rocker look, at a quicker rate than the spread of earlier styles such as the Teddy Boy look. Whereas the Rockers followed the American style for jeans, white T-shirts, leather jackets, long sideburns and motorbikes, the Mods (short for modern) drew their inspiration from Italian fashion, with tight, smart trousers, elongated 'winkle picker' shoes, Ben Sherman shirts and Vespa mopeds.

Newspapers

Newspapers had an odd love-hate relationship with rock and roll and all the pop stars that the music gave rise to. The *Daily Mirror* was so keen to be associated with Bill Haley that it even sponsored a train to collect him from Portsmouth and take him to his first performance in London. However, the same newspaper published a series of terrifying stories about the menace of juvenile delinquents from the Teddy Boys through to the Mods and Rockers of the mid-1960s. Source M is a typical headline about Mods and Rockers from 1964.

Source M

Daily Mirror

Monday, May 18, 1964

After Clacton .. a new battlefield

WILD ONES 'BEAT UP' MARGATE

30 arrested in all-day clashes

By MIRROR REPORTER

THE wild ones—self-styled Mods and Rockers—picked the Kent resort of Margate to beat up for Whitsun. All day yesterday the rival teenagers fought and smashed their way around the town.

When it got dark, about [illegible] Mods were parading around Margate. Two hundred Rockers were lurking in a quiet corner of the town.

At least thirty youths had been arrested. And there was blood on the sands.

Most of the Mods had arrived on scooters bristling with headlights and badges. Most of the leather-jacketed Rockers had roared into town on shiny motor-cycles.

Wrecking

Many of the teenagers turned up late on Saturday night. They got down to the wrecking and smashing right away.

At 10.30 yesterday morning the big battle broke out—as [illegible] Mods attacked 100 Rockers.

Six policemen stepped in, truncheons waving—and both mobs turned on them.

Soon after that raging Mods swarmed through Margate's High-street, smashing windows.

All afternoon, the rival gangs fought small skirmishes.

Extra police poured into the town from as far as fifty miles away.

But at Kent's county police headquarters, at Maidstone, a spokesman said: "The situation at Margate is in hand."

Clashed

At Clacton, Essex—beaten up by 1,000 teenagers at Easter—no trouble was reported yesterday.

In Skegness, Lincs, about fifty youths clashed with eleven police on Saturday night. Four youths will appear in court.

At Devil's Dyke, a Sussex beauty spot near Brighton, twenty Mods beat up a cafe early yesterday.

Later, ten boys were arrested in Brighton and charged with stealing food.

Girls who followed the wild ones—Page 3

The Battle of Margate Sands —Centre Pages

HEAD WELL DOWN .. An arrested youth is carried off, head down, by policemen at Margate. The constable on the left has a black eye. And the sergeant has lost his helmet in the scuffle.

HANDS FULL One policeman, truncheon out, struggles to hold two youths at once on Margate sands.

3.6 The front cover of the *Daily Mirror*, published on 18 May 1964

Question

Of the mass media discussed above, which one had the greatest impact on:

a) the spread of rock and roll among young people
b) popular reactions to rock and roll by older people?

Explain your answer.

Newspapers therefore contributed to the growth of fan mania, but also turned whole sections of British youth into 'folk devils', blamed for driving society towards catastrophe with their rude, outlandish behaviour.

Enquiry 1: what was the nature and significance of the impact of The Beatles on popular culture in Britain in the 1960s?

After a brief overview of The Beatles' rise to prominence, there follow a number of sources that discuss the nature and extent of the band's impact on the way that British people thought and acted in the 1960s. As you go through the enquiry, keep in mind the key themes of the 'impact' of rock and roll on British society and popular culture that you have come across in this unit:

- rebellion, verging on violence, of teenage boys
- increased sexualisation of teenage girls
- the growth of commercialised youth leisure pursuits
- the reaction of older people to these trends
- the role of the press and other mass media in reporting and furthering these trends.

The Beatles remain one of the most famous icons of the 1960s. They started off in Liverpool in 1957 as a skiffle band called the Quarry Men. In 1960, after a lack of success in Liverpool, they changed their name to The Beatles and went to Hamburg where they were assured of regular gigs for American servicemen and German audiences. In Hamburg, they developed into a loud, exuberant band and became more popular than the other expatriate bands out there. After their return to Britain, they secured a regular slot at the Cavern Club in Liverpool from February 1961. There were over 400 similar bands in Liverpool at this time, and the Mersey Beat scene was far from unique, with similar bands playing in similar clubs across the country.

It was two meetings, one in November 1961 with businessman and entrepreneur Brian Epstein, and another in June 1962 with record producer George Martin, that caused the Beatles' to triumph over contemporary rivals. Epstein, who became the band's manager, secured a record deal with Parlophone Records, while Martin gave lots of advice that greatly influenced The Beatles' music. The band, with John Lennon on vocals and rhythm guitar, Paul McCartney on vocals and bass guitar, George Harrison on lead guitar, and Ringo Starr (who only joined the band on Martin's insistence in June 1961) on drums, first entered the charts in October 1962 with 'Love Me Do', a song written by Paul McCartney when he was only 16. From then on, Lennon and McCartney worked extremely hard to write and release their own songs; they went on to have 17 number one hits in Britain between 1963 and 1969.

The quality of their songs, together with their smart, iconic look (see Source A on page 31) ensured that 'Beatlemania' had spread across the country by mid-1963. In 1964, they led the 'British Invasion' of the American charts: in April 1964 The Beatles had no fewer than 12 records in *Billboard* magazine's Hot 100. In 1965, the Beatles were awarded MBEs for their services to British exports.

As the noise of female fans often drowned out the music at live performances, the band grew tired of touring; they played their last concert in August 1966. After this they spent much more time in the recording studio and began to develop much more experimental music; some critics argue that albums such as *Sergeant Pepper's Lonely Hearts Club Band* (1967) were so complex and innovative that they broke down barriers between elite and popular music. By 1970, only Paul McCartney wanted to keep the Beatles going and the band broke up in that year.

In his 1981 book *Shout! The True Story of the Beatles*, Philip Norman estimates that by 1970, in addition to the huge sales of singles and albums, Beatles merchandise, including hats, bags, badges, shirts, jackets, socks, handkerchiefs, tea towels, mugs, ashtrays and jigsaw puzzles, had sold for more than £100 million.

Enquiry source 1A

According to the *Daily Mirror*, the 'police had to hold back 1000 squealing teenagers as the Beatles made their getaway after their Palladium TV show . . . A police motorcade stood by as the four pop idols dashed for their car. Then the fans went wild, breaking through a cordon of more than 60 policemen.' *The Express* agreed, although it thought that the mob of screaming girls was only five hundred strong, and amended the number of policemen to twenty. In fact, both versions were probably exaggerated: a photographer who accompanied the band to the theatre later recalled that they saw no more than eight girls, and a photograph printed in the *Daily Mail* showed McCartney leaving the theatre watched by one policeman and three girls.

Three weeks later, however, the crowds that awaited the Beatles outside the Prince of Wales Theatre in Leicester Square were certainly no figment of an editor's imagination. . . . If there was one event that confirmed the Beatles' popularity with the general public, this [the Royal Variety Performance] was it. When ITV broadcast a tape of the concert a few days later, almost twenty-six million people tuned in to watch.

From Dominic Sandbrook, *Never Had it so Good*, published in 2005

Enquiry source 1B

YEAH! YEAH! YEAH!

You have to be a real square not to love the nutty, noisy, happy, handsome Beatles. If they don't sweep your blues away – brother, you're a lost cause. If they don't put a beat in your feet – sister, you're not living. How refreshing to see these rumbustious young Beatles take a middle-aged Royal Variety performance by the scruff of their necks and have them Beatling like teenagers. Fact is that Beatle People are everywhere. From Wapping to Windsor. Aged seven to seventy. And it's plain to see why these four cheeky, energetic lads from Liverpool go down so big. They're young, new. They're high-spirited, cheerful. What a change from the self-pitying moaners, crooning their lovelorn tunes from the tortured shallows of lukewarm hearts. The Beatles are whacky. They wear their hair like a mop –but it's WASHED, it's super clean. So is their fresh young act. They don't have to rely on off-colour jokes about homos for their fun . . . Youngsters like the Beatles are doing a good turn for show business and the rest of us – with their new sounds, new looks. *Good luck Beatles!*

From the *Daily Mirror*, published on 6 November 1963

Definition

Vacuity
Vacancy of mind, thought, from 'vacuous' meaning unintelligent.

Enquiry source 1C

Those who flock round the Beatles, who scream themselves into hysteria, whose vacant faces flicker over the TV screen, are the least fortunate of their generation, the dull, the idle, the failures . . . a bottomless pit of **vacuity** . . . the huge faces bloated with cheap confectionary and smeared with chain store make-up, the open, sagging mouths and glazed eyes, the hands mindlessly drumming in time to the music, the broken stiletto heels, the shoddy, stereotyped 'with-it' clothes: here apparently, is a collective portrait of a generation enslaved by a commercial machine . . . Bewildered by a rapidly changing society, excessively fearful of becoming out of date, our leaders are increasingly turning to young people as guides and mentors . . . Indeed whatever youth likes must be good: the supreme crime, in politics and culture alike, is not to be 'with-it'.

From Paul Johnson, 'The Menace of Beatlism', published in *New Statesman* magazine on 28 February 1965

Enquiry source 1D

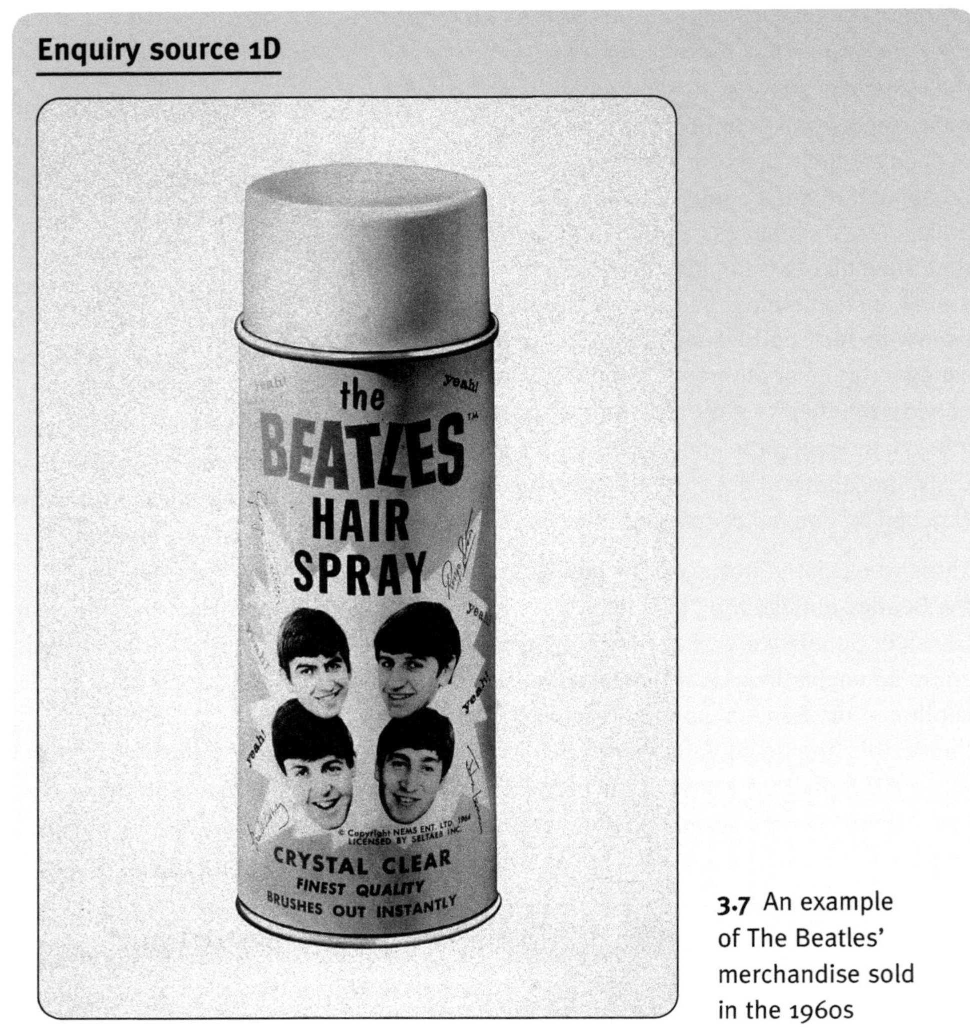

3.7 An example of The Beatles' merchandise sold in the 1960s

Enquiry source 1E

[Beatlemania] is one way of flinging off teenage restraints and letting themselves go . . . The fact that thousands of others are screaming along with her makes the girl feel she is living life to the full with people her own age . . . this emotional outlook is very necessary at her age. It is also innocent and harmless. The girls are subconsciously preparing for motherhood. Their frenzied screams are a rehearsal for that moment. Even the jelly babies [which girls threw on stage] are symbolic.

From the *News of the World*, published on 17 November 1963

Enquiry source 1G

We're more popular than Jesus now. I don't know which will go first – rock'n'roll or Christianity. Jesus was all right, but his disciples were thick and ordinary. It's twisting it that ruins it for me.

From an interview with John Lennon, published in the *Evening Standard* on 4 March 1966

Enquiry source 1F

In later years the teenagers of the sixties often remembered their formative years as the decade of the Beatles and the Rolling Stones. This is true up to a point, in that these characters monopolised the attention of the press, but . . . it is easily overstated . . . The dreadful reception of [the album] Magical Mystery Tour illustrates the fact that . . . the Beatles were never universally or unconditionally popular. Plenty of people hated them; millions more, probably a majority were generally indifferent to them and their music. And the more the Beatles departed from their conservative image of 1963, the more people disliked them . . . Show tunes, light classical music, jazz and cabaret music all thrived during the sixties . . . It was no accident that the most successful chart act of the sixties was not the Beatles, but Cliff Richard . . . The most popular Beatles' album, Please Please Me, spent forty-three weeks in the Top Ten. By comparison . . . The Sound of Music film soundtrack of 1965 remained in the Top Ten for more than five years . . . and held the number one spot for a staggering 69 weeks.

From Dominic Sandbrook, *White Heat: A History of Britain in the Swinging Sixties*, published in 2006

Enquiry source 1H

As a rebellion against restraints, the Sixties began with a flood of youthful energy bursting through the psychic dam of the Fifties. The driving force of this rebellion was The Beatles. The true revolution of the Sixties . . . was an inner one of feeling and assumption: a revolution in the head. In effect, the 'generation gap' that opened in the Fifties turned out not to be a quarrel with a particular set of parents and children, but an historical chasm between one way of life and another. The Sixties witnessed a shift from an assumption of hierarchy and fixed values to an era of multiple viewpoints and levelled standards.

From Ian MacDonald, *Revolution in the Head: The Beatles' Records and the Sixties*, published in 1994

Practice source evaluation

- List the different types of source used in Enquiry 1. Give each source a rank out of five for reliability as evidence for the impact of The Beatles on popular culture and British society, where 5 is extremely useful or reliable and 1 is not useful or is unreliable.
- Take the two sources you have ranked as the least useful or reliable and, for each one, explain why.
- Take the two sources you have ranked as the most useful or reliable and, for each one, explain why.

The whole point of evaluating sources is to determine the extent to which we can use the information provided by those sources as evidence to support our conclusions about historical problems. The more reliable or useful the source is, the more weight the information in that source should be given in our answers. Now that you have evaluated the sources in this enquiry, use the information with the appropriate weighting to answer this question:

To what extent do the sources show that The Beatles had a dramatic impact on British society between 1963 and 1970?

SKILLS BUILDER

1 Study Sources 1A, 1B, 1C and 1D and use your own knowledge.

To what extent would it be true to say that the rise of The Beatles was driven by the manipulation of young people by commercial interests?

2 Study Sources 1E, 1F, 1G and 1H and use your own knowledge.

Do you agree with the view that the Beatles were a 'driving force of . . . rebellion'?

Unit summary

What have you learned in this unit?

Youth culture existed in Britain before the arrival of rock and roll. However, rock and roll music appealed to the young in particular; it allowed record executives, clothing and merchandise sellers to tap into the lucrative youth market and to shape the style that youth culture adopted.

While mass media did popularise certain styles of music and dress, at the same time it responded to trends that already existed among certain sections of the young population. While radio and television increasingly portrayed the fresh, fun image of youth culture, and some of their programmes were aimed more specifically at a teenage audience, cinema and newspapers often dwelt on the more worrying effects of the new styles on the behaviour and attitude of young people.

The Beatles were a tremendously successful rock/pop band that benefited in many ways from the same trends that gave rise to youth culture more generally: the rising numbers and disposable wealth of young people, and their desire to create a separate image for themselves based on consumption. The Beatles influenced popular culture through their music, but also through their style and merchandise; however, their appeal was not universal and many people were indifferent to the band.

What skills have you used in this unit?

You have evaluated many different types of source to decide how far their content should be used to answer questions about the past. You have used the cross-referencing of these sources to help build an argument in answer to historical questions.

Exam tips

This is the sort of question you will find on your examination paper as an (a) question:

Study Sources G, M and 1E.

How far do Sources M and 1E support the opinion given in Source G that the different nature of teenagers was 'emphasised too much' by mass media?

Explain your answer, using the evidence of Sources G, M and 1E. (20)

Look back at the tips from Unit 2; build upon them with the tips below.

- Make sure you have a clear idea of what the question is asking: how far do Sources M and 1A suggest that mass media helped to create or exaggerated the existence of a 'generation gap'?
- Go through Sources M and 1E looking for ways in which they do support Source G, but also considering limits to this support.
- Remember to consider the provenance of the source – who wrote it, for what audience, when, the type of source it is – when deciding how much emphasis to place on the source in your answer.
- Finish your answer with a conclusion that clearly weighs up the extent to which Sources M and 1E support Source G.

RESEARCH TOPIC

The Beatles, The Rolling Stones, The Kinks, The Hollies, The Yardbirds . . .

- Go to www.pearsonhotlinks.co.uk (express code 5063P) and click on Unit 3 Research Topic. Use the websites on there to find out more about the music and fashion of some of the leading British bands of the 1960s.
- Split into groups to research a particular band and create a presentation about their impact on British popular culture.

UNIT

4 Did mass media undermine deference and promote the growth of a 'permissive society' in Britain 1954–69?

What is this unit about?

This unit explores the relationship between mass media and the relaxation of the austere attitudes discussed in Unit 2. The key question is whether cinema, television and the press exaggerated, or contributed towards, more liberal attitudes to sex, social hierarchy and authority, or whether they merely reflected changes caused by more significant, underlying factors.

Key questions

- Was there a 'cultural revolution' in Britain 1954–69?
- How far did mass media undermine a social hierarchy in this period?
- How far did mass media change British attitudes to sex between 1954 and 1969?
- Mass media 1954–69: moulder or mirror of popular culture and society?

Timeline

1954	Television Act allows the creation of commercial Independent Television
1956	John Osborne's play *Look Back in Anger* is first performed
1957	Wolfenden Committee Report recommends the liberalisation of laws that made homosexuality illegal
1959	Obscene Publications Act allows serious works of art to use 'obscene' words and images
1960	*Lady Chatterley's Lover* trial allows publication of this 'pornographic' novel
1961	*Private Eye* launches
	Suicide Act means that suicide ceases to be a crime and those who fail to kill themselves will no longer be prosecuted
1962	Colour supplements first appear in Sunday newspapers
	The Pilkington Committee Report on television is published
1964	Mary Whitehouse launches her Clean-Up TV campaign
	Television Act increases the regulatory strength of the Independent Television Authority and calls for the creation of BBC2
1965	Murder (Abolition of the Death Penalty) Act is passed. This initially suspends hanging for 5 years, before it is abolished in 1969

1967 First colour television broadcasts begin

Sexual Offences Act legalises homosexual acts between men over the age of 21, in private, in England and Wales (not in Scotland until 1980 or in Northern Ireland until 1982)

Abortion Act legalises abortion through the NHS during the first 28 weeks of pregnancy

Family Planning Act allows local health authorities to provide birth control devices. The contraceptive pill has been on sale since 1961

1968 Theatres Act abolishes censorship of plays on stage in the UK

1969 Divorce Reform Act allows divorce to be granted after 2 years of separation if both parties want it, and after 5 years if one party wants it, on the sole grounds of 'irreconcilable differences'

SKILLS BUILDER

1. What words would you use to describe these fashionable looks from 1954 and 1967?
2. Can the change in women's fashion tell us anything about broader changes in British society during these years?
3. How far do the clothes people wear today indicate their values or attitudes?

Sources A and B

4.1 and **4.2** Examples of women's fashion from 1954 and 1967

Was there a 'cultural revolution' in Britain 1954–69?

The historian Arthur Marwick has argued that the 1960s marked the end of 'Victorianism' and the rise of a more '**permissive** society'. Many right wing politicians have agreed with this interpretation and blame the 1960s for a lot of current social problems. Other historians, including Joanna Burke, have more recently argued that the 'permissive' values we so often associate with the 1960s were only really held by a small minority of the population: she argues that instead of talking about 'the Swinging Sixties' we really ought to refer to the 'cautious sixties'. Before looking at the way the media portrayed social hierarchy and sex, it is first necessary to consider the legal, financial and technological contexts in which the British people experienced the media. If a 'cultural revolution' did happen in the 1960s, it could be the case that these contextual factors were more important than the effects of mass media.

Definitions

Permissive

An attitude that allows something to be done; in particular tolerates sexual freedom.

Liberal

Broad-minded, without prejudice. Respect for individual rights and freedoms.

De jure

According to the law.

De facto

In fact, in reality, whether by right or not.

Private members' bills

Pieces of legislation that are not official government policy, or part of an election manifesto. The bills may be introduced by backbenchers from any side of the House.

Intrinsically

In itself, as opposed to extrinsic, meaning in terms of its possible effects.

The legal context

The timeline at the start of the unit gives an overview of the **liberal** legislation passed by British governments between 1959 and 1969. These laws decriminalised certain acts and relaxed the laws on other crimes relating to sex. However, just because the laws relating to abortion or homosexuality changed, it does not necessarily follow that people's attitudes towards these things changed; things may change ***de jure*** but this does not always equate to ***de facto*** changes. The journalist Peter Hitchens sees the abolition of hanging in particular as 'a victory for the elite over the people': only 18 per cent of people supported abolition in June 1966. Polls from the later 1960s consistently revealed that most people, young or old, did not welcome the more relaxed laws on homosexuality, divorce and abortion. Source C is the conclusion of historian Dominic Sandbrook.

Source C

At least as far as the transformation of public opinion is concerned, then, the concept of a permissive sixties makes little sense.

From Dominic Sandbrook, *White Heat*, published in 2006

Demand for these liberal laws came not from the people, but from certain backbench MPs who based their **private members' bills** on campaigns that had gone back several decades. Pressure for reform of the laws on homosexuality had gone back to the 1890s, for divorce laws to the 1910s, for birth control to the 1920s and abortion to the 1930s. David Steel's Abortion Act or Leo Abse's Sexual Offences Act were not the result of pressure from their constituents, but were issues that they had felt strongly about for a long time before the 1960s. Many MPs came to agree with Steel, Abse and others that laws should be based on the practical consequences of the legislation, rather than on the grounds of moral ethics. For example, rather than debate whether abortion was **intrinsically** right or wrong, Steel asked the House to consider the high number of deaths and injuries that resulted from dangerous 'back street' abortions (about 40 deaths and 100,000 injuries in 1966). Members of Parliament were allowed to vote according to their conscience on these bills, rather than having to vote according to the party line. Although these bills officially had nothing to do with the government, Roy Jenkins, Home Secretary from 1965–67, unofficially encouraged Labour support for the liberal laws. While conservatives (from all parties, hence the small 'c') worried that such laws would create a 'permissive society', he saw the changes as the measure of a 'civilised society' as shown in Source D.

Source D

Let us be on the side of people who want to be free to live their own lives, to make their own mistakes, and to decide, in an adult way and provided they do not infringe the rights of others, the code by which they wish to live; and on the side too of experiment and brightness . . . of fuller lives and greater freedom.

From Roy Jenkins, *The Labour Case*, published in 1959. Labour were in opposition at the time and did not come to power until October 1964

In his 1975 book, *Permissive Britain: Social Change in the Sixties and Seventies*, Christie Davies argued that the '**causalist**' MPs failed to consider the long-term consequences of more liberal laws; they assumed, in his view incorrectly, that moral values in society would be unaffected by these Acts of Parliament. Davies believes that it is the removal of strict, clearly defined boundaries of decent behaviour that have contributed most significantly to the 'strange death of moral and respectable Britain' since the 1970s.

Definition

Causalist

Davies invented this term to mean a view of legislation based on its social consequences rather than a 'moralist' view based on a moral code.

SKILLS BUILDER

1 In what ways does Source D show Roy Jenkins to have been a 'causalist' MP?

2 Using Source D, and the other information in this unit thus far, how far do you think it is fair to blame permissive attitudes in the 1960s for the passing of so many liberal laws during these years?

3 Do you think these laws should have been passed?

The context of greater affluence

The historian Eric Hobsbawn called the period between the 1950s and early 1970s the 'golden era' of Western capitalism. The huge growth in wealth across the Western world allowed the people of these countries to afford ever more luxuries. In Britain, almost every household had a television by 1970. Ownership of cars doubled between 1960 and 1970 from 5,650,000 to 11,802,000. During the same period the number of supermarkets grew from around 800 to over 5000; this led to the closure of around 60,000 smaller shops and gradually changed the look of the traditional high street. The table on page 52 gives a broad overview of the expansion in consumer acquisition of luxuries.

Source E

	1955	*1975*	*1995*
Vacuum cleaner	51	90	96
Washing machine	18	70	91
Refrigerator	8	85	98
Freezer	n/a (not available)	15	79
Television	35	96	98
Telephone	19	52	92
Central heating	5	47	85
Dishwasher	1	2	12
Microwave oven	n/a	n/a	47
Video recorder	n/a	n/a	70
CD player	n/a	n/a	63
Home computer	n/a	n/a	20

4.3 A table showing the percentage of British homes that had a range of consumer durable products in 1955, 1975 and 1995. From Derrick Murphy (ed.), *Britain 1914–2000*, published in 2000

Questions

1 During which years did ownership of consumer durables increase the most?
2 In your opinion do levels of wealth or material comfort have an impact on people's attitudes?

By 1970, the Central Statistical Office recorded that watching television was one of the most popular leisure activities among all social groups: men and women spent around 23 per cent of their free time in front of the small screen, twice as much as people in Belgium, Italy or Sweden. To an even greater extent than radio, the huge growth in the popularity of television in the 1950s and 1960s increased the amount of leisure time that people chose to spend in their own homes. This domestication of spare time had some important consequences for British society: in particular, class divisions that had been reinforced by more public leisure pursuits such as dog racing (working class) or playing tennis (middle class) became more blurred. Now anyone could watch the same programmes from their own homes regardless of their occupation, wealth or place of residence. To a degree, television undermined the separation of elite and popular culture: working-class people could watch shows with artistic merit (such as *The Wednesday Play*), while it was widely rumoured that even the Queen greatly enjoyed watching the music hall antics of comedians Morecambe and Wise in the 1970s. The rise of television, together with a general rise in wealth and consumerism, also spread certain fashions more quickly; it became less obvious which class a person belonged to based on dress alone. However, to say that television completely changed things would be an exaggeration: British people continued to go out for recreation, especially at the weekends. Class divisions did persist in the choice of such recreation: in 2009 there were still around 2500 working men's clubs in Britain while the Royal Opera House in Covent Garden still struggles to attract those outside the upper-middle class!

New fashions, such as **Op Art** and 'the Look', inspired by designers such as Mary Quant, with their boutiques clustered around London's King's Road and Carnaby Street, and made accessible to many by the mass production and sale of such designs in high streets across the country, meant that from the mid-1960s it was almost impossible to tell a young woman's class from the way she dressed. Barbara Hulanicki's fashion company Biba sold cheap clothes from her shops in London and across the country via mail order. The most famous model of the 1960s, Twiggy, said that whereas Mary Quant's clothes were for 'rich girls', Biba 'was for anyone'. The clothes were given a good deal of publicity in newspapers, in part because of the launch of colour sections after February 1962, and in part because of the work of a new breed of dashing photographer, including David Bailey, Brian Duffy and Terence Donovan. Mary Quant thought fashion attracted so much attention in the newspapers because it 'reflects what is really in the air': the growth of affluence, consumerism, the new confidence of youth and the changing role of women (see Unit 9). Opinion was divided about such innovations as the mini-skirt, first brought to prominence by the model Jean 'the Shrimp' Shrimpton at a racecourse in Melbourne in October 1965. Source F is a photograph of Twiggy in a mini-dress, while Sources G and H are two opinions about fashion in the mid- to late-1960s.

Definition

Op Art

A style of painting pioneered in Britain by Bridget Riley that made use of black and white (later bold colours) and geometric shapes. This style was thought to be very modern and influenced not only fashion, but design more generally.

Source F

4.4 One of the photographs that helped to establish Twiggy (Lesley Hornby) as 'the face of 1966'

Source G

The way girls model clothes . . . it's provocative. She's standing there defiantly with her legs apart saying, 'I'm very sexy, I enjoy sex, I feel provocative, but you're going to have a job to get me. You've got to excite me and you've got to be jolly marvellous to attract me. I can't be bought, but if I want you, I'll have you.'

From an interview with Mary Quant, published in *The Guardian* on 10 October 1967

Source H

Of the 17 women in my [London Underground] compartment, 12 were wearing cardigans of some sort, 10 had chosen navy blue as their colour, and 13 were wearing sandals or sandal type shoes. They all had fairly ordinary haircuts and there wasn't a mini-skirt in sight. Most people are interested in being comfortable rather than smart.

From an article by Prudence Glynn, fashion editor, published in *The Times* on 16 September 1966

SKILLS BUILDER

1 How far does Source H support Mary Quant's views about the importance of fashion in the 1960s?

2 How reliable are Quant's views about the importance of fashion to British people's attitudes in the 1960s?

3 Are Prudence Glynn's observations a more reliable guide to people's taste in fashion and attitudes more generally? Why?

Definition

Family Planning Association

A charity, founded in 1930, that provides contraceptives and advice (at first to married couples only).

The technological context: the Pill

One of the most commonly held views about the 1960s is that there was a 'sexual revolution': young people in particular are thought to have had sex more often and with more people. Many historians have sought to explain this change through the rise of the contraceptive pill: the historians Akhtar and Humphries argue, 'The years between 1965 and 1969 were when the sexual revolution began in Britain. The pace of change was astonishing – and the Pill made it all possible.' The Pill was developed in America in the mid-1950s and was first prescribed by British doctors in January 1961. By 1964, around 480,000 women were taking the Pill. However, at the discretion of many GPs, and as a rule by the **Family Planning Association**, access to the Pill was restricted to married women until 1970; it was not until the 1970s and 1980s that the Pill rivalled the condom as the contraceptive of choice for most Britons.

Two major surveys, Michael Schofield's *The Sexual Behaviour of Young People* (1965) and Geoffrey Gorer's *Sex and Marriage in England Today* (1971), suggest that notions of a 'sexual revolution' in the 1960s are hugely exaggerated and greatly misleading. Schofield found that only 18 per cent of girls and 10 per cent of boys in his sample of 2000 teenagers had had sex with more than three people, and that 17 per cent of girls and 33 per cent of boys had had sex by the age of 19. He concluded that while promiscuity existed among teenagers, this was far from normal behaviour. Gorer's study revealed that 96 per cent of women and 95 percent of men were married by the age of 45, and that the average age of marriage for women fell below 23 in 1970, down from 25 in 1946. As mentioned above, most people continued to hold conservative attitudes towards divorce and homosexuality; the only significant change was that young people were more tolerant of sex before marriage than their parents' generation had been. These surveys hardly reveal a popular revolution in attitude to sex in the 1960s.

How far did mass media undermine a rigid social hierarchy 1954–69?

Television

We have already seen that television developed rapidly as a mass medium after the Queen's coronation in 1953; 4 per cent of households had a television set in 1950, rising to 40 per cent in 1955, 80 per cent in 1960 and 95 per cent in 1969. In 1955, the BBC monopoly on television ended when 14 independent companies were allowed to begin broadcasting funded by advertising. The 1954 Television Act had only given ITV a licence to broadcast for 10 years and a review was needed to extend this; in 1962 the **BBC Charter** was also due for renewal. In July 1960, the government set up a Committee of Inquiry on Broadcasting to assess the impact of television thus far, and to make recommendations for its future. The Committee was chaired by Sir Harry Pilkington and its members included Richard Hoggart, whose views strongly influenced much of the report. Source I is a collection of extracts from the report that the committee delivered in 1962.

Source I

Paragraph 38

For television . . . A large volume of sharply critical submissions reached us. Such a volume of critical interest was to be expected since television now plays so great a part in the lives of many millions. Here, as in sound broadcasting, we find that people are disposed to criticise what they dislike rather than to praise what they admire. But this rapidly developing medium has also inspired great hopes . . . It was perhaps largely because they realised what television had done, and could do, that people and organisations which wrote to us as viewers were conscious of what it had done badly, or failed to do at all; of how it had abused its power, and failed to realise its possibilities.

Paragraph 206

Foreign programmes, usually of American origin, were . . . criticised not because they were foreign, but because of their content . . . It is not enough to satisfy the statutory requirement as to the amount of foreign material if the quality is ignored.

Paragraph 254

Advertisements which appeal to human weakness could well in the long run have a deplorable individual and social effect . . . More exacting standards would not necessarily make advertising too restricted, drab and unexciting.

From the *Report of the Committee on Broadcasting, 1960*, published in 1962

Hoggart was particularly worried about the effects of 'vulgar' American-style programmes on ITV. He thought that game shows such as *Double Your Money* and *Take Your Pick* (both 1955–68) would erode traditional British culture, and that crime dramas and Westerns would make people more violent. He also worried that advertising would increase the materialism and commercialisation of British people and popular culture. A good number of the Report's recommendations were ignored by the government, but the 1964 Television Act did increase the power of the ITV

Definition

BBC Charter

A series of rules by which the BBC must operate to justify its funding by licence fee. Legally this is renewed every 10 years by the monarch, but some feel that governments have put ever greater pressure on the BBC to conform to its needs before the Charter is now renewed.

SKILLS BUILDER

1. What can we learn from Source I about the concerns of the Pilkington Committee?
2. Look back at Richard Hoggart's views on popular culture in *The Uses of Literature* on page 38. What evidence is there in Source I that his opinions dominated the Pilkington Report?
3. How much can we learn about the impact of television on British people before 1962 from these extracts from the Pilkington Report?

regulator, the Independent Television Authority: after 1964, ITV companies had to screen two plays and two current affairs programmes in addition to the news each week to fulfil their public service obligation. The Report also led to the creation of BBC2 in April 1964 to further increase public service broadcasting.

The Report's emphasis on the need for quality drama on television led to a demand for new plays from British playwrights. The *Wednesday Play* (BBC1 1964–70) helped launch the career of influential writers Dennis Potter and Nell Dunn, and director Ken Loach. Sydney Newman, the head of drama at the BBC at the time, insisted that 'great art has to stem from . . . the period in which it is created'. Writers responded with hard-hitting, '**social realist**' plays such as *Up the Junction* (1965) with a powerful home abortion scene and *Cathy Come Home* (1966) about homelessness. Producers and directors were hugely innovative in this period. At the start of the 1960s, plays on television, such as those of *Armchair Theatre* (ITV 1956–63), were broadcast live and were essentially the same as plays at the theatre. By the mid-1960s, Loach and others had begun to shoot many scenes on location and 'vision mix' them with live studio footage. This made the films much more realistic: many viewers were unsure whether the scenes shot on location were fiction or news clips. The BBC Board of Governors was so concerned about this that in 1965 it banned *The War Game*, a play about a nuclear attack on Britain; it was not broadcast until 1985.

Definition

Social realist

An artistic style that portrays ordinary people going about their everyday lives. It often focuses on the working classes, hardship and struggle.

While these plays had a tremendous impact on the 6–10 million people who saw them, they did not directly change things very much. The passage of the 1967 Abortion Act was possibly eased by the popular reaction to *Up the Junction*, but clearly had far more to do with David Steel's campaign. Similarly, the launch of Shelter, a charity for homeless people, on 1 December 1966, had been planned for a long time; it was sheer co-incidence that *Cathy Come Home* had only been screened two weeks before this. Shelter acknowledges that it did gain a surge of support in the light of public discussion of the play. Birmingham City Council also relaxed its rules about husbands and wives staying together in their shelters, after the play was screened.

While *The Wednesday Play* discussed controversial topics, they did not portray or inspire a rebellion of working-class opinion against their social superiors. On the contrary, the working classes generally held the most conservative opinions about liberal reforms. The programme that working-class viewers identified with the most was the soap opera *Coronation Street*. Launched in December 1960, it had a twice weekly audience of 20 million within its first year. Northern viewers in particular identified with the ordinary backdrop to the drama – the home, the shop, the pub – and the strong female characters, such as Elsie Tanner, who evoked a feeling of nostalgia for wartime community. *Coronation Street* represented a genuine working-class culture; it portrayed those who longed for change and advancement, such as Ken Barlow (see the Introduction), as exceptional in a community where people may have grumbled about life but got on with things in a practical fashion.

A programme that did genuinely challenge social superiors and figures of authority was *That Was The Week That Was* (*TW3*), launched in November 1962. It represented the pinnacle of the '**satire** boom' that had begun in the late 1950s with comedians such as Peter Cook and Dudley Moore, and evolved in the early 1960s through their contribution to the highly successful *Beyond the Fringe* stage show. *TW3* combined current affairs with stand-up comedy; at its peak it received 12 million viewers a week and was said to empty many pubs late on Saturday night when it was screened. Reginald Bevins, the Postmaster General who oversaw broadcasting, tried to have *TW3* stopped; he was prevented by Prime Minister Harold MacMillan (even though he was the target of many jokes) who recognised the damage that would be done by attacking such a popular programme. Despite its short run of two series, *TW3* did help to make journalists less deferential to politicians. In doing so, it paved the way for investigative journalists who subsequently unearthed many political scandals. It was not popular with everyone as the two interviews in Source J show.

Definition

Satire

Humour that makes fun of (usually famous) people; it often exposes their vices.

Source J

Something new was happening in the way that the general public was allowed to perceive its rulers . . . Television opened up politics and the political debate to everybody. You opened the door between the servants' quarters and the respectable folk and allowing the servants to see what was going on. That I think was what offended people who wrote in to the newspapers and shouted that this kind of television shouldn't be allowed.

I think a lot of people are just outraged. I occasionally watch it with my parents. After a while my father would say, 'Do we have to watch this stuff'. It got your teeth on edge sometimes when it started being rude about the Queen. I think that was something that really upset people. It was one thing to discuss the monarchy as an institution, quite another to be personal about the Queen.

From John Bassett and Mary Balmer, interviewed on *Carry on Up the Zeitgeist: Saturday Night Saturnalia*, first broadcast on Radio 2 on 17 April 1992

TW3 was one of the programmes that inspired Mary Whitehouse (see Biography on page 79), a housewife from Nuneaton, to launch her Clean-Up TV campaign on 27 January 1964. The first meeting, held on 5 May in Birmingham Town Hall, was attended by around 2000 people, mostly middle-aged women. By this time, she claimed that she already had 120,000 signatures in support of her Manifesto, of which Source K is an extract.

Source K

We women of Britain believe in a Christian way of life . . . [We shall] fight for the right to bring up our own children in the truth of the Christian faith, and to protect our homes from the exhibitions of violence. We object to the propaganda of disbelief, doubt and dirt that the BBC projects into millions of homes through the television screen. [The BBC should] encourage and sustain faith in God and bring Him back to the heart of our family and our national life.

From Mary Whitehouse and Norah Buckland, *Manifesto* of Clean-Up TV, written in 1964

In 1965, she renamed the organisation the National Viewers and Listeners Association (NVLA); she continued to attack all sorts of programmes but toned down the Christian basis of her criticism to attract more supporters.

SKILLS BUILDER

1 How far does Source J support the idea that television undermined figures of authority in the 1960s?

2 How far do Sources I, J and K agree about the impact of television on British society in the 1960s?

3 Using Sources I, K and the other information from this unit, which do you think had the greater effect on class relations in Britain in the 1960s: satire or social realism on television?

Cinema

We have already seen that cinema attendance began to fall after 1946. Despite the government's abolition of the Entertainments Tax on cinema tickets in 1960, attendance figures fell even further between 1954 and 1969 as the table below shows.

Question

What do you think was the major reason for the fall in cinema admissions during this period?

Source L

Year	*Total cinema admissions (in millions)*
1954	1276
1964	343
1974	138
1984	53
1994	106
2004	160

4.5 A table showing total cinema attendance figures in the UK, published in 1998 and 2005. Source: Office for National Statistics

Shrinking audiences meant that over half the cinemas in the country were forced to close between 1955 and 1963. Despite this, a number of memorable British films were made in this period. One of major genres of British film in the late 1950s and 1960s was the 'New Wave'. These were hard, gritty films about the everyday life of working-class people, usually in the north of England, shot in black and white. Part of their inspiration came from the stage, where John Osbourne's play, *Look Back in Anger*, was first performed in May 1956. The play, the first example of what became known as 'kitchen sink' drama, was different from anything else around at the time, as shown in the interviews in Sources M, N and O.

Source M

I was living in London and one morning one of my friends said let's go to the theatre. It was *Look Back in Anger*. We heard so much about it we just had to see this play. I was just transfixed. The curtains drew back and the first shock was the stage: it was just so depressing. Normally when the curtains open we'd seen the drawing room, the rather elegant furniture, the desk, the windows, the long curtains, charming furniture, charming people. We knew it wasn't that sort of play, but it was the first time I saw this rather dingy room, and there was this rather drably dressed woman at an ironing board. I was sitting in my chair getting really incensed. I couldn't wait for it to be over so I could give my friend a piece of my mind! He was rude, coarse and his poor wife was standing there ironing; he couldn't stand that she had an upper class accent and upper class manners. She was so patient that it made the viewer really impatient.

From Bernice Coup, a London housewife, interviewed on *Carry on up the Zeitgeist*, first broadcast on Radio 2 on 3 April 1992

Source N

[Jimmy Porter] was a hero! He was right! His discontent, his anguish, his disgust at the world is the proper way to regard a disgusting world. I thought it absolutely wonderful! Terrific – witty, fast, it gave a young man like me a modish aggression. Lots of young artists, writers, rebels suddenly found their rebellion licensed and suddenly found a behaviour pattern for their aggression.

From Edward Pearce, a student in London in the late 1950s, interviewed on *Carry on up the Zeitgeist*, first broadcast on Radio 2 on 3 April 1992. Jimmy Porter was the lead character, a young man who shouts angrily about the monarchy, the church, the middle classes, and even his mum. He famously says 'People of our generation aren't able to die for good causes any longer. There aren't any good, brave causes left'

Source O

For the first time I was recognising people on stage that I lived with . . . For the first time my own generation was on stage by right, saying the kinds of things that we argued about at university, but saying them in public to an audience that were not used to hearing them. This was a challenge, a confrontation with a generation that was saying to their generation 'What kind of a mess have you made and what are you going to do about it?' And not saying it tragically, saying it with a cock-sure, derisory self-confidence.

From *The Guardian* theatre critic Kenneth Tynan, interviewed on *Carry on up the Zeitgeist*, first broadcast on Radio 2 on 3 April 1992

In 1958, *Look Back in Anger* was made into a film. A number of other 'New Wave' films followed:

- *Room at the Top* (1959)
- *Saturday Night and Sunday Morning* (1960)
- *A Taste of Honey* (1961) (The only one with a female lead character)
- *A Kind of Loving* (1962)
- *The Loneliness of a Long Distance Runner* (1962)
- *Billy Liar* (1963)
- *This Sporting Life* (1963)
- *Kes* (1970).

While the 'New Wave' films placed working-class lives, concerns and accents on the big screen, many working-class people did not enjoy them, preferring the comedies discussed on page 62. One reason is that these films were written and directed by middle-class men. The films presented a stereotyped view of the working classes as earthy and pleasure seeking. The films were also dominated by tough men, and did not deal with important issues of race, gender or sexuality. As such, the films tell the historian more about middle-class concerns about 'the state of the nation', than about the working classes.

SKILLS BUILDER

1 What do Sources M, N and O suggest about the way in which men and women reacted to *Look Back in Anger?*

2 The interview extracts in Sources M, N and O are all responses to the stage version of the play; does this limit the value of these sources as evidence of the impact of 'kitchen sink' drama on British people in the late 1950s?

3 What features do 'New Wave' films have in common with social realist television from the 1960s?

4 Does the fact that 'New Wave' films were made by middle-class directors make them entirely useless to historians trying to find out about the lives and attitudes of the British working classes in the 1960s?

The press

Between 1951 and 1970, newspaper circulation fell from 16.8 million to 14.6 million; five national daily newspapers were forced to close after 1960. The table below gives figures for the sales of the leading national newspapers between 1939 and 1999.

Source P

	1939	*1951*	*1960*	*1970*	*1980*	*1990*	*1999*
Daily Express	2486	4193	4130	3607	2325	1585	1091
Daily Herald	2000	2071	1467				
Daily Mail	1510	2245	2084	1917	1985	1708	2357
The Sun				1509	3873	3855	3701
Daily Mirror	1367	4567	4545	4697	3651	3083	2341
Daily Sketch	850	777	1152	806			
Daily Star					1033	833	613
The Daily Telegraph	640	976	1155	1402	1456	1076	1044
The Guardian	51	140	190	303	375	424	393
The Independent						411	224
News Chronicle	1317	1586	1206				
The Times	213	245	255	402	316	420	727
Today						540	
TOTAL circulation	10,434	16,809	16,184	14,643	14,978	13,935	12,491

4.6 A table showing the circulation of British national newspapers in thousands of copies from 1939 to 1999. Source: Audit Bureau of Circulations

In a bid to boost sales, and attract some of the huge amount of advertising revenue that had gone to commercial television since 1955, newspapers tried ever more populist tactics. News headlines became punchier and an ever greater share of the front page was given over to images rather than words. A further innovation to attract advertising revenue was the introduction of colour supplements in Sunday newspapers in 1962. In the wake of the satire boom, tabloid newspapers in particular became more scathing in their treatment of politicians and political scandal. A good example of this is the treatment in the press of John Profumo, Conservative Minister for War, in June 1963.

Whereas in the past politicians had usually been allowed to keep their private lives out of the media (for example David Lloyd George, Prime Minister 1916–22 had an affair with his secretary for years), this was increasingly no longer the case. Not only had Profumo had an affair with a 'call-girl', Christine Keeler, but there were rumours she was simultaneously having an affair with a Soviet spy, hardly good for national security. Even so, Profumo might have escaped the attention of the national press, which only ran the story after his resignation on 5 June, had it not been for the satirical stories run by *Private Eye* magazine. The *Eye*, founded by Richard Ingrams, Christopher Booker and Willy Rushden in October 1961, did not target one political party in particular, but wanted to 'simply poke fun at the powers that be'. Although it only had 10,000 readers at the time, its exposé of the scandal in March 1963 led Labour politicians to demand that Profumo deny the allegations in parliament, and that a Commission of Enquiry be set up to investigate the affair. Profumo did deny the rumours on 4 June, which made his resignation the next day all the more scandalous: he had lied to parliament.

Prime Minister Harold Macmillan asked Lord Denning to lead the Commission of Enquiry. When his report was published on 26 September 1963, it became a best-seller. When *The Daily Telegraph* published the report in full, readers were amazed by such scandalous stories about political elites as 'The Man in the Mask', a member of the Cabinet who had served dinner at a private party while naked except for a mask, a small lace apron, and a card around his neck reading 'If my services don't please you, whip me'. The publication of the report did a great deal of damage to the reputation of the Conservative Party; although Macmillan had been ill for some time, the scandal surely contributed to his resignation in October 1963.

Politicians had generally not been held in high regard by the British people since 1945, but this was usually due to what people saw as their self-interest or untrustworthiness. The 1960s, because of the increased willingness of the press to attack political elites on a personal level, saw the association of political elites with 'sleaze'. As we shall see, this trend increased in the 1970s and 1980s, and began to extend even to members of the royal family.

How far did mass media change British attitudes to sex between 1954 and 1969?

Television

We have already seen that Mary Whitehouse felt that there was too much violence on television, but she also complained about 'sexy innuendoes, suggestive clothing and behaviour' on the BBC. While some of *The Wednesday Play* dramas did deal with sexually related issues, and you could see girls in mini-skirts on the pop music shows such as *Ready! Steady! Go!* (ITV 1963–66), there was no sex on television in this period. Possibly the most sexualised element of all broadcasting were the advertisements on ITV: see the research task in Unit 9.

Cinema

While the 'New Wave' films were artistically important, they were not the biggest hits at the box office. The most successful film of those listed on page 59 was *Saturday Night and Sunday Morning*, and even this was only the fourth most popular film of 1960. The biggest British hits of the 1960s, the *Carry On* comedies and James Bond films, were overtly sexual in very different ways. At least one, and sometimes two, *Carry On* films were released every year between 1958 and 1976. The jokes were largely centred on the music hall staples of slapstick, toilet humour and sexual innuendo, with busty Barbara Windsor often the centre of attention. Sean Connery starred in five hugely successful Bond films in the 1960s, starting with *Dr. No* (1962). The key to Bond's success was undoubtedly the backdrop of the Cold War, with the Cuban Missile Crisis in 1962, the Vietnam War from 1965 to 1975, and, in Britain, the discovery of a spy ring in the highest positions of authority in the secret service between 1955 and 1979. However, the powerful glamour of Bond, and the scantily clad Bond girls, such as Ursula Andress as Honey Ryder in *Dr. No*, contributed to the films' success. Other British films that had a sexual focus included *A Taste of Honey* (1961) about single parents, *Victim* (1961) on homosexuality and *Darling* (1965), starring Julie Christie as Diana, a **socialite** who uses sex to get to the top. Source Q is how one modern film reviewer summarised the film.

Source Q

Its portrayal of a fashionable London 'jet-set' through Diana, Robert and their on/off relationship, covers subjects such as sex, homosexuality, age difference, fidelity, betrayal, jealousy, pregnancy and abortion, though even by the standards of the time *Darling* is not especially daring or realistic.

From Ewan Davidson's 2003 review of *Darling* which can be viewed on the Screenonline website

Question

Does Source Q suggest that films in the 1960s were very modest with regard to their sexual content?

Definition

Socialite

A prominent person in fashionable society; a modern example is the 'it girl'.

In terms of their influence on British people's attitudes to sex, it is highly questionable whether these films had much of an impact at all. As discussed in Unit 2, such films are usually about escapism and the values depicted on screen are not necessarily those by which people live in the real world. The popularity of such films suggests the British were far from prudish about sex on screen.

The press

The launch of colour supplements, sexualised adverts and scandalous news stories contributed to a generally more permissive air in the media. However, it was not until 1969 that the first exposed female nipple was published in a British newspaper; media tycoon Rupert Murdoch (see Biography Box on page 92), clearly thought this was one way to boost the circulation of his new newspaper, *The Sun*. Like cinema however, it is questionable how far the press altered British attitudes to sex. Source R shows the opinion of two anonymous 'men on the street' from 1971.

Source R

As far as I'm concerned, permissive society is a mass media thing . . . Everyone believes we're living in a permissive society when nobody actually knows what it is.

I think there was just as much sex 50 years ago as there is today; it's more permissive in what it allows people to know. Things that were hidden 50 years ago have come out into the open. It's no better or worse than it has ever been.

From anonymous members of the public, interviewed on *Everything you need to know about the Permissive Society*, first broadcast on Radio 4 on 22 July 1971

Unit summary

What have you learned in this unit?

The years 1954–69 did see a number of changes in British popular culture. These changes were in large measure driven by the greater affluence of a society that enjoyed the 'golden era' of capitalism. British people bought more luxuries and increasingly came to define themselves in terms of what they bought. Mass media encouraged this through advertising and the depiction of glamour. However, while the media was more permissive in what it portrayed, it is not clear how far this altered people's morals and attitudes.

There were a number of important liberal laws passed in this period, but this does not necessarily mean that the British people themselves became more liberal in their outlook. While young people may have gone for the latest, more revealing look, and a minority had promiscuous sex lives, most people continued to dress and think conservatively.

Mass media did begin to **democratise** society through its portrayal of the working classes, more so on television than at the cinema, and through its attacks, especially satirical ones, on political elites.

What skills have you used in this unit?

You have not only analysed the information contained in a range of sources, but also made inferences from suggestions raised by those sources. You have compared and contrasted sources to try and arrive at a convincing conclusion about the impact of mass media on British society and popular culture between 1954 and 1969. You have weighed up the significance of mass media when compared with other important factors that may have influenced British attitudes on a range of issues in this period.

Definition

Democratise

The removal of barriers of class or rank in society.

SKILLS BUILDER

1 Which mass medium do you think had the greatest impact on British society and popular culture between 1954 and 1969: television, cinema or the press?

2 Set up a debate: 'This class believes the 1960s were swinging'. Remember to use people's views from the time (for and against) when you set out your case.

3 Look back over Units 3 and 4. What evidence is there that the British people became commercialised between 1954 and 1969? What role did mass media play in this?

Exam tips

This is the sort of question you will find appearing on the examination paper as a (b) question.

Study Sources C, K and R and use your own knowledge.

Do you agree with the view, expressed in Source R, that the existence of a 'permissive society' in the 1960s was 'a mass media thing'?

Even before you read them, make a list of the possible points that could crop up in the sources. In what ways could mass media have contributed to a more permissive society? How far did mass media *exaggerate* the existence of a permissive society? What criteria could you use to judge this? You could make a table like the one shown below to set down these points before you look at the sources.

	Point 1	Point 2	Point 3	Point 4
Details from the sources that support this point				
Details from the sources that go against this point				
Overall paragraph shape				

- With your possible points in mind, look at Source R. Pick out different bits of information that support or challenge the importance of each point; note these extracts in your table under the appropriate point heading.
- Now do the same for Sources C and K.
- Not all the columns of the table will be filled as some points may not crop up in the sources. In your essay, focus on the points that *have* cropped up in the sources.

You are now ready to write your essay, using each column of the table as the basis of a paragraph.

Remember to:

- directly answer the question in the first line of each paragraph
- use cross-referenced extracts from the sources to support the point
- include some of your own background knowledge to further illustrate which sources give a more accurate view of the historical question in hand: remember, sources are generally only *representations* of 'the truth'!
- use your own knowledge to add key points which are not raised in the sources.

RESEARCH TOPIC

1 Watch clips from one of the 'New Wave' films listed on page 59. If possible, watch the whole film. As you watch the film, make notes on the following questions:

- Which problems face the working-class characters in this film?
- How does the director emphasise the focus of the audience on the working classes?
- Which characters do the audience sympathise with most and why?
- What can we learn from this film about working-class life and attitudes in the 1960s (for example, living conditions, jobs, leisure pursuits, family relationships, attitudes to sex and gender)?

2 Once you have seen the film, compare your notes with others in groups of four, or as a whole class.

3 If possible, split into groups to research the same questions and feed back to the class on each film listed on page 59.

UNIT

5 Anarchy in the UK? Media, popular culture and society in the 1970s

What is this unit about?

The 1970s are usually regarded as a disastrous decade for Britain. This unit focuses on how mass media and popular culture responded to the economic problems, violence and terrorism that marred these years. This unit also considers the extent to which mass media contributed to a further liberalisation of moral codes that had begun to occur in the 1960s.

Key questions

- How far were the 1970s a disastrous decade for the British?
- How far did mass media and popular culture reflect or **exacerbate** the social and economic tensions of the 1970s?
- How far did mass media spread permissive attitudes in British society?
- How far did mass media undermine authority in the 1970s?

Definition

Exacerbate

To make things worse.

Timeline

1969		The Troubles begin in Northern Ireland and continue throughout the 1970s
		Voting age is reduced from 21 to 18 years
1970		Equal Pay Act prohibits different pay or working conditions according to gender. It comes into force in 1975
		Matrimonial Property Act takes into account the work that women do in the home to ensure that they get a fair division of wealth in divorce
	June	Conservatives win General Election. Edward Heath becomes Prime Minister
1971	**February**	Currency is decimalised: end of shillings and 240 pence in the pound
	March	Women's Liberation march in London
	June	The *Oz* magazine obscenity trial. The owners of this magazine are found guilty of breaking the obscenity laws with their 'School Kids' edition, but are released from prison on appeal
		Widespread protests over Margaret Thatcher's decision to ban free school milk
1972	**January**	Miners go on strike for 47 days

Year	Date	Event
	30 January	'Bloody Sunday': 27 protesters are shot and 14 of these are killed by British troops in the Bogside area of Londonderry, Northern Ireland
		BBC introduces Ceefax
		Lord Longford publishes his self-funded report into the pornography industry
1973		Britain joins the European Economic Community, the forerunner of the European Union
		Independent Broadcasting Authority Act allows the establishment of commercial radio stations in Britain
1974	**February**	Miners' strike. Heath orders a 3-day week to conserve energy from January to March
	October	Harold Wilson secures the backing of the Liberals to form a Labour government after the return of a hung parliament in the General Election
	21 November	The IRA kill 21 people in an explosion in Birmingham
		Prevention of Terrorism Act gives emergency powers to police forces where they suspect terrorism
1975		Sex Discrimination Act establishes the Equal Opportunities Commission to enforce the Equal Pay Act
		First punk rock bands emerge in London. The Sex Pistols form in December
1976	**April**	Wilson resigns and James Callaghan becomes Prime Minister
		Race Relations Acts sets up the Commission for Racial Equality to enforce laws that prevent racial discrimination
1977		The Committee on the Future of Broadcasting submits its report. This leads to launch of Channel 4 in 1980
		Queen Elizabeth II's Silver Jubilee
		Obscene Publications Act is amended to include the showing and distribution of films
1978		Louise Brown, the first test-tube baby is born
1979		Many public sector workers go on strike over low pay: the 'Winter of Discontent' begins
	May	Conservatives win the General Election. Margaret Thatcher becomes the first female Prime Minister of the UK

Source A

5.1 Front cover of a fanzine used to promote the Sex Pistols' 1976 **Anarchy** in the UK tour

SKILLS BUILDER

1 What words would you use to describe the woman's image in Source A?

2 What values or attitudes does this image suggest the woman had?

3 How far does this image suggest that British society was anarchic in the 1970s?

Definitions

Anarchy

Literally 'without government', it can more generally mean a state of social confusion.

Nostalgia

A longing for conditions or things from the recent past.

How far were the 1970s a disastrous decade for the British?

Until recently, the 1970s were thought to be a time best forgotten: a decade full of tension and an absence of good taste. The historian Arthur Marwick has suggested that 'Perhaps violence, racial tension and terrorism are the most important social phenomena of the 1970s'. While there are grounds for such judgement, many people who lived through the 1970s look back on those years with a keen sense of **nostalgia**. There was a quick succession of distinctive styles, from the hippies' flared trousers at the start of the decade, through to the punks' ripped, safety-pinned clothes at the end of the decade, which challenged the status quo. The 1970s could be seen as the decade when the permissive values of a small minority in the 1960s became more widely discussed, experienced and, perhaps, accepted by British people. If this is the case, then it must be assessed whether mass media and popular culture drove such changes in people's attitudes, or whether the changes reflected the impact of more significant, underlying factors.

The financial context

1973 saw the end of the 'golden era' of capitalism. In October that year, a number of Arab states invaded Israel. In retaliation for American support for Israel, the Arab members of the Organization of the Petroleum Exporting Countries (OPEC) stopped the supply of oil to the USA.

The price of oil soon quadrupled as a result. The pound had already been devalued in 1967, so the cost of all imports rose. The 'oil shock', the devaluation of the pound and huge cuts in government spending sent the British economy into a damaging recession. Between 1974 and 1978 the standard of living fell for the first time since the start of the 1950s; unemployment rose from 2 per cent to 4.7 per cent of the population. Inflation, usually not a problem in a stagnant economy, averaged 13 per cent in the 1970s and rose as high as 25 per cent in 1975: a weekly shop that had cost £25 in 1970 cost £115 in 1983. The price rises led trade unions to demand higher wages, which further worsened inflation: a truly vicious cycle! Government efforts to limit pay increases led to a tense struggle with the unions; this was widely reported in the media. Miners caused power cuts and even a 3-day working week when they went on strike in 1972 and 1974. Things grew even worse in the winter of 1978–79 when public sector workers went on strike: litter was not collected by dustmen and piled up in the streets; in one Liverpool graveyard the workers refused to bury the dead! The inflation, unemployment and strikes all contributed to a general feeling that Britain was in a state of serious, perhaps terminal decline. Source B is one historian's view of the 1970s.

Questions

1. How does Source B suggest that economic problems affected the British people in the 1970s?
2. Do you think economic problems could affect popular culture or mass media?

Source B

Almost everyone who has reflected seriously about Britain in the 1970s agrees that the decade was little short of a disaster . . . Britain was beset by economic failure. The trade unions acted like robber barons, holding the rest of the country to ransom. Inflation stalked the land destroying the social fabric. Ordinary people constantly found themselves bullied by powers outside their control. This was a period of strikes, power cuts and discontents.

From Nick Tiratsoo, *From Blitz to Blair: a New History of Britain Since 1939*, published in 1997

The political context

The financial problems of the 1970s undermined the economic consensus that had existed between the Labour and Conservative parties since the end of the Second World War. Instead of **Butskellism**, British people seemed to face an increasingly stark choice between the strongly left-wing rule of the trade unions and a strongly right-wing, perhaps even fascist, government. On the left, union leaders such as Jack Jones of the Transport and General Workers Union and Joe Gormley of the National Union of Miners, seemed to be the most powerful men in the country: in every instance the government had to give in to union demands for wage increases. On the right, Margaret Thatcher, leader of the Conservative Party from 1975, gradually emerged as the voice of reaction against the 'mob rule' of the unions. Many people sympathised with the unions at the start of the decade, but the disruption to everyday life caused by the strikes led to a loss of support as the decade wore on.

Definition

Butskellism

A blend of R. **But**ler (Conservative Chancellor 1951–55) and H. Gait**skell** (Labour Chancellor 1950–51); economic policies acceptable to both parties.

The other major source of tension was Northern Ireland. Tension between Protestants and Catholics erupted into violence in 1969; the British government sent in troops to try and restore order. However, events such

Definitions

Bloody Sunday

27 protesters were shot and 14 of these killed by British troops in the Bogside area of Londonderry, Northern Ireland.

Draconian

Named after Draco, a law-maker in ancient Athens, it means severe, harsh or strict.

Women's lib

A movement for the recognition and extension of women's rights.

Question

Around 2 million women listened to *Women's Hour* in the 1970s. How far do you think interviews with women such as Germaine Greer would affect British society?

as **Bloody Sunday** only inflamed the situation: the violence escalated in the 1970s and spread to mainland Britain, with Provisional IRA bombs set off in London, Birmingham and Guildford. The government saw this as the biggest threat to British security since the Second World War and passed the Prevention of Terrorism Act. This was a **draconian** piece of legislation that, among other things, allowed the police to arrest people merely on suspicion that they were plotting acts of terrorism.

Both the trade union disputes and the violence in Northern Ireland had deep, complex roots. However, it must be assessed whether the British media and popular culture reflected or perhaps fuelled these tensions with slanted views or representations.

The social context

There were a number of significant social changes that began to take place in the 1970s. The 1969 Divorce Reform Act and the 1970 Matrimonial Property Act made it easier for women in particular to seek a divorce. Within a year the rate of divorce doubled to 100,000. In 1965, there were only 2.8 divorces per 1000 population; by 1975 this had increased to 9.6 and by 1980 there were 12 per 1000, a figure only slightly less than the number of marriages. At the same time, an increasing number of married women went out to work: in 1951, only a quarter did so; this rose to half by 1970 and three-quarters by 1990. The 1970s saw the growth of '**women's lib**': the National Women's Conference first met in February 1970 to demand equal pay, free contraception and childcare. In 1972, the feminist magazine *Spare Rib* was launched. The founders of the magazine also staged a demonstration against the Miss World competition that year. In October 1970, the Australian academic Germaine Greer published *The Female Eunuch*, in which, among other things, she argued for an end to marriage. The book was widely discussed, not only because it reflected the experiences and emotions of many women, but also because Greer made frequent appearances on television and radio.

By the start of the 1970s, the era of mass black and Asian immigration to Britain was over: their combined population had already risen from 337,000 in 1961 to 650,000 in 1971. The only significant influx after this was when 30,000 Ugandan Asians were granted refuge after they were forced to flee by dictator Idi Amin. However, immigrants continued to settle in only a few towns and cities; in such places, racial tension developed (see Unit 9). Source C comments on racial tension in Birmingham and the relationship between this tension and mass media and popular culture.

Source C

It did a tremendous amount of good having an ordinary character in there who happened to be black. It is important to remember that this happened around the time that Enoch Powell [see Unit 9] was making all those terrible 'rivers of blood' speeches, and British television audiences needed to see someone like Melanie every week. She was someone they could identify with. I remember feeling apprehensive about appearing on television every week. Powell caused a great deal of racial tension and I was worried people in the street would recognise me, and be hostile towards me. But when I went into Birmingham, fans of the show would stop me and ask about Crossroads. They loved the programme and obviously liked Melanie. I never had any trouble.

From an interview with Cleo Sylvestre, who played Melanie Harper in the ITV soap opera *Crossroads*, in Stephen Bourne, *Black in the British Frame*, published in 2005

Questions

1 What can we learn about the impact of mass media on race relations in Britain in the 1970s from Source C?
2 What type of television programme do you think would have the most impact on the way that women or racial minorities were perceived by the British?

How far did mass media and popular culture reflect or exacerbate the social and economic tensions of the 1970s?

Television

Of all mass media in the 1970s, television was possibly the most important. There were only three television channels, BBC1, BBC2 and the ITV **franchises**, and, as 95 per cent of British households had a television set, the potential audience for a popular programme was very large. On average, between 1977 and 1979, people watched 16 hours of television per week in the summer and 20 hours in the winter; children and the elderly watched the most television, while women saw more than men. As so many people saw the same programmes, the content of these shows formed an important part of the next day's conversations at school, work or home. The impact of television was further enhanced by the spread of broadcasts and reception in colour: BBC2 began colour broadcasts in 1967, with BBC1 following in November 1969. The percentage of colour television sets increased from 1.7 in 1970 to 70 in 1979. Some authorities were worried about the impact of gory colour reports on the Troubles in Northern Ireland or the Vietnam War that dragged on until 1975, but this did not stop the rise of colour television as the norm.

Definition

Franchise

The authorisation given by a company to sell its goods or services in a particular area.

The 1970s were a relatively healthy time for the commercial broadcasters. Between 1971 and 1975, the government taxed ITV's profits, an annual figure of somewhere between £15 million and £27 million per franchise, rather than its advertising revenue. To limit the amount of tax they had to pay the government, many franchises decided to invest their revenue in new programmes. ITV began to produce some high quality shows, such as *The World at War* (1973–74) and current affairs programmes such as *This Week* and *World in Action*. At the same time, the BBC struggled with its costs: the licence fee was kept at a fixed rate in a time of high inflation and increased costs due to colour transmission. ITV's audience share was over 70 per cent at the start of the decade. Charles Curran, the Director General from 1969 to 1977 had to make BBC1 more competitive in order to justify the licence fee. Partly as a result of this, the 1970s are remembered as a golden age of the **sit-com**, with many classic series, such as *Till Death Do Us Part, Fawlty Towers, Porridge* and *The Good Life* all made by the BBC in these years. With weekly audiences as high as 20 million, the values and images shown in such programmes may have had a large impact on British people's attitudes to authority, morality and on a range of social issues.

Definitions

Sit-com

Short for situation comedy, a programme where the humour derives from putting together certain characters in certain places.

Rag and bone men

Men who went around town in a horse-drawn cart asking for any unwanted items that they could sell on.

Nouveau riche

From the French for 'new rich'; someone who has made a lot of money in their own lifetime rather than inherited their wealth. It is usually used as an insult to draw attention to a person's lack of taste or refinement.

Sit-coms

Many sit-coms of the 1970s share a number of common traits. The table on page 73 is an overview of some of the most popular sit-coms: their main characters, typical plot lines and locations. Look at the table and then answer the questions below.

SKILLS BUILDER

1 What similarities are there between
- the main characters
- the main settings
- the typical plots

in these popular sit-coms?

2 How many of the 'tensions' outlined in the 'contexts' above are reflected in these sit-coms? Which are ignored?

3 What can the popularity of these programmes tell us about British society in the 1970s?

4 How far do you think these programmes would affect groups within society or people's views of contemporary issues?

Name of sit-com	*Peak audience*	*Main characters*	*Main setting*	*Typical plot*	*Potential to influence?*
Steptoe and Son BBC 1962–65 and 1970–74	28 million	Harold (in his 30s) and his father Albert (in his 60s). They are **rag and bone** men.	Harold's flat in Shepherd's Bush, London, crammed with old bits and pieces.	Harold wants to make something of his life but Albert prevents him through a mixture of reliance on his care, bullying, and being disgusting (hence Harold's catchphrase, 'you dirty old man!').	Attitudes to authority (in this case elders).
Porridge BBC 1974–77	16.8 million	Fletch, an habitual criminal in his 40s, and his cell-mate Godber, in his early 20s, in prison for the first time, and who wants to go straight.	The fictional Slade Prison, mostly in Fletch and Godber's cell.	Fletch knows everything there is to know about prison and is usually involved in a scam at the expense of the prison guards or trying to help Godber.	Attitudes to authority (police and prison wardens).
Rising Damp ITV (Yorkshire) 1974–78	18.6 million	Rigsby, the right-wing landlord, and his tenants: Alan, a trendy left-wing student, Philip, a sophisticated black student from Croydon and Miss Jones, a middle-class spinster.	The flats.	Rigsby, trying to show how intelligent he is, has arguments about important issues with Alan and Philip. He invariably ends up looking pompous and prejudiced. Rigsby also tries, almost always unsuccessfully, to woo Miss Jones.	Attitudes to racial minorities and class.
The Good Life BBC 1975–78	15.7 million	Husband and wife Tom and Barbara Good, who decide to give up their jobs and live off the land in their back garden in Surbiton, and their **nouveau riche** neighbours, Margot and Jerry Leadbetter.	The Good's house and garden.	Although they fundamentally get on very well, the Leadbetters look down upon the Goods' attempts to grow vegetables and rear livestock in their garden and the Goods criticise the Leadbetter's materialism.	Attitudes towards class and consumerism.
Fawlty Towers BBC2 1975–76, repeated 1985	12.5 million	Hotel manager Basil Fawlty, his wife Sybil and a Spanish waiter, Manuel.	Fawlty Towers Hotel in Torquay, Devon.	Basil is at the centre of a stressful situation. Manuel makes things worse before Sybil sorts everything out.	Attitudes towards women.
Likely Lads/ Whatever Happened to the Likely Lads? BBC 1964–66 and 1973–74	27 million	Bob Ferris and Terry Collier, both from working-class backgrounds in Newcastle. Terry is happy with his working-class life, but Bob wants to become part of the middle class.	Bob and Terry's homes, the pub and locations around the North East.	Bob and Terry get into various scrapes and are generally hen-pecked by the various women in their lives.	Attitudes towards women and the family.
Till Death Do Us Part BBC 1965–68 and 1972–75	12 million	Alf Garnett, a right-wing, racist docker from the East End of London, his wife Else, daughter Rita and his socialist son-in-law Mike from Liverpool.	The Garnett home, generally the dining table or the lounge.	Alf rants and raves about his prejudices, often calling his wife a 'silly moo' and arguing with Mike.	Attitudes towards women and the family, racial minorities and class.
Are You Being Served? BBC 1972–85	22 million	Shop assistants Captain Peacock, a pompous city gent, the camp Mr Humphries, snobby Mrs Slocombe, and attractive working-class girl Miss Brahms.	Grace Brothers, a department store in London.	Some project is being worked towards or some disaster coped with, with lots of innuendo and slap-stick humour.	Attitudes towards homosexuals, class and consumerism.

5.2 A table showing some of the most popular 1970s sit-coms, with their main characters, typical plot lines and locations

Soaps and dramas

Coronation Street remained the most popular soap of the decade. Although it was still clearly steeped in nostalgia, a number of the story lines did reflect the more troubled times in the 1970s. Where once Ken Barlow (see Introduction) had been the angry young man of the working classes, by the 1970s he had become an optimistic, liberal member of *The Street*. In real life, while 50 per cent of workers were members of trade unions, the other half, including many self-employed or unskilled workers, were not. Their pessimistic fears are articulated by photo shop owner Ernie Bishop in Source D. Ernie's business collapsed and he was forced into the embarrassing position of having to live off his wife's earnings for a while. In 1978 he was shot dead by burglars.

Source D

Why, if you're ordinary and honest and you slave away, why does life become more and more impossible every day? And don't tell me it's not the government. They don't care. If the TUC barks, they throw them a bone. And where does that bone come from? From the skeletons of all the rest of us. Labour, Conservative, they're all the same, they've all got their nests nicely feathered. And I defy Callaghan [the Prime Minister] to come here and tell me any different.

From an episode of *Coronation Street*, broadcast in 1976

Question

The views in Source D were articulated by a fictional character. Does this mean that this document is of no value to historians who want to find out about British society in the 1970s?

Definition

The Sweeny

From the Cockney rhyming slang 'Sweeny Todd' for Flying Squad, a branch of the Metropolitan Police that responds to and investigates serious armed crime.

The most popular dramas were either based on the past, such as ITV's *Upstairs Downstairs*, set in England between 1903 and 1930, or on contemporary policing. *The Professionals*, and especially ***The Sweeny***, reflected the modern side of tough policing. Compared to *Dixon of Dock Green* or *Z Cars*, *The Sweeny* depicted a rough, tough police force that was not afraid to hit first and ask questions later to get an arrest. At a time when suspicions were raised about corruption within the police force, Detectives Jack Reagan and George Carter were shown as hard, but honest men. In 1969, *The Times* had tape-recorded three officers who were willing to take a bribe to let criminals go. An internal enquiry into corruption was launched, but only one officer was demoted as a result. In 1977, it emerged that Bill Moody, the detective in charge of the enquiry, was himself guilty of corruption and sentenced to 12 years in prison. However, a poll in 1977 revealed that 75 per cent of British people thought the police were honest. *The Sweeny* reflected the reality exposed by *The Times* report scandal, that police might bend the rules to get results, but it's overwhelmingly positive presentation of tough policing was very popular, with audiences of around 19 million between 1975 and 1978.

News and documentaries

The 1970s saw the rise of hard-hitting investigative journalism on television. The trend was started on ITV, with programmes such as *This Week* and *World in Action*. The aim of the producers and directors was to 'grab the audience by the lapels', with a 'fast and dirty style' of camera work. Both shows regularly gained audiences of over 10 million with probing investigations into such scandals as the use of toxic asbestos in housing, the damage done by the drug **Thalidomide**, corruption in Westminster, and with reports from Vietnam and Northern Ireland. The Independent Broadcast Authority (IBA, which replaced the ITA after the launch of commercial radio in 1973) often criticised TV journalists, such as *This Week*'s Jonathan Dimbleby or *World in Action*'s John Pilger. The IBA accused them of 'campaigning' with slanted stories, rather than offering neutral reports. The biggest source of controversy was over reports on Northern Ireland. The IBA banned two programmes from transmission: *World in Action*'s 'South of the Border' in 1971 and the same show's 1978 report on the alleged use of torture by security forces in Northern Ireland. The IBA urged ITV to 'lay off Northern Ireland'.

The BBC also faced threats, this time from its Board of Governors and even directly from the government, over its news programmes on Northern Ireland. Threats included a call (not acted upon) by then Prime Minister James Callaghan for 'Service Management Boards' to secure greater government control over broadcasts. Source E is a selection of quotations on the position of the BBC on Northern Ireland.

Definition

Thalidomide

A sedative that caused the malformation or absence of a baby's limbs when taken during the mother's pregnancy.

Source E

[The BBC should remember] the values and the objectives of the society that they are there to serve.

From an interview with Christopher Chataway, the Postmaster General (the Minister with responsibility for broadcasting), in 1971

Between the British Army and the gunmen, the BBC is not and cannot be impartial.

From a letter from Lord Hill, Chairman of the BBC Board of Governors, to the Home Secretary in 1971

My Right Honourable friend the Home Secretary, believes it is time the BBC put its house in order.

From a speech by Prime Minister Margaret Thatcher in October 1979, after a controversial *Panorama* programme about the use of roadblocks in Northern Ireland

Source F is how one historian has summed up the news and documentary output on television in the 1970s. He compares such programmes favourably with the more 'commercialised' output of documentaries over the next two decades.

Source F

The 1970s was also a decade when highly constraining, not to say misleading, notions of 'balance' and 'objectivity' were challenged, despite persistent and often unreasonable opposition from broadcasting regulators. This challenge came in its sharpest form from producers and journalists, supported by television executives.

From David McQueen, '1970s Current Affairs: a Golden Age?', a conference paper, written in 2008

SKILLS BUILDER

1. What do you think Mrs Thatcher meant by the phrase 'put its house in order'?
2. How far do Christopher Chataway and Lord Hill agree on the way the BBC should report news from Northern Ireland?
3. How far do the statements in Source E support the conclusions made in Source F?

Radio and popular music

Pirate radio stations had already forced the BBC to make some concessions to popular music in the 1960s. After the 1973 Independent Broadcasting Authority Act, BBC radio had to compete with a range of UK-based commercial stations. Despite the restrictions on licence fee increases, the BBC invested more money in its local radio stations and began broadcasting on am and fm. However, while Radio 3 was allowed to keep its large budget for live concerts and lectures, Radio 1 was forced to cut its broadcast time and to share airtime with Radio 2. This clearly showed the Board of Governors' persistent bias against popular music. Despite this, audiences for Radio 1 rose throughout the 1970s, with DJ Tony Blackburn's *Breakfast Show* attracting 20 million listeners.

There were a number of different trends in popular music that can either be seen as escapist or reflective of the troubling times. In the early 1970s, 'glam rock' rose to the fore with artists such as Slade, Marc Bolan and Gary Glitter. By the mid-1970s, this was going out of fashion and performers such as David Bowie had to contend with the rise of New York-inspired disco. Just at the point when *Saturday Night Fever* (1977) marked the high point of disco, its ultra smooth style was rivaled by the rise of the home-made, anarchistic style of punk. The leading punk band, with hits such as 'Anarchy in the UK' and (in the year of the Silver Jubilee) 'God Save the Queen', were the Sex Pistols. The band rapidly rose to fame through press attention, particularly after they swore at interviewer Bill Grundy on Thames Television's *Today Show* on 1 December 1976. Apart from the raw anger of the music, the band also made famous the ripped and safety-pinned clothes of designer Vivienne Westwood. Like Mary Quant in the 1960s, in November 1974 Westwood had opened a boutique in London (called Sex) that sold clothes to fashionable young Londoners. Appearances in the press and on television spread the fashion to other young people across the country into the 1980s. While punk style remained limited to a minority of young people, it has had a large impact on subsequent mainstream music and fashions.

Punk did more than just give rise to provocative new fashions: it could also be seen as further promoting female independence and confidence. Bands such as The Slits were among the first all-female bands to write and perform their own music, while bands such as X-Ray Spex and The Banshees were fronted by formidable female singers like Poly Styrene and Siouxsie Sioux. One ex-punk, Adam Ant, observed that, 'punk was the first youth movement in which women played as big a part as men. For the first time bands had female members who were not there solely as sex objects'. While some commentators feel that the shifts in style strongly reflect the times in which they were created, others doubt that such a link really exists. Sources G and H give two contrasting views on the significance of punk culture in the 1970s.

Source G

It was surely no coincidence that punk rock arrived on the streets of Britain in 1976 and 1977, for this period represents the fault line between . . . the post-war social-democratic consensus and Thatcherism [see Unit 6] . . . British punk rock became successful and notorious in the space of a few months. This is because British punk rock seemed to be designed to articulate young people's dissatisfaction with the post-war social-democratic consensus . . . The Prime Minister of the time James Callaghan suggested that 'amid the debris of political controversy we yearn for the symbols of national unity' . . . Whilst this was true for the majority of the population in 1977, a significant minority looked towards the politics of the punk rock scene to feel that they were not alone in feeling distinctly uncomfortable with the direction in which Britain was sailing.

From Stuart Borthwick, 'Punk Rock: Artifice or Authenticity' in *Popular Music Genres: An Introduction*, published in 2004. Borthwick is a lecturer in Popular Music Studies

Source H

The seventies were an extreme decade; the extreme left and extreme right were reflected even in its music. Any art follows its own internal logic and much of what happened to British music and fashion during the seventies was driven by the straightforward need to adopt and then outpace what had happened the day before. Clipped, hard-edged fashions appear on the street to mock floppy romantic ones, and then it happens in reverse. The high gloss extravagance of the Teds is answered by the neat, fresh, cool look of the Mods, which will be met by the psychedelic extravagance and hairiness of the hippies. They are answered by the super-Mod working class cool of the first skinheads, though in due course, wannabe Ziggy Stardusts will bring androgyny and excess back to the pavement and playing ground. Leather-bound punks find a new trump card to offend the old rockers . . . Shoes, shirts, haircuts, mutate and compete. For much of the time, this game doesn't mean anything outside its own rhetoric, it simply is – and then isn't.

From Andrew Marr, *History of Modern Britain*, published in 2008

SKILLS BUILDER

1 How far do Sources G and H agree on the reasons for the emergence of punk?

2 How far do Sources G and H agree about the significance of punk music in British society in the 1970s?

3 Which source offers the more convincing view on the importance and impact of punk?

The press

We have already seen that newspapers tend to offer slanted versions of news stories, depending upon the political views of the owner and the readers that the paper hopes to attract. However, in the case of war or terrorism, many reporters have prided themselves on their ability to expose the truth, regardless of political bias. We also saw that the satire boom of the 1960s encouraged a more confrontational approach to government in the press. With the exception of one or two publications, the coverage of the Troubles in Northern Ireland tended to be heavily in favour of the British government. Source I is the view of one media specialist.

Question

Why would the British press have reported the events in Northern Ireland in the way suggested in Source I?

Source I

Not only does violence, reported in a non-explanatory manner, dominate the coverage: it is also presented as if it were the almost exclusive preserve of republicans. The IRA violence comes to appear the **alpha and omega** of the problem and Britain's historical and contemporary responsibility is obscured.

From Liz Curtis, 'Reporting Republican Violence' in B. Rolston and D. Miller (eds), *War and Words*, published in 1996

Definitions

Alpha and omega
The first and last letters of the Greek alphabet; it means 'the beginning and the end'.

Wildcat strike
A strike without the authorisation of trade union officials.

Flying picket
Workers on strike who move from place to place to stop other workers going to work.

As one would expect, the more left-wing newspapers, such as *The Guardian*, showed greater sympathy to workers who went on strike than the right-wing press, including the *Daily Mail* and the *News of the World*, which strongly criticised the unions. Some historians have speculated that press coverage of '**wildcat strikes**' and '**flying pickets**' encouraged other unions to adopt these tactics in their own struggles. The press not only reported on industrial disputes, they were at times severely affected by them: *The Times* was forced to close for almost a year from December 1978 to November 1979 when its print workers went on strike. Circulation figures continued to fall, particularly for the broadsheets. One newspaper which was able to buck this trend was *The Sun*. The paper had been failing under its old owners, but new owner Rupert Murdoch boosted sales throughout the 1970s by copying its arch rival, the *Daily Mirror*, with a tabloid format, a white on red logo and large sensationalist headlines. In addition, it simplified its language, advertised on television and reported stories from soap operas, a large reason for the growth of 'celebrity news'. *The Sun* now appealed to its working-class readers, not on the grounds of class identity, but in terms of their taste in popular culture. In November 1970, the paper also introduced the first nude 'page three girl', a draw for many male readers. In doing so, some critics have argued that *The Sun* made pornography more acceptable to the British. Partly in reaction to this, Mary Whitehouse and Lord Longford were amongst those who attended the National Festival of Light, a Christian gathering of around 10,000 people in September 1971, to campaign against 'sexploitation' and violence in the media. Lord Longford went further and compiled his own report about pornography. He went to Copenhagen to see the effects of a total lack of censorship; in *The Sun* he became known as 'Lord Porn' for his research, which included seeing a live sex show.

Cinema

The 1970s were a turbulent time for British cinema. Mounting debts in American film studios led to a withdrawal of investment. In 1968, American money had funded 85 per cent of British films; within 2 years this was reduced to 66 per cent. At the same time, the Conservative government cut the funds available to the National Film Finance Corporation, one of the major British sources of investment. The number of British films made each year fell from 49 in 1968 to 31 in 1980; after the

Biography

Mary Whitehouse (1910–2001)

Mary Whitehouse was born in Nuneaton. After leaving school, she became an art teacher. It was while she was teaching that she first became concerned about her pupils' views on sex and morals, and their lack of knowledge of Christian values. She joined a group called Moral Rearmament that sought to spread Christian values. In 1963, she decided to focus specifically on the damage done to British morals by mass media, in particular by Hugh Carleton-Greene, Director General of the BBC from 1960–69, whom she blamed for the growth of liberal, permissive values on television. She managed to gain 500,000 signatures for her Clean-Up TV petition, which she sent to the Queen. In 1965, this campaign was merged into the National Viewers' and Listeners' Association (NVLA). Whitehouse was especially critical of television plays, the frequent use of the word 'bloody' in *Till Death Do Us Part*, but also programmes such as *Doctor Who* and the children's story show *Jackanory*. In 1977 she launched a legal case against *Gay News* magazine for publishing a 'blasphemous' poem about a Roman soldier having sex with Jesus. She won the case and magazine owner Denis Lemon was fined and given a suspended prison sentence. In her 1977 book, *Whatever happened to sex?*, Whitehouse said that 'being gay was like having acne'. She campaigned against pornography and her letters to government officials may have had some part in the passage of a law in 1981 to force sex shops to have blacked out windows. In 1984 she campaigned against 'video nasties' (see Unit 7) and this helped to pass the Video Recordings Act that placed age restrictions on videos. She spoke a great deal at meetings across the country, with around 250 engagements every year from the mid-1960s to the end of the 1970s. The NVLA is still going, under the name of Mediawatch-uk since 2001. Her life's work became the subject of a 2008 BBC film, *Filth, the Mary Whitehouse Story*, starring Julie Walters in the lead role. Her reputation still divides people, with many supporting her strong moral stand, while others see her as interfering, reactionary and out of touch with the real world.

boom years of British film in the 1960s, the mid-1970s saw the dominance of American films such as *The Sting* (1974) and *Towering Inferno* (1975). James Bond continued to be commercially successful, with *Live and Let Die*, *The Spy Who Loved Me* and *Moonraker* the most popular films of 1973, 1975 and 1979.

Comedy and horror films remained the staple of British film production into the mid-1970s. The Obscenity Act of 1959 and Theatres Act of September 1968 led to greater permissiveness at the British Board of Film

Censors (or Certification after 1984). The Theatres Act virtually ended the censorship of plays on British stages. However, while controversial musicals such as *Jesus Christ Superstar* (1972–) were now allowed to run, it did not lead to a deluge of depraved, permissive plays. By the early 1970s, the BBFC classified films with much stronger violent or sexual content for release. Films such as *Get Carter* (1971), *A Clockwork Orange* (1971) and *Straw Dogs* (1971) contained scenes of extreme violence, while *Last Tango In Paris* (1972), *Confessions of a Window Cleaner* (1974), and the *Emmanuel* films (1974, 1975) contained nudity and sex. Some local authorities banned these films from their cinemas regardless of the BBFC classification. Stanley Kubrick, director of *A Clockwork Orange*, withdrew the film himself after reports in newspapers that a man had murdered a tramp having watched a similar scene in the film. It emerged afterwards that the murderer had read the book but not seen the film. *Emmanuel* (soft porn) was the fourth most popular film in 1974, perhaps an indication that liberal views on sex were becoming more widespread.

The most popular foreign films also shared these themes of crisis and breakdown of established order. Martin Scorsese's *Mean Streets* and *Taxi Driver* both concerned the struggle of individuals against society. Francis Ford Coppola's *Apocalypse Now* conveyed the loss of decency and morality in American soldiers in Vietnam. Roman Polanski's *Chinatown* showed a bleak, violent world controlled by a powerful business tycoon. As discussed in previous units, it is questionable whether these films made British society any more violent. Source J is the poster used to advertise *Confessions of a Window Cleaner* and Source K features extracts from the *Report of the Committee on Obscenity and Film Censorship*.

Source J

5.3 The poster used to advertise *Confessions of a Window Cleaner* in 1974

Source K

[The Committee was] totally unprepared for the sadistic material that some film makers are prepared to produce . . . [Film] is a uniquely powerful instrument: the close-up, fast cutting, the sophistication of modern makeup and special effects techniques, the heightening effect of sound effects and music, all combine on this large screen to produce an impact which no other medium can create . . . Given the amount of explicit sexual material in circulation, and the allegations often made about its effects, it is striking that one can find case after case of sex crimes and murder without any hint at all that pornography was present in the background . . . The role of pornography in influencing society is not very important . . . to think anything else is to get the problem of pornography out of proportion with the many other problems that face our society today.

From Committee On Obscenity and Film Censorship, *The Report of the Committee On Obscenity and Film Censorship*, published in 1979

SKILLS BUILDER

1 How useful is Source J for historians who wish to find out whether British cinema in the 1970s made permissive values more widespread in Britain?

2 Does Source K contradict itself about the power and significance of film in altering people's attitudes and behaviour?

3 Bernard Williams, the chairman of the Committee, was a liberal moral philosopher who believed nothing should be banned by law unless it harmed someone. How far does this affect the reliability of the report's findings?

How far did mass media change British society in the 1970s?

Economic and social tensions, and changes in the law, directly affected the lives of many British people in the 1970s. However, as mass media reflected many of these problems, they may have made things seem worse than they really were: bad events are more newsworthy. They may also have spread or shaped ways in which to think about, or respond to, the problems that faced society. Sources L and M are two summaries about British society in the 1970s. Read the sources and then answer the questions that follow.

Source L

. . . it sometimes seemed as though Britain was effectively talking itself into having a crisis, as though it somehow felt more comfortable with its back to the wall, imbibing the spirit of the Blitz. Having spent the whole decade making its flesh creep with horror stories about how bad things were, steeping itself in a popular culture that frequently verged on the apocalyptic, the nation finally found its nightmares coming true with the winter of discontent in 1979.

From Alwyn Turner, *Crisis? What Crisis? Britain in the 1970s*, published in 2008

SKILLS BUILDER

1 How far do Sources L and M agree that the 1970s was a time of great change for the British?

2 In pairs, look back over this unit for evidence that supports the view of either Source L or Source M.

3 Having compared the evidence in support of the two sources, which one do you think more accurately reflects the impact of mass media and popular culture on British society in the 1970s?

Source M

The British in 1979 were poised between a reverence for old historic symbols which had provided order and cohesion over the centuries, and an uneasy awareness that such reverence had become a recipe for immobilism. Polls . . . suggested that, despite everything, most British people remained calm. A poll commissioned by the EEC in 1977 showed that 82 per cent of the population declared themselves to be broadly satisfied with living in Britain, compared to 68 per cent in France and 59 per cent in Germany.

From Kenneth Morgan, *British History Since 1945: The People's Peace*, published in 1990

Unit summary

What have you learned in this unit?

The 1970s were a time of financial hardship compared to the prosperous years of the 1960s. Rising unemployment, and above all inflation, caused tension between trade unions and the government. The Troubles in Northern Ireland also gave a backdrop of violence to the decade.

Mass media reflected these developments to different degrees and in different ways. While the newspapers were full of news about violence in Northern Ireland and bomb attacks on Britain, there was very little reference to the causes of the Troubles on television apart from a few controversial documentaries. Newspapers tended to be self-censoring in that they did not tend to investigate allegations of wrongdoing by British troops. Producers and executives were keen to promote investigative journalism in the 1970s, but television authorities did ban a few programmes from transmission.

In popular culture, while the clash between the unions and the government was rarely mentioned in dramas and sit-coms, tension between left-wing and right-wing views played a key part in many plot lines. Tension and violence in society was also the subject matter of many films in this period, although comedies remained popular. The escapism or violence of some genres of popular music in this period can also be seen as a reaction to the troubled times.

It is not clear whether mass media changed British society in this decade. Depictions of racial minorities on television may have changed the attitudes of the white majority to a degree and the more liberal censorship of the BBFC may have spread permissive attitudes via the cinema. Media coverage may also have raised awareness of campaigns that had previously been fringe phenomena such as the women's lib movement. There were some backlashes against depictions of sex and violence in mass media, but only from a small minority of the population.

What skills have you used in this unit?

As well as practising the skills you have developed in the previous units, you have also begun to think more carefully about the provenance of a source when evaluating its reliability or use to the historian. By considering who wrote a particular source you have gauged the extent to which its views and judgements may be relied upon when forming your own conclusions.

Exam tips

This is the sort of question you will find appearing on the examination paper as an (a) question.

Study Sources E, J and K.

How far do Sources J and K support the view expressed in Source E that some mass media were failing to uphold 'the values and the objectives of society'?

Explain your answer, using the evidence of Sources E, J and K. (20)

You tackled an (a) style question in Units 2 and 3. Look back at the exam tips you were given there. Now build upon those tips with the advice below.

- Make sure you understand what the question is asking: the focus is clearly on the relationship between mass media and values in society.
- With questions such as this one, you should apply your background knowledge to work out which values Source E is specifically referring to. Remember to consider the provenance of the source when you do this.
- Remember that you should not just rely on what the source directly says: you should also consider what the source *suggests* but does not specifically mention.
- Remember to conclude with a statement that directly answers the question: 'how far' do Sources J and K support the views in Source E.

RESEARCH TOPIC

1 Pick one of the television programmes mentioned in this Unit. Use the Internet to research the programme and watch DVDs of the show to make notes on how the programme depicts or addresses, if at all, the following areas on which British people formed opinions in the 1970s:

- racial minorities
- women
- homosexuality
- the family
- class differences
- consumerism.

2 Once you have completed your research, give a short presentation about the programme. Use a number of short clips that you have found that sum up the values and attitudes depicted in this show. Explain how far you think the programme would have affected British society in the 1970s.

Questions

1 Which mass medium do you think experienced the most censorship in the 1970s: television, cinema or the press?

2 How far could mass media be blamed for increasing tensions within British society?

3 At the start of the unit it was suggested that the 1970s saw the spread of permissive attitudes from a minority to a much wider proportion of British people. How far do you agree with this assessment?

UNIT

6 How far was mass media, popular culture and British society 'Thatcherised' after 1979?

What is this unit about?

The legacy of Margaret Thatcher's time as Prime Minister from 1979 to 1990 still divides opinion. To some, she saved Britain from ruin and made the country prosperous; to others, she promoted greedy individualism and eroded the social unity of the country. Thatcher believed that the free market was better than the state at generating wealth and allocating resources, and that individuals, rather than society as a whole, should take greater responsibility for their own welfare. This unit explores the extent to which these ideas affected mass media, popular culture and British society, and the extent to which mass media supported and spread Thatcher's values among the British people.

Key questions

- What was Thatcherism?
- How far did Thatcherism affect mass media after 1979?
- How far did mass media promote Thatcherism after 1979?
- What was the impact of investigative journalism on political figures of authority after 1979?

Timeline

Year	Date	Event
1979		Conservatives win the General Election in May. Margaret Thatcher becomes the first female Prime Minister of the UK
1980		Housing Act allows people to buy the homes that they had previously rented from councils
1981		Rupert Murdoch buys *The Times* and *The Sunday Times*
	April	Race riots occur in Brixton, London
	July	Race riots in Toxteth, Liverpool
1982		Channel 4 and its Welsh equivalent S4C begin television broadcasts
	2 April	The Falklands war with Argentina starts and lasts for 74 days
		Hunt Report into the provision of cable television
1984		Band Aid raises money for victims of famine in Ethiopia. It is followed by the Live Aid concert at Wembley in 1985
	March	The Miners' Strike begins and lasts almost a year in some areas

	October	The IRA bomb the Grand Hotel in Brighton where the Conservatives are holding their annual conference. Five people are killed
		Cable and Broadcasting Act set up the Cable Authority
		Video Act classifies films for release on video and bans the sale of videos to children below the classification age
1985		Comic Relief makes the first of its annual appearances on television
1986		Rupert Murdoch moves his printing operations to Wapping despite a printers strike
		The Peacock Committee publishes its Report on Financing the BBC
1989		Debates in the House of Commons are televised for the first time
1990		The Broadcasting Act abolishes the IBA, allows the expansion of satellite channels and causes a big shake-up of the ITV franchises

Source A

6.1 A photo of the comedian Harry Enfield as one of his characters, 'Loadsamoney', in 1988

SKILLS BUILDER

1. How would you describe the character shown in Source A?
2. 'Loadsamoney' was a fictional character created for a comedy programme. Can Source A therefore tell us anything about British society in the 1980s?
3. 'Loadsamoney' launched Enfield on a national tour, and even gave him a number 5 chart hit in May 1988. Does the success of 'Loadsamoney' mean that mass media promoted greed?

Harry Enfield wanted people to laugh *at* his character, the Essex plasterer 'Loadsamoney', as a vulgar, greedy lout. However, he became so concerned that people laughed *with* 'Loadsamoney' and saw him as a positive role model, that he had the character squashed under a steam roller during the 1989 televised Comic Relief show! Did the British become vastly more selfish and materialistic in the years after 1979, and if so, did mass media encourage this, or merely reflect the impact of more significant factors? One invaluable source of information to explore these issues is the British Social Attitudes surveys. The surveys were first carried out in 1983; there is now a very useful website called BritSocAt that gives online access and analysis of over 20,000 survey questions asked in British Social Attitudes surveys over the last 25 years.

Questions

1 Having read Margaret Thatcher's biography, how would you sum up Thatcherism?

2 In what ways could such aims and values affect mass media and popular culture in Britain under Thatcher? Explain your answer.

The political context: what was Thatcherism?

In Unit 5 we saw how the political backdrop could affect mass media and popular culture. The years after 1979 bore this out even further with the rise of 'Thatcherism'. Although Thatcher resigned in 1990, no government since then, including the New Labour governments of Tony Blair and Gordon Brown, has seriously challenged the general thrust of Thatcher's policies. The Biography Box below gives an overview of Margaret Thatcher's career and some of the values she stood for.

Biography

Margaret Thatcher (1925–)

Margaret Thatcher was born in Grantham, Lincolnshire, where her father Alfred owned two grocery shops. He was very active in local politics and used to take his daughter to many meetings. Margaret was brought up with a Christian faith that informed a strongly held set of conservative moral values throughout her life. Having studied Chemistry at Oxford University, she worked for a few years as a research chemist, but later trained to be a barrister. In 1951, she married Denis Thatcher, a wealthy businessman. She never lost her interest in politics and, having lost in the 1950 election, and not been selected as a candidate in the 1955 election, she won the seat of Finchley and became a Conservative MP in 1959. She gradually rose through the ranks of the Party, until in 1970 she was made Education Secretary. In this role, she became notorious as 'Margaret Thatcher, milk snatcher' for stopping the free provision of milk for 7–11-year olds. In 1975, she became leader of the Conservative Party, then in opposition and, when her party won the 1979 election, became the first female Prime Minister. Once in power, her first priority was the economy. She wanted to reduce government interference in the economy and to use the law to smash the power of the trade unions. Manufacturing output fell 30 per cent and unemployment doubled between 1978 and 1983, with 3.6 million out of work. Many commentators felt that it was only success in the 1982 Falklands war that saw Thatcher re-elected in the 1983 General Election. In her second term in office, she privatised many state-owned companies, such as British Telecom and British Rail, and sold 1.5 million council houses to their tenants. By the mid-1980s, the number of people who owned stocks and shares had tripled since 1979, from 7 to 25 per cent of the population. Thatcher centralised more power in Whitehall at the expense of local authorities, such as Liverpool Council, who resisted her policies. She also promoted unelected 'political advisers' from the world of business to advance her policies. She took a tough line against the year-long miners' strike in 1984, against the Provisional IRA throughout the 1980s, and against the Soviet Union in the last years of the Cold War. These stands were very popular with many British people. In 1987, she was re-elected for a third time, the only Prime Minister to achieve this in the twentieth century. However, a number of policies in her third term, most notably the introduction of the 'Poll Tax' in 1989–90, were very unpopular. She resigned in November 1990. In 1992, she entered the House of Lords as Baroness Thatcher. Although she has maintained a fairly low profile since then, just as Butskellism dominated post-war politics, her ideology remains in British politics today.

The financial context

Thatcher's policies to promote the free market and individual wealth affected the British people in a number of ways.

- On average, the British people became wealthier, but the gap between the richest and poorest members of society grew larger. Thatcher cut the standard and higher rates of income tax. Partly as a result of this, and partly due to the windfall from the sale of North Sea oil, average disposable income rose by 37 per cent between 1982 and 1992. Between 1997 and 2002, 3 million more Britons earned incomes that were taxed at the highest rate. However, she also increased value added tax (VAT) from 8 to 15 per cent; many felt that this **regressive tax** was unfair on the poor.
- British people became more used to borrowing to pay for consumer goods. In 1986, in what became known as 'Big Bang', a great deal of government regulation on the financial industry was scrapped; this modernised the stock market and allowed banks to take more risks with their lending and investments. This contributed to the rise in private household debt from £16 billion in 1980 to £47 billion in 1989, and in mortgages from £43 billion to £235 billion. By 2003, personal debt, including mortgages, stood at £1.3 trillion – by far the highest in Europe. While banks made huge profits, a 2003 Financial Services Authority report estimated that 6 million families, around 20 per cent of the total, faced problems with debt. The rise of credit cards also contributed to this problem: the first credit card was launched in June 1966; by 1980 there were 10 million credit cards in Britain, a figure that had risen to 27 million by 1990.
- There were fewer Britons who were typical members of the old working class. After a bitter struggle with the miners' union in 1984, a series of Employment Acts in 1988, 1989 and 1990 weakened trade unions. Trade Union membership fell from 13.5 million in 1979 to 6.7 million in 1997. The removal of government subsidies for struggling older industries also saw a decline in the percentage of the labour force employed in manual labour from 47 per cent in 1974 to 36 per cent in 1991. The number of miners fell from 200,000 to 10,000 in the same period. Many local communities were greatly affected by the end of a major local industry, such as ship building in Sunderland and steel manufacturing in Sheffield (as depicted in the 1997 film *The Full Monty*).

Definition

Regressive tax

A tax which takes a higher percentage of a person's income the poorer they are.

Question

How might the average increase in disposable income affect popular culture? Think back to the effects it had on teenagers in the 1950s – these 'baby boomer' teens had grown up to become adult workers by the 1980s.

The media context: how far did Thatcherism affect mass media after 1979?

How far did Thatcherism affect television?

In Unit 1 we discussed how different forms of ownership could affect media output and hence a good deal of popular culture. Thatcher introduced a number of changes that sought to promote competition in the media industry. These changes were designed to be at the expense of the

BBC, which she saw as a wasteful organisation, producing 'liberal' programmes that the British public did not want or like. Competition was increased by:

- the launch of Channel 4 in 1982
- the liberalisation of laws on **cable** broadcasting in 1984
- the deregulation of television and the expansion of satellite television in 1990.

A fourth channel was first recommended in the 1977 *Report of the Committee on the Future of Broadcasting* by the Committee on the Future of Broadcasting, chaired by Lord Annan. The Report recommended that the new channel would commission programmes made by independent companies, rather than make its own shows like the BBC and ITV. The aim was to improve the diversity of programmes on television. As Source B explains, Thatcher approved of the free market element of this Report.

Source B

. . . Channel Four was creating small businesses, the economic foundation of Thatcherism. In giving viability to the independent sector, Channel Four was taking filmmakers who had lived on subsidy, and sometimes dreamed of revolution, and was turning them into entrepreneurs, lean and hungry companies competing in the marketplace for their next commission, negotiating over producer fees . . . and intellectual property rights . . . It became apparent through the 1980s that the system of commissioning was to be the norm rather than the exception in the new age of broadcasting.

From John Caughie, *Television Drama: Realism, Modernism and British Culture*, published in 2000

However, Thatcher was not so pleased with the liberal aspects of the 1980 Broadcasting Act, based on the Annan Report. One of her **'wet'** ministers, the Home Secretary William Whitelaw, ensured that Channel 4 would be subsidised by ITV advertising, and that it would have a legal **remit** to educate, innovate and provide for minority tastes, rather than chase advertising revenue with populist shows. This role for Channel 4 was confirmed by the decision in 1990 to convert the original limited company into a corporation like the BBC.

Some of the programmes on Channel 4 that fulfilled the remit included:

- *The Tube* (1982–87): a live pop and rock music programme that gave many bands, and alternative comedians, their big break. The show's format was revived in an even more outlandish fashion by *The Word* (1990–95).
- *Brookside* (1982–2003): a soap opera set in Liverpool that tackled socially challenging storylines such as the effects of rape and drug abuse. It had the first black and gay lead characters.

Definitions

Cable

Cable had been laid since the 1920s to transmit radio signals in areas with poor reception. In 1951 Gloucester became the first town to receive television signals via cable. For many years both the BBC and ITV argued against allowing commercial cable operators to bring in signals from other regions or even abroad. Ironically, when this was finally allowed to happen in 1985, the expansion of cable television was small because of the rise of satellite television!

'Wet'

This was Thatcher's term for more liberal members of her Cabinet who favoured less censorship and less extreme free market policies.

Remit

A set of instructions or an area of responsibility.

- *Dispatches* (1987–): a documentary programme that has broadcast investigative journalists' work on a range of controversial topics such as government corruption and Islamic extremism.

Another way in which Thatcher increased competition in television was the introduction of the Cable and Broadcasting Act in 1984. This allowed cables to carry as many new television channels into the homes of subscribers as possible. By 1990, cable television was available to 15 million out of 22 million homes in Britain. New television companies such as Sky Channel were only loosely regulated by the Cable Authority.

The most significant introduction of competition in television broadcasting stemmed from the 1990 Broadcasting Act. The terms of this Act meant:

- every terrestrial channel had to commission 25 per cent of its programmes from independent production companies
- the launch of a fifth terrestrial channel (carried out in 1997)
- the growth of satellite television (see Unit 7)
- the replacement of the Cable Authority and the IBA with the Independent Television Commission (ITC), a 'light touch' regulator. The ITC and a whole host of other regulating bodies were themselves replaced by the Office for Communications (Ofcom) in 2003
- companies had to bid for the 15 regional ITV broadcast contracts. The sums of money required for a successful bid varied from region to region. Carlton TV Ltd bid £43,170,000 to replace Thames Television as the weekday broadcaster in London, while Channel Television only had to bid £1000 to secure the contract for the Channel Islands! The successful companies were awarded contracts that lasted for 10 years
- acquisitions and mergers were allowed between ITV franchises; the rules concerning such mergers and acquisitions by other media companies were further relaxed in the 1990s and 2000s. This has led to some significant **cross-media ownership**.

These mergers had a number of impacts on television production in Britain. As part of the new **economies of scale**, ITV Plc closed down many regional production centres in places such as Newcastle, Nottingham, Norwich and Southampton. The need to make profits in order to survive has had an impact on programming; many critics allege that there has been a 'dumbing down' of programmes to sell advertising to as many viewers as possible; 'dumbed down' television and the rise of commercial sponsorship for television shows has fuelled greater consumerism. Source C discusses the impact of these changes on the types of programme shown on television.

SKILLS BUILDER

1 What can we learn from Source B about how far Thatcherism affected television in the 1980s?

2 Did the Channel 4 remit make television more of a moulder of British attitudes? Explain your answer.

Definitions

Cross-media ownership

The result of a merger or take-over between companies in different areas of mass media.

Economies of scale

Larger firms tend to be more efficient and profitable than smaller ones for a range of reasons; for example, a television studio has fixed costs but a production company with more workers could make more programmes to sell than a smaller company with the same studio.

Source C

One piece of research by the ITV Network Centre published in January last year showed that, since the 1990 Broadcasting Act, the amount of current affairs programming across the four main terrestrial channels fell by 35 per cent, the number of arts programmes more than halved and religious programmes were cut by nearly 75 per cent. All of those areas were once where important documentary work could be done. It also showed that in peak time there has been a 133 per cent increase in shows devoted to hobbies and leisure and a 125 per cent increase in soaps . . . I think what's actually happened here is that regulations that were in place to preserve and to further citizen values or public service values on television have increasingly been replaced by regulations that are designed to further corporate values.

From Professor Julian Petley's discussion on documentary filmmaking held in Birmingham in January 2004. Petley is professor of Screen Media and Journalism at Brunel University

Question

At the time of writing, many people were complaining about the loss of their local radio station brand to one of the networks (for example Peterborough's Hereward FM became one of the Heart stations). Why do you think such complaints were made? Are such complaints justified in your opinion?

Definition

Blockbuster

This was originally American slang used to describe a successful play, possibly because of the numbers of people who would swamp the 'block' (a mass of buildings between two streets) where the theatre was. It was then taken to mean a very successful film. Nowadays it has come to mean a film with very high production and marketing costs geared towards huge audiences and merchandising.

Questions

1 For what reasons would the 1990 Broadcasting Act have led to the changes in programming discussed by Professor Petley?
2 How might this change in programming have affected popular culture?
3 Would the changes in programming make television more a moulder or mirror of British attitudes? Explain your answer.

How far did Thatcherism affect radio?

Many of the changes that affected commercial television also affected commercial radio. The 1990 Broadcasting Act led to the establishment of many more local and regional commercial stations. By 2007, almost all of these had been bought by groups associated with the three independent national stations that the Act also allowed to be set up: Classic FM (established in 1992), Virgin Radio (now Absolute Radio, 1993–) and Talk Radio UK (now talkSPORT, 1995–). All of these stations have themselves been sold to larger media companies: for example, Virgin Radio was sold to the Times of India Group in April 2007! The Times of India Group also owns 29 magazine titles and another 31 radio stations, mainly in India.

How far did Thatcherism affect cinema?

It is sometimes claimed that the Thatcher years saw a 'renaissance' in British cinema. There is some truth to this: as Source L on page 58 showed, audience figures rose after the mid-1980s for the first time since the 1950s. This recovery had nothing to do with Thatcher who did much to undermine the British film industry. In part, interest in the cinema may have been rekindled by the rise of television shows about cinema, such as Barry Norman's (later Jonathan Ross') *Film* (BBC1 1972–) and Alex Cox's *Moviedrome* (BBC2 1987–94). The increased audiences were primarily driven by the popularity of American **blockbusters** and their sequels made up around 85 per cent of all films shown in British cinemas after 1979.

Thatcher wanted filmmaking to be treated like any other British industry: to remove government subsidies and promote the free market. The 1985 Film Act scrapped the **Eady Levy** that had subsidised British studios from the total takings at box offices. Domestic investment in British films also fell after Thatcher privatised the National Film Finance Corporation and removed a 25 per cent tax break on investments in film. British filmmakers, still a highly talented bunch, were forced to become Thatcherite entrepreneurs to get their films made. Many, such as director Ridley Scott, went to work in America where he made films such as *Blade Runner* and *Gladiator*. Those who stayed in Britain worked with independent production companies such as Handmade Films, Merchant Ivory Productions and Working Title Films. In order to produce films with a Hollywood production value, i.e. films that attracted mass audiences, many British filmmakers sought American financial backing. They increasingly received this backing, especially after the success of Working Title's *Four Weddings and a Funeral* (1994) which made $244 million. Domestic investment mainly came from television companies such as Film on Four and BBC Film. After the National Lottery was set up in 1994, some of its proceeds also funded British filmmaking. In 2000, the Labour government set up the UK Film Council to 'stimulate a competitive, successful and vibrant UK film industry and culture, and to promote the widest possible enjoyment and understanding of cinema throughout the nations and regions of the UK.' It distributes around £17 million of Lottery funds to British filmmakers each year and helps to distribute independent films in cinemas across the country. The impact of these changes, and of Thatcherism more broadly, on British films as popular culture are discussed on pages 96–97.

Definition

Eady Levy

The tax, which started in 1957, was named after Sir Wilfred Eady, a treasury official.

Question

Given the way in which Thatcher undermined the British film industry, how far would you expect to see a scathing attack on her and her values in British films after 1979? Explain your answer.

How far did Thatcherism affect the press?

Both Thatcher and Thatcherism affected the press in a number of ways. Firstly, the tough line taken against trade unions allowed newspaper owners to modernise their printing operations. In 1983, newspaper owner Eddy Shah defeated the National Graphical Association's attempt to stop the introduction of new print machines for his chain of local newspapers in the Manchester area. The greater efficiency and profitability of the new system allowed him to set up one of only two new national daily newspapers since the 1960s: as the first colour newspaper, *Today* set a trend but folded in 1995 after poor circulation figures. Shah's 1983 victory emboldened Rupert Murdoch (see Biography Box on page 92) who moved his printing operations from Fleet Street to a new complex at Wapping in 1986. The move meant that journalists could put together the newspaper and print it electronically without having to use specialist print workers. Murdoch sacked the printers who went on strike (he wanted to sack them anyway but because they went on strike he did not have to pay them any redundancy money!). For a whole year many of these workers demonstrated outside the Wapping plant; Murdoch enjoyed the full support of the government with the protection of a sizeable police presence. The demonstrations occasionally turned violent and over 1000 arrests were made. Partly because of this assistance, and partly because of his political views, the Murdoch press strongly supported Mrs Thatcher. Source D describes Murdoch's style as a newspaper **proprietor**.

Definitions

Proprietor

An owner of a business or shop.

Monopolies Commission

Now called the Competition Commission, it investigates any mergers or take-overs that would result in one firm having more than a quarter of a particular market and too much influence over that market.

Source D

It was Mrs Thatcher who arranged for Rupert Murdoch's acquisition to escape a reference to the **Monopolies Commission** . . . A newspaper merger unprecedented in newspaper history went through in three days. He [Murdoch] guaranteed that the editors would have control of the political policy of their newspapers; that they would have freedom within fixed annual budgets; that the editors would not be subject to instruction from either the proprietor or management on the selection or balance of news and opinion; that instructions to journalists would only be given by the editor . . . In my year as editor of *The Times*, Murdoch broke all these guarantees . . . he was reminded of these undertakings to the Secretary of State. 'They're not worth the paper they are written on' Murdoch replied.

From Harold Evans, *Good Times, Bad Times*, published in 1983

Questions

1 How far would it have been in Thatcher's interests to allow the merger between Murdoch's News Group and Times Newspapers in 1981?

2 Why do you think Evans was so concerned about Murdoch's style of proprietorship?

Biography

Rupert Murdoch 1931–

Rupert Murdoch was born in Melbourne, Australia. His father Keith had been a journalist and, on his death in 1952, left shares in a number of Australian newspapers. Rupert was at Oxford University at the time, but returned home in 1953 to take over as managing director of his father's company, News Limited. He was highly ambitious and an extremely shrewd businessman. Over the next few years, he bought a number of newspapers across Australia; in 1964, he launched Australia's first national newspaper, and bought his first newspaper outside Australia: *The Dominion* in New Zealand. His major ambition was to get into the British media. He achieved this in 1969 when he bought the *News of World*, then one of the highest selling newspapers in the world, and *The Sun*. He soon began to interfere in editorial decisions at both newspapers, saying to the *News of the World* editor 'I did not come all this way not to interfere'. With the revenue from *The Sun* he was able to found his company News Corporation, and to purchase *The Times* and *The Sunday Times* in 1981. The previous owners of the newspaper had been forced to sell because of the increased cost of printing in the 1970s. Murdoch overcame these costs with the move to Wapping in 1986. Murdoch had begun to acquire newspapers in America in 1973, but, having obtained American citizenship in 1985, moved into television through the establishment of the Fox Network. In addition to Fox News and the other Fox Channels, News Corporation also owns Sky, Star TV, Twentieth Century Fox film studios and Myspace among many other firms. *Private Eye* (see page 61) regularly draws attention to Murdoch's cross-media ownership with a column called 'I-Sky': it charts occasions when *The Sun* or *The Times* promote Sky television. Murdoch is now estimated to be the 132nd most wealthy person in the world, with assets of over $4 billion!

As Source E describes, Thatcher also used the law to restrict media reporting on issues of national security far more than previous governments.

Source E

The Thatcher Government's legal actions against newspapers and broadcasters have resulted in a significant erosion of freedom of the press in Britain in 1987, in the view of journalists, civil libertarians and the handful of politicians interested in the issue. Throughout the year, the Government pursued its efforts to inhibit British publication of and news reporting about 'Spycatcher', an account of misconduct in the British security services by Peter Wright, a former intelligence agent . . . 'Britain is sinking further into that league of nations where press freedom is barely understood, let alone protected,' said Kenneth Morgan, director of the Council . . . For her part, Prime Minister Margaret Thatcher very early on condemned investigative reporters as 'people who use freedom in order to destroy freedom.' A senior official insists that there is no vendetta against the press, but he described Mrs Thatcher as committed to enforcing the laws regulating its activities . . . The BBC and *The Independent*, for example, are each tied up in litigation with the Government on three fronts.

From Howell Raines, 'British Press Freedom Erodes Under Thatcher, Critics Say', published in *The New York Times* on 19 December 1987

Although the word '**spin**' was not coined until the 1990s, it was under Thatcher that carefully selected information began to be presented (or often leaked) to the press by her close ally and Chief Press Officer Bernard Ingham. Public Relations (PR) officials, or 'spin doctors', such as former tabloid journalist Alastair Campbell, have since become familiar, yet shadowy, figures. There have been occasional outbursts against their influence, such as when government press officer Jo Moore said in an email 'It's now a very good day to get out anything we want to bury' on 11 September 2001, the same day as the terrorist attacks on the World Trade Centre in New York. It is not just government that employs PR people; most large organisations now have dedicated PR workers. The author of Source F has argued that the rise of PR and spin, together with financial pressures on newspapers, has led to the rise of 'churnalism'.

Source F

[Researchers at Cardiff University's school of journalism] found that a massive 60 per cent of . . . quality-print stories consisted wholly or mainly of **wire copy** and/or PR material, and a further 20 per cent contained clear elements of wire copy and/or PR to which more or less other material had been added. With 8 per cent of the stories, they were unable to be sure about their source. That left only 12 per cent of stories where the researchers could say that all the material was generated by the reporters themselves. The highest quota proved to be in *The Times*, where 69 per cent of news stories were wholly or mainly wire copy and/or PR . . . The researchers went on to look at those stories which relied on a specific statement of fact and found that with a staggering 70 per cent of them, the claimed fact passed into print without any corroboration at all. Only 12 per cent of these stories showed evidence that the central statement had been thoroughly checked.

From Nick Davies, *Flat Earth News*, published in 2008. Davies had worked as a journalist for many years before he published this book

Definitions

Spin

A slant on information used to create a favourable impression when it is presented to the public.

Wire copy

The 'wires' are items of news that are sent to journalists by press agencies such as the Press Association or Reuters. These agencies have their own reporters on the ground but also feed PR releases to the journalists. Wire copy is the direct use of this information in newspaper stories.

SKILLS BUILDER

1 What do you think Thatcher meant when she said that investigative journalists 'use freedom in order to destroy freedom'?

2 Why do you think Davies is so concerned about the large proportion of stories that are based on 'wire copy and/or PR'?

3 Would Source E or Source F be more useful to an historian who wants to find out about the impact of Thatcherism on the press? Explain your answer with reference to content and provenance!

4 You have now seen several examples of cross-media ownership; is it a cause for concern?

How far did mass media promote Thatcherism after 1979?

Did television programmes promote Thatcherism?

Although Thatcher never directly said that 'greed is good', she certainly encouraged people to make as much money as they could. Many television shows in the 1980s and into the 1990s could be seen as promoting and glamorising wealth and materialism. Many drama series imported from America, such as *Dynasty*, *Falcon Crest*, and most famously *Dallas*, with a peak audience of 21 million in November 1980, focused on the lives of rich, selfish characters. Source G is a photograph used to promote *Dynasty* which, like *Dallas*, was mainly about an oil tycoon.

Source G

6.2 A photograph used to advertise *Dynasty*, taken in 1983

While the lifestyle of American millionaires was beyond the vast majority of Britons, shows such as *Dynasty* did inspire fashion trends such as padded shoulders in women's jackets and made people reflect on their own living conditions. Source H is one man's view about the impact of these television shows.

Source H

. . . in the old days you felt differently. There are no poor people if you're all poor people. It's only when you see the rich that you realise 'God I'm poor'. [Lifestyles of the rich were] continually flaunted in glowing colour on 21-inch screens in every Port Talbot house.

From an interview with Owen Reynolds, a Welsh steel worker, in Ian Jack, *Before the Oil Ran Out: Britain 1977–86*, published in 1987

Questions

1 How far does Source G suggest that soap operas like *Dynasty* promoted Thatcherism?

2 How far does Source G support the view in Source H?

Television not only portrayed the lives of the super wealthy, a trend that continued into the 1990s and 2000s with shows such as *Beverly Hills 90210* (FOX Network, shown on Channel 4 1990–2000) and *The O.C.* (FOX Network, shown on Channel 4 2003–07), but also increasingly catered for viewers with increased disposable income who wanted to improve their lifestyles. The trend began with celebrity chefs such as Delia Smith, Gary Rhodes, Ainsley Harriot and later Jamie Oliver and Nigella Lawson. Television programmes catered for people's aspirations for their (now increasingly privately owned) homes with programmes such as *Location Location Location*, *Escape to the Country*, *Property Ladder* and *Grand Designs*. Gardening was also extremely popular and television shows such as *Gardeners' World* encouraged people to improve their gardens. Although these programmes can clearly be seen to have fuelled consumerism, a more positive interpretation is that they have been a democratising force: they suggested ways in which ordinary people could attain the sophistication and luxury that had been the preserve of the rich. A large number of out-of-town garden centres opened to cater for the demand for products. Shopping itself became a leisure activity with cafés in garden centres. Critics would argue that 'lifestyle' programmes and quizzes have mushroomed on daytime and early evening television because they are cheap to produce.

Question

Do you think the amount of 'lifestyle' programming means that television has been 'dumbed down'?

How far did cinema promote Thatcherism after 1979?

Films may not have such a direct relationship with Thatcherism: unlike the press or television, which deal far more with reports, investigation, and satire, films are primarily rooted in action, escapism and **allegory**. However, they can be seen to promote, criticise or otherwise react to the values that Thatcher stood for through the analysis of their storylines.

Definition

Allegory

A symbolic representation.

Thatcher's economic views were largely derived from American attitudes to business and the economy. It is therefore no surprise to see such

Thatcherite values such as individualism, freedom and ambition reflected in American films. The most explicit exhibition of Thatcherism was in the 1987 film *Wall Street*. The story focused on the morally bankrupt business activities of Gordon Gekko, a New York entrepreneur and asset stripper, who claimed that 'greed is good'. Other films that are directly critical of or satirise ruthless capitalists include *American Psycho* (2000) and the British film *How to Get Ahead in Advertising* (1989). You can use the Internet to research these films.

British films reacted to Thatcherism in two divergent ways which can be referred to as 'us' and 'them' films. 'Us' films were produced by smaller, domestically funded companies and were primarily intended for a domestic audience. These films presented Britain 'as the British saw it'; they overwhelmingly attacked Thatcherism, either through the realistic depiction of social tension that resulted from the increased gap between rich and poor, or through satire and allegory. Film Four funded several such films, including *The Ploughman's Lunch* (1983), *My Beautiful Laundrette* (1988), and *High Hopes* (1988). More recent films in this genre include *This is England* (2007). Sources I and J are two reactions to such films.

Question

On the surface of things, American blockbusters, such as *Star Wars* or *Indiana Jones*, have nothing to do with Thatcherism. However, many critics see Thatcherite values strongly promoted in such films. Can you think of any ways in which such films might have promoted Thatcherism in Britain?

Source I

They are all very depressing, and are no doubt meant to be. The rain pours down; skinheads beat people up; there are race riots; there are drug fixes in squalid corners; there is much explicit sex, a surprising amount of it homosexual and sadistic; greed and violence abound; there is much grim concrete and much footage of 'urban decay'; on and off there are voice-overs by Mrs Thatcher, Hitler etc. . . . The done thing is to run down Mrs Thatcher, to assume that capitalism is parasitism, that the established order of this country is imperialist, racist, profiteering.

From Professor Norman Stone, 'Through a Lens Darkly', published in *The Sunday Times* on 10 January 1988

Source J

Independent filmmakers of the 1980s reacted strongly against the effects of Thatcherism. They responded to the imposition of market criteria in every sector of society, to political authoritarianism . . . and the leading role of the City . . . It can be seen, I believe, as a 'British New Wave', coming long after the idea of a New Wave had crumbled away in most other European countries.

From Peter Wollen, 'The Last New Wave: Modernism in the British Films of the Thatcher Era', in L. D. Friedman (ed.) *Fires Were Started: British Cinema and Thatcherism*, published in 2006

Questions

1 When was the original New Wave British cinema? How far do you agree with the view in Source J that the films mentioned above were another 'New Wave'?
2 How do you account for the vastly different reactions to British films in the 1980s by the authors of Sources I and J? Explain your answer with reference to the provenance of each source.

'Them' films depict a romanticised, historical image of Britishness to appeal to American perceptions of Britain and maximise profits from US filmgoers. The result of this was the growth of American-financed 'heritage' films such as A *Passage to India* (1984), *Howard's End* (1992), *The Remains of the Day* (1993). More recent films that have updated this winning 'heritage' Britishness formula include *Four Weddings and a Funeral* (1994), *Notting Hill* (1999) and *Love Actually* (2003). While most Americans now think that the actor Hugh Grant is a typical Brit, the impact of these popular films on British audiences is less clear. One cultural critic has summarised the impact of such films in Source K.

Source K

During the 1980s, British films and television have successfully marketed and packaged the national literary heritage, the war years, the countryside, the upper classes and elite education. Like natives in Third World countries who impersonate themselves for the sake of the tourists, Britain appears the victim of its own sophisticated media-making: the imaginary has become reality . . . Britishness in the cinema may thus be a myth, but it remains no less powerful for that . . .

From Thomas Elsaesser, *European Cinema: Face to Face With Hollywood*, published in 2003

SKILLS BUILDER

1 What do you think the author of Source K means by 'the imaginary has become reality'?

2 How far do Sources J and K support the view that cinema promoted Thatcherism in Britain after 1979?

Questions

1. Why would *The Sun* back Blair in 1997?
2. Do you find such an open declaration of support for one political party a cause for concern?
3. Do *The Sun*'s switches of support in 1997 and 2009 suggest that it has been more of a moulder or mirror of British political opinions?

How far did the press promote Thatcherism?

We have already seen how press ownership could affect the content of British newspapers. Throughout the 1980s and 1990s, around 70 per cent of newspapers in circulation backed the Conservative Party, with only the *Daily Mirror* backing the Labour Party on a large scale. However, in 1997, *The Sun* switched allegiance from the Conservatives to Labour, a fact clearly announced by the headline in Source L. Labour leader Tony Blair had met Murdoch on several occasions and had made a favourable impression: Blair was clearly a Thatcherite in his political outlook, and in particular promised not to impose controls on cross-media ownership. Such was the size of *The Sun*'s circulation (3.8 million copies daily in 1997) that only 33 per cent of newspapers now backed the Conservative Party. In October 2009, long after opinion polls suggested that David Cameron's Conservatives would win the 2010 election, *The Sun* announced that it was switching sides again!

Source L

THE Sun

MAY 1st

An historic announcement from Britain's No1 newspaper

Tuesday, March 18, 1997 28p THE PAPER OF THE PEOPLE

THE SUN BACKS BLAIR

Give change a chance

Historic . . Blair reads early copy of today's Sun

THIS is the election for the millennium.

In six weeks' time Britain will vote for a government to take it into the 21st century.

The people need a leader with vision, purpose and courage who can inspire them and fire their imaginations.

The Sun believes that man is Tony Blair. He is the best man for the job, for our ten million readers and for the country.

It is a momentous decision which we have not taken lightly because we still have reservations about some of New Labour's policies. But for all the Tories' achievements of the past 18 years, they no longer deserve our support.

They are tired, divided and rudderless. They need a rest and so does the country. Blair is the breath of fresh air this great country needs.

On Pages 6 and 7 we explain why we are putting our trust in him.

Election special – Pages 2, 4, 5, 6 and 7

6.3 The front page of *The Sun*, published on 18 March 1997. The Labour Party went on to win a landslide in the General Election on 1 May that year

Some media critics have described the history of the press since the 1980s as a process of 'tabloidisation'. In the 1980s and 1990s, front covers contained fewer stories and had increasingly large headlines. In a bid to boost sales, many 'broadsheets' began to adopt this strategy and even switched to the 'tabloid' size; only *The Daily Telegraph* and the *Financial Times* have retained the genuine broadsheet format. In addition, virtually every newspaper, especially Sunday papers, began to include supplements that catered to different interests: money, home, travel and motoring sections all attracted targeted advertising and promoted consumerism. All of these trends, together with the rise of 'churnalism' discussed above, have weakened the role of newspapers as a 'fourth Estate' in the eyes of many critics. However, the enquiries about investigative journalism below indicate that the press has not entirely become a willing tool of government since the 1980s.

Enquiry 2: Investigative journalism and the government after 1979

Thatcher and investigative journalism

Thatcher did not just promote competition to undermine the BBC: she also tried to directly intervene by banning some programmes and appointing Governors of the Board who sympathised with her political views. In February 1987, as part of the *Secret Society* series, the BBC planned to broadcast six programmes made by the investigative journalist Duncan Campbell. One of the shows was about a secret new spy satellite, code-named Zircon. The BBC, on the advice of the government, banned the programme. Even after the programme had been pulled, the police raided BBC offices in Glasgow and removed all material from the series. The 'liberal' Director General Alasdair Milne was forced to resign in favour of the much more compliant Sir Michael Checkland. The fact that the Governor of the Board was the Conservative Marmeduke Hussey made the BBC more compliant with government wishes. Thatcher also disliked the 'neutral' way in which the BBC reported on Northern Ireland. In 1988, a government White Paper led to a ban on all interviews with members of Sinn Fein; the BBC was forced to disguise the voice and face of Sinn Fein leaders such as Gerry Adams if they wanted to get around the law. Such intrusion led to the formation of Charter '88, a civil liberties pressure group that opposed such censorship.

ITV was not immune from this attempted interference into its news broadcasting. On 28 April 1988 ITV screened an episode of *This Week* entitled 'Death on the Rock'. The show investigated the killing of three members of the Provisional IRA earlier that year on Gibraltar by the SAS (special armed services). The SAS were authorised to use lethal force if the suspects made any move to detonate a bomb they had planted on the island; the SAS claimed that the three suspects did make such moves, while eye-witnesses said that the SAS shot them 'in cold blood'. Thatcher's Home Secretary, Douglas Howe, tried to ban the show from being broadcast. However, the IBA refused, and stated that 'the issues as we see them relate to free speech and free inquiry which underpin individual liberty in a democracy'. Enquiries 3 and 4 below further explore the relationship between the government and investigative journalism.

Enquiry 3: Gotcha! The media, the government and the Falklands war 1982

The Falkland Islands lie 300 miles off the coast of the southern tip of Argentina, 7500 miles from Britain. The islands have no valuable resources, but were strategically important as a stop-off point on voyages around the southern tip of Africa on the way to India. The French, Spanish, Argentines and British had all laid claim to the islands before the British established permanent control from 1833. In 1945, the Argentines began to press their claim to the islands at the UN. The British said that they would only withdraw once the inhabitants of the island had voted for this to happen; as the population were British, this was never likely to happen.

On 2 April 1982, the **Falklands war** began when Argentine forces occupied the islands. They had invaded upon the orders of General Galtieri who led the military **junta** in charge of Argentina. He wanted to gain a swift military victory to distract attention away from domestic economic problems and to bolster his own power. While diplomatic negotiations continued with the Argentinians, a British Task Force was dispatched. British ships arrived on 19 April and began to land troops on the islands. On 2 May, Margaret Thatcher ordered the submarine *HMS Conqueror* to attack an Argentinian light cruiser called the *General Belgrano*. The *Belgrano* was torpedoed and sunk with the loss of 368 crew members. This divided opinion in Britain: while some approved of her action to protect British troops, reports came back that the *Belgrano* was not in the **Total Exclusion Zone (TEZ)**, and was sailing away from the islands. Some critics, notably the Labour MP Tom Dalyell, suspected that Mrs Thatcher had ordered the attack to boost her popularity, and to stop any possibility of success for a new diplomatic settlement announced by the Peruvians 14 hours earlier. Thatcher insisted that she did not learn of this plan until after the *Belgrano* had been sunk. On 21 May SAS troops began to land on the islands and, after some tough fighting, proceeded to recapture the airstrip at Goose Green. By mid-June they had recaptured the capital, Port Stanley, and taken almost ten thousand Argentine prisoners.

Definitions

Falklands war

A brief, undeclared war, fought between Argentina and Great Britain in 1982 over the control of the Falkland Islands. Also referred to as the Falklands conflict.

Junta

A political or military faction that has seized power following a revolution or coup.

Total Exclusion Zone (TEZ)

An area of around 200 miles around the Falkland Islands within which the British, on 30 April 1982, declared they would attack any Argentine vessel.

The war resulted in the deaths of 635 Argentines and 255 British people and had cost the British almost £3 billion. It led to a surge of pride and patriotism among the British, and contributed to the success of Mrs Thatcher in the 1983 election. However, disputes over the sinking of the *Belgrano* and the way the media had reported the Falklands war dragged on into the mid-1980s. In particular, scandal erupted in 1984 when Clive Ponting, a civil servant at the Ministry of Defence, leaked two key documents to Tom Dalyell that confirmed that the ship was outside the TEZ and heading away from the Falklands, and that the government had misled a Select

Committee enquiry into the *Belgrano* case. The government arrested Ponting and had him charged with breaking the 1911 Official Secrets Act; he was found not guilty by the jury because they felt the documents were in the public interest. The following documents give an overview of the way in which mass media reported the war and the sinking of the *Belgrano*.

Enquiry source 3A

THE Sun

Tuesday, May 4, 1982 14p TODAY'S TV: PAGE 12

QE2 IS SET TO SAIL FOR WAR

Liner may be turned back from a cruise

We told you first

NINE days ago The Sun said that the QE2 was to be called up. Everybody denied it. Yesterday the Ministry of Defence confirmed it. If you really want to know what's going on in the war buy The Sun. We try harder. See Page 2.

GOTCHA

Our lads sink gunboat and hole cruiser

SUNK *AN Argie patrol boat like this one was sunk by missiles from Royal Navy helicopters after first opening fire on our lads*

CRIPPLED *THE Argie cruiser General Belgrano . . . put out of action by Tigerfish torpedoes from our super nuclear sub Conqueror*

From TONY SNOW aboard HMS Invincible

THE NAVY had the Argies on their knees last night after a devastating double punch.

WALLOP: They torpedoed the 14,000-ton Argentina cruiser General Belgrano and left it a useless wreck.

WALLOP: Task Force helicopters sank one Argentine patrol boat and severely damaged another.

BATTLE FOR THE ISLANDS

The Belgrano, which survived the Pearl Harbour attack when it belonged to the U.S. Navy, had been asking for trouble all day.

The cruiser, second largest in the Argy fleet, had been skirting the 200-mile war zone that Britain has set up around the Falkland Islands.

MAJOR

With its 15 six-inch guns our Navy high command were certain that it would have played a major part in any battle to retain the Falklands.

But the Belgrano and its 1,000 crew needn't worry about the war for some time now.

For the nuclear submarine Conqueror, captained by Commander Richard Wraith, let fly with two torpedoes.

The ship was not sunk and it is not clear how many casualties there were.

HMS Conqueror was built at Cammell Laird's shipyard in Birkenhead for £30million. She was launched in 1969 and

Continued on Page Two

UNION BOYCOTTS WAR

A UNION chief is telling seamen on two ships taken over by the Government: "Don't go to war—the union can't protect you."

The astonishing advice comes from George Cartwright the Communist leader of the National Union of Seamen at Felixstowe Port in Suffolk.

The Government has just requisitioned the Townsend Thoresen roll-on, roll-off vessels Baltic Ferry and Nordic Ferry.

'Folly'

The ferries will carry troops and battle equipment in support of the QE2.

Mr Cartwright told the 150 seamen: "Our advice is that it would be folly to go off on a dangerous adventure.

"I'm old enough to remember that one in three merchant seamen were killed in the last war.

"It is not a case of being unpatriotic. We are not at war and our advice is based on union practicalities.

"What we are saying is that if seamen put themselves under military command, they will no longer have our protection.

Question

"There is no question of politics being behind the recommendation. We were asked for our view and gave our best advice."

He believes the majority of crew members will decide not to sail to the South Atlantic.

So far I have heard from three seamen who want to go, the rest are non-committal or against joining the task force," Mr Cartwright said.

6.4 The front cover of *The Sun*, published on 4 May 1982. This front cover was only published on the early edition; the headline was replaced with 'Did 1200 Argies drown?' on the later edition

Enquiry source 3B

The situation was that you were a propagandist; that's how it turned out. So there wasn't any need to put pressure on anyone to write gung-ho copy because everyone was doing it without any stimulus from the military. And that's how most of the reporters felt. They were all very patriotic and 'positive' about the whole thing. So the military didn't have to lean on them.

From an interview with *Observer* journalist Patrick Bishop, shortly after the war in 1982. Bishop was one of the 16 newspaper reporters who travelled to the Falklands with the Navy taskforce

Enquiry source 3C

In April 1982 I took over as the *Observer*'s television critic. I anticipated a cosy period of acclimatisation: a new American soap called *Dynasty* was soon to start, followed by the year's main event, the stirring quasi-warfare of the World Cup in Spain. Instead, at coffee time on the Monday morning of my second week, ITV brought us the real thing live: the departure of a British military force to recapture a piece of colonial territory 8000 miles away . . . Little did we guess that these were the last sunny, honest, unspun images we were likely to get for some time; or that the Falklands war would turn out to be the worst-reported war since the Crimean . . . All the significant news, good or bad, was announced or leaked from London. Reporters in the south Atlantic had the sour experience of hearing 'their' news being broken for them on the World Service. Reports were censored, delayed, occasionally lost . . . In the age of image, the Falklands war remained image-free for much of its length – no British pictures for 54 of the 74 days the conflict lasted – and image-weak thereafter . . . when the action on land began, the images were limited and controlled . . .

The fact that we'd been trying for decades to offload the islands, with the ardent Thatcherite Nicholas Ridley presenting a leaseback solution to the House of Commons only two years previously, was forgotten. The fact that we'd traded with the junta, welcomed its leaders and sold arms to them, but now realised that it was a filthy dictatorship after all, was swallowed without a burp. The fact that there were a mere 1800 islanders, and that their way of life was preserved at the cost of 1000 British casualties and 1800 Argentinian ones did not seem a grossly stupid and expensive way of conducting foreign policy.

From Julian Barnes, 'The worst reported war since the Crimean', published in *The Guardian* on 25 February 2002

Enquiry source 3D

Britain took account of the perceived lessons from Vietnam during the war with Argentina in 1982, the Falklands war. This was Britain's 'first taste of a campaign fought in the full glare of modern media attention'. The remoteness of this war . . . facilitated media management. Places on Royal Navy taskforce ships were limited [to 16 reporters, 2 radio reporters, 3 TV reporters (and crew) and 2 photographers], and the government and military leadership decided which organisations should be allowed to report the war at first hand, excluded non-British correspondents, and controlled communications from the war zone. The Falklands war highlighted the conflict between, on the one hand, the perceived public right in any democratic system to be informed and, on the other, government and military needs to withhold information for reasons of operational security. The British government . . . practiced a policy of 'deception, misinformation, disinformation and media manipulation through denial of access, control of communications and politically based censorship'.

From Lyn Gorman and David McLean, *Mass Media and Society into the 21st Century*, published in 2009

Enquiry source 3E

Ponting did not deny what he had done, but claimed in court the higher duty to reveal the truth, rather than conceal it to preserve the embarrassing fact that the public had been consistently and intentionally lied to, not only during the war (which might have been excusable), but for as long after it as ministers could get away with. Despite the strongest possible hint from the judge in his summing-up that the evidence against Ponting justified a conviction, twelve randomly selected members of the public ignored his advice.

Ponting's acquittal did Thatcher no political damage. Detailed raking over the embers of what the overwhelming majority of the British public wanted to consider an unalloyed triumph was of interest only to political opponents, pedants and intellectuals.

From Eric J. Evans, *Thatcher and Thatcherism*, published in 2004

Practice source evaluation

- How reliable are these sources for historians who wish to find out about how the media covered the Falklands war and the sinking of the *Belgrano*? Consider the provenance of each source and then rank them in order of their reliability.
- Take the source you find the most and least reliable and for each explain why.
- Which of these sources offers the best and the worst evidence for the way the media reported the Falklands war and the sinking of the *Belgrano*? Consider the content of the sources when you explain your answer.

You may also wish to view footage of an argument between Mrs Thatcher and Mrs Gould, a viewer from Cirencester, on *Nationwide*, broadcast by the BBC shortly before the General Election in May 1983.

Now that you have analysed and evaluated the sources, you are in a strong position to use them effectively to answer the following question:

To what extent do the sources show that mass media provided effective investigative journalism into the Falklands war and the sinking of the *Belgrano*?

SKILLS BUILDER

1 Study Sources 3A, 3B, 3C, 3D and use your own knowledge.

To what extent would it be fair to say that mass media had no choice but to report what the government wanted it to report during the Falklands war?

2 Study Sources 3A, 3C and 3E and use your own knowledge.

To what extent do you agree that mass media were the willing partners in a government cover-up of the circumstances which led to the sinking of the *Belgrano*?

Enquiry 4: Dr David Kelly and the 'Dodgy Dossier'

Although the following events took place over a decade after the retirement of Margaret Thatcher, the 'Dodgy Dossier' case raises similar, important issues about the relationship between mass media and government. On 18 July 2003, Dr David Kelly was found dead in woods near his home in Oxfordshire. He had apparently committed suicide by taking painkillers and then cutting his left wrist. The Labour government launched an enquiry into his death; on 28 January 2004, the Hutton Committee confirmed that Dr Kelly had committed suicide. Although he had been under a great deal of pressure at the time, many people did not believe the report and saw it as part of a government whitewash (cover-up).

Dr Kelly was employed by the Ministry of Defence as an expert in biological warfare. He played a major role in uncovering biological weapons in Iraq after the first Gulf War (1990–91). As a leading expert, he was asked to read over sections about weapons inspections in Iraq in a Defence Intelligence Staff dossier on 'weapons of mass destruction' in 2002. A key claim in the report that was used to justify the invasion of Iraq in March 2003 was that Iraq had weapons of mass destruction that could be fired 'within 45 minutes' of an order for their use. No such weapons were found after the invasion took place.

On 22 May 2003, Dr Kelly met BBC journalist Andrew Gilligan with the assurance that Gilligan would not name his source in any stories. He told Gilligan that he thought the '45-minute claim' had been put into the report by Alastair Campbell, Tony Blair's Director of Communications. Gilligan broadcasted the story on radio and the press began to write about a 'dodgy dossier' or a 'sexed-up report'; the government denied the claim and began to search for the source of the story. Given Dr Kelly's expertise, it was not long before the Ministry of Defence confirmed to the press that he was the source. He was made to appear in front of a televised Committee enquiry into the affair on 15 and 16 July 2003, which put him under great stress. On the morning of 18 July, he was found dead in the woods. After an extensive investigation, the Hutton Report found the government totally innocent of any involvement with Dr Kelly's death or of 'sexing-up' the dossier, but blamed Gilligan's 'unfounded' reporting and 'defective' management at the BBC. Following the Report's publication the Director General of the BBC, Greg Dyke, Chairman of the Board of Governors, Gavyn Davies, and Andrew Gilligan all resigned. There have been many stories in the press since 2004 that have poured doubt on the accuracy of the Report.

The documents below relate to Dr Kelly's death, the Hutton Enquiry and the way the media covered the story in 2003 and 2004. In addition, you may also find it useful to watch a BBC documentary about Dr Kelly's death and use the Internet to research Professor Petley's views on the media and the press.

Enquiry source 4A

MONTHS of frustration boiled over as Greg Dyke elbowed aside his lieutenants. The BBC director-general, lampooned as a Labour lackey, insisted that the time had come for the corporation to retaliate against No. 10's bombardment. His anger poured out into the BBC's 3500-word retort to Alastair Campbell. 'It is our firm view,' he dictated, 'that No. 10 tried to intimidate the BBC in its reporting of events leading up to the war and during the course of the war itself.' Dyke, the former Labour donor whose appointment in 1999 had called into question the corporation's editorial independence, had crossed a line. Later that day the BBC sent the letter to Campbell and included the further accusation that he had turned his complaints about the BBC into a 'personal vendetta' against Andrew Gilligan, its defence correspondent.

The effect on Campbell was electric. He was already determined to extract an apology for reports that he had forced the intelligence services to exaggerate the case for war against Iraq. Now he accused the BBC of 'weasel words' and 'outrageous allegations', before bursting into the studios of *Channel 4 News* to launch a finger-jabbing diatribe against the standards of BBC journalism.

Although Dyke did not seek the row, its timing is opportune. It comes ahead of a meeting on Tuesday with Theresa May, the Conservative party chairman, to deal with accusations that the BBC is biased against the Tories. In the midst of the most serious clash between the BBC and Labour since it came to power, who now could challenge Dyke's independence?

There is a deep anger among the foot soldiers of the BBC's news division at the almost daily 'bombardment' they encounter from Labour. One said: 'During the war it got to a stage where it was difficult for editors to edit because there was a constant stream of complaints. The *Today* programme (on Radio 4) was attacked with complaints from No. 10 all the time during the war.'

From Nicholas Hellen and Jonathan Carr-Brown, 'Barons of BBC Relish Chance of a Sexed-Up Row', published in *The Times* on 29 June 2003

Enquiry source 4B

Campbell used it as a decoy to distract attention from a highly embarrassing story, which was emerging slowly in May and June 2003, that the long-debated Iraqi weapons of mass destruction did not exist . . . This move [Campbell attacked the BBC on *Channel Four News* on 27 June 2003] finally established the decoy story as the main media line. The original questions about the Iraqi weapons of mass destruction were shunted into the sidings. Several political reporters wrote at the time that this looked like a diversionary tactic. Nonetheless, all of them agreed to be diverted. PR works.

From Nick Davies, *Flat Earth News*, published in 2008

Enquiry source 4C

. . . the BBC collectively has been the victim of a grave injustice. If Lord Hutton had fairly considered the evidence he heard, he would have concluded that most of my story was right. The government did sex up the dossier, transforming possibilities and probabilities into certainties, removing vital caveats; the 45-minute claim was the 'classic example' of this; and many in the intelligence services, including the leading expert in WMD, were unhappy about it . . . This report casts a chill over all journalism, not just the BBC's. It seeks to hold reporters, with all the difficulties they face, to a standard that it does not appear to demand of, for instance, government dossiers. I am comforted by the fact that public opinion appears to disagree with Lord Hutton and I hope this will strengthen the resolve of the BBC. I repeatedly said also that I did not accuse the government of fabrication, but of exaggeration. I stand by that charge, and it will not go away. I love the BBC and I am resigning because I want to protect it. I accept my part in the crisis which has befallen the organisation. But a greater part has been played by the unbalanced judgements of Lord Hutton.

From Andrew Gilligan's resignation speech on 30 January 2004

Enquiry source 4D

THE INDEPENDENT

No 5,392 www.independent.co.uk THURSDAY 29 JANUARY 2004 60p

WHITEWASH?
THE HUTTON REPORT
A SPECIAL ISSUE

Eight months ago, BBC reporter Andrew Gilligan broadcast his now infamous report casting doubt on the Government's dossier on Iraq's weapons capability, a vital plank in its case for war. In the ensuing furore between No 10 and the BBC, Government scientist David Kelly, who was revealed to be Gilligan's source, was found dead in the woods. Tony Blair appointed Lord Hutton, a former Lord Chief Justice of Northern Ireland, to hold an inquiry into the circumstances surrounding Dr Kelly's death. He listened to 74 witnesses over 25 days, and yesterday published his 740-page report. In it, he said Gilligan's assertions were unfounded and criticised the BBC, whose chairman has now resigned. He said that Dr Kelly had broken the rules governing civil servants in talking to journalists. He exonerated Tony Blair, cleared Alastair Campbell and attached no blame to the government for the naming of Dr Kelly. So was this all an establishment whitewash? And what of the central issue which Lord Hutton felt he could not address? If the September 2002 dossier which helped persuade the nation of the urgent need for war (and triggered this tragic chain of events) was indeed reliable, where, exactly, are Iraq's weapons of mass destruction?

6.5 The front cover of *The Independent* published on 28 January 2004

Enquiry source 4E

In the aftermath of the suicide, British commentators were divided as to whether the lion's share of blame for Kelly's suicide rested with the government or the BBC. Some blamed the news agency for refusing to release Kelly's name sooner; other fingers pointed at the MoD for violating its normal rules of secrecy by telling reporters that it would confirm the mole's name if they submitted it to the ministry. For its part, the government accused the BBC of having an antiwar bias that had led to sensationalist reporting. Britain's conservative tabloids were eager to point fingers at the BBC. 'Are the BBC to blame?' asked the conservative, mass-circulation *News of the World* (20 July). 'Maybe . . . It is the reputation of the BBC that will be covered in Kelly's blood.' *The Sun* (21 July) was even more damning in its rhetorical questions: 'The BBC is in the gutter . . . How can we ever trust them again?' But others argued that it wasn't clear exactly what the BBC could have done to save Kelly. Writing in the liberal *Guardian* on 21 July, Jackie Ashley offered an explanation for the conservative attacks on the corporation. 'The attacks on the BBC have been led by two groups – Rupert Murdoch's newspapers and New Labour spin-doctors – which have been closely intertwined in recent years. The covert Murdoch message is clear enough: Tony, we are your real, reliable supporters, not the dodgy lefties of the BBC.' Others cautioned against making too much of the battle between the BBC and press secretary Alistair Campbell, saying that they were simply actors in a larger drama. 'Blair went to war arguing that Iraq posed an imminent threat,' said an editorial in London's liberal *Independent on Sunday* (20 July). 'It is not scientific advisors, or Campbell, or the BBC . . . who should be in the dock but the prime minister . . . We need [an inquiry] into the real reasons why this country was taken into a war that has claimed not only too many lives as its victims but the nation's trust in its leaders as well.'

From Barry Shelby and Sarah Colman, 'Suicide and Suspicions over War in Iraq', posted on the Worldpress website on 13 August 2003. The website was founded in 1997 to provide (chiefly American) readers with an objective account of the way foreign media report current news events

Practice source evaluation

- Study Sources 4A and 4B. How far does the contemporary report in Source 4A support the later views of Source 4B?
- How far does the speech in Source 4C justify the bold front page decided upon by the editors of *The Independent* in Source 4D?
- Source 4E is from an American website. Does this mean it is the most useful source for an historian who wants to find out about the death of Dr Kelly and the way the British media reported this? Explain your answer with reference to the provenance of the other sources.

SKILLS BUILDER

1 Read Sources 4A, 4B and 4C.

How far do Sources 4A and 4B support the view in Source 4C that 'the BBC collectively has been the victim of a grave injustice' during the David Kelly affair?

2 Use Sources 4A, 4B, 4D and 4E and use your own knowledge.

How far do you agree that mass media reported the events concerning the 'dodgy dossier' and the death of Dr Kelly in an objective fashion?

Unit summary

What have you learned in this unit?

Margaret Thatcher had a large impact on all mass media, both in terms of the rules concerning their operation and ownership, and on their content. Competition was encouraged in a bid to make the BBC more responsive to the demands of the free market, and to make media firms more efficient and profitable. Independent television and radio companies sought to maximise profits in a (generally unsuccessful) attempt to avoid being bought by larger companies. This was a key factor in the growth of 'lifestyle' television on all terrestrial channels. Such programmes were also a reflection of the greater material aspirations of many British people that resulted from Thatcher's financial policies.

While the press had divided opinions about Thatcher depending upon its political loyalties, both television and cinema had a love-hate relationship with Thatcherism. Many of its popular cultural products glamorised material wealth while others were critical of the social impact of an increasing gap between rich and poor.

What skills have you used in this unit?

You have furthered the sophistication of your source evaluation. You have assessed the comparative reliability of a source by considering the chronological context in which the source was produced. You have used this process to weigh up with sharper focus and greater accuracy the extent to which a source supports a proposition, or the view of another source.

RESEARCH TOPIC

Use the Internet to conduct research into one of the following controversial topics and the way in which the media reported it. As you conduct your research, consider how far your findings support the view that 'the connection between politics and mass media has become too close for comfort for a democracy such as Britain'.

- The Poulson affair that concerned corruption in local government 1970–74.
- The Thalidomide affair that erupted in 1972.
- The DC-10 air crash of 1974.
- Police corruption: there are several important cases of this including the Soho pornography ring of the 1970s, the investigation of the murder of Stephen Lawrence in 1993 and the shooting of Jean Charles de Menezes in 2005.
- The alleged 'shoot to kill' policy of the British Army in Northern Ireland during the Troubles.
- The Zircon Affair of 1986.
- The trial and 'wrongful' imprisonment of Abdel Baset Megrahi for the bombing of Pan-Am flight 103 which exploded over Lockerbie on 21 December 1988.
- The 'Cash for Questions' or 'Sleaze' affair 1994–97, especially concerning Jonathan Aitken and Neil and Christine Hamilton.
- The expenses scandal of 2009.

You might also find it useful to use the Internet to research the following television programmes: *Panorama, Private Investigations, Taking Liberties, Rough Justice, Here and Now, Correspondent* (all BBC); *The Cook Report, Disguises, World in Action* (ITV); and *Cutting Edge, Dispatches* (Channel 4).

UNIT

7 Britain 2.0? New media and its impact on popular culture and British society

What is this unit about?

This unit focuses on the rise of new media and the effect this has had on popular culture and British society since the 1980s. New media refers to innovations in the way that information can be broadcast, shared or stored. There have been two waves of new media technology: the first in the 1980s and 1990s included video recorders, and cable and satellite television. The second, ongoing since the 1990s, includes digital technology, mobile phones and the Internet. The key question is whether new media have begun to empower individuals and promote a more democratic society, or whether they have reinforced the cultural and economic dominance of a few big businesses.

Key questions

- What was the impact of the first wave of new media in the 1980s and 1990s?
- What has been the impact of the second wave of new media since 1998?
- How far is it possible to talk of a 'Britain 2.0'?
- Has digital technology been a force for democratisation in Britain?

Timeline

1962	NASA launches Telstar, the first commercially used communications satellite partly backed by the British General Post Office
1963	Sony launches the first home video recorder. The first video cassette went on sale in 1969
1969	Scientists working for the US military create ARPANET, the first version of the Internet. The first email is sent in 1970
1972	First games consoles go on sale in America. They become widely available in the UK in the early 1980s with the launch of the Sinclair ZX Spectrum, the Commodore 64 and the Nintendo Entertainment System
1977	Apple launches the first mass produced personal computer
1979	Sony launches the Walkman personal stereo. The compact cassette had been created in 1965 by Philips
1980	Sony launches the first consumer camcorder
1982	Creation of the first digital audio compact disc (CD). CD sales overtake those of vinyl records in 1988

1984 Cable and Broadcasting Act sets up the Cable Authority. The first 'broadband' cable system is laid in Swindon

Video Act classifies films for release on video and bans the sale of videos to children below the classification age after widespread concern about the impact of 'video nasties'

1986 Launch of British Satellite Broadcasting. The company is bought by Rupert Murdoch's Sky Television in 1990

1988 Société Européenne des Satellites, a firm based in Luxembourg, launches the Astra 1A satellite. It carries four Sky channels from 1989–2001

1990 Production of the first commercially available digital camera. The first megapixel camera is launched in 1997

Broadcasting Act abolishes the IBA, and allows the expansion of satellite channels

1991 Tim Berners-Lee creates the first website using his invention, the World Wide Web

Launch of the Groupe Special Mobile (GSM) communication system in Europe. It now covers 80 per cent of the world. The first mobile phone had been launched in 1973, but GSM allows second generation (2G) mobile phones to send digital signals, including Short Message Service (SMS) or 'text' messages

1992 The first text message in the world is sent via computer in the UK; it said 'Merry Christmas'

1993 Creation of the Digital Versatile Disc (DVD). A range of firms agree on a standard format in 1995. DVDs outsold video cassettes for the first time in 2002

1995 Ward Cunningham launches the WikiWikiWeb, the first example of a **wiki** application on the Internet. Wikipedia is launched in 2001 and 'wiki' enters the Oxford English Dictionary in 2007, meaning 'a form of collaborative website'

1997 Production of the first commercially available MP3 player

1998 Americans Sergey Brin and Lawrence Page launch Google. In 2006, 'to google' enters the Oxford English Dictionary, meaning 'to search for information on the Internet'

Launch of digital satellite broadcasting

2001 Apple launches the iPod

2005 Americans Steve Chen, Chad Hurley and Jawad Karim launch YouTube. By 2009, 20 hours of video are uploaded to the site every minute

2007 Channel 4, ITV and BBC all launch websites that allow people to watch current and past programmes online

2008 The BBC and ITV launch Freesat, a subscription-free satellite TV service

2009 The government publishes its *Digital Britain* report

2012 Analogue television transmission stops in UK

Definition

Wiki

Comes from the Hawaiian language for fast. The idea of a wiki web page is that it is able to be edited quickly by its users.

Questions

1 What do you think the person who created this image is trying to say about the nature of the Internet?

2 How far do you think this image gives an accurate view of the Internet? Explain your answer.

Source A

7.1 An image used on several websites to illustrate ways in which the Internet is used

What was the impact of the first wave of new media in the 1980s and 1990s?

Videos and video recorders

The rise of video recorders and video cassettes in the 1980s meant that people could increasingly watch programmes when they wanted, rather than when schedulers wanted them to watch them. Perhaps more importantly, people could opt out of television altogether and buy or rent films to watch at home. Indeed, choice has expanded so far that soon it might not be possible to refer to all but a few successful television shows as popular culture. Unlike films at the cinema, there was no legislation that censored films on video until the 1984 Video Act. Before the Act was passed, many people were concerned about the impact of cheap, foreign horror films on children who had managed to get hold of them on video. Films such as *Driller Killer* (1979) and *The Evil Dead* (1982) led Mary Whitehouse (see Biography Box on page 79) to speak about what she called 'video nasties' in 1982. The *Daily Mail* ran a campaign against 'video nasties' with a series of bold headlines in 1983; these included: 'BAN VIDEO SADISM NOW', 'YOUTH "KILLED AFTER A VIDEO SESSION"' and 'CRUEL MOVIES FAN HACKS 4 TO DEATH'.

Questions

1 Why do you think the editor of the *Daily Mail* chose to run such headlines on the front page?

2 How far are these headlines, promoted as a '*Mail* campaign', a useful guide to public opinion about violent or 'obscene' videos in the early 1980s?

The Director of Public Prosecution (DPP – now head of the Crown Prosecution Service) authorised the police to seize 'obscene' material under the 1959 and 1977 Obscenity Acts. One devout Christian Chief Inspector in Manchester ordered the seizure of *The Best Little Whorehouse in Texas* in the belief that it was a pornographic film; it was, in fact, a musical starring Dolly Parton! By 1984, video shops were just as pleased about the new legislation as Mrs Whitehouse: after film classification for videos, they now knew which titles they could stock without the threat of them being confiscated. Sales of video cassettes rose throughout the 1980s and 1990s, until they were overtaken by the sale of DVDs in 2004; videos are now virtually obsolete. Since 2000, there has been a relaxation on censorship of videos: many of the 39 titles banned by the DPP have now been passed for release with a few minor cuts.

Satellite television

Even more than cable, the rise of **satellite** television in the 1980s led to:

- an increase in the number of channels available to many British people. Many channels were now available from abroad with the correct satellite dish
- the rise of channels that were dedicated to just one genre of programme
- the establishment of 'pay-TV' in Britain
- the transmission of real-time images of events from around the world.

Together with the relaxation of regulations in the 1990 Broadcasting Act, these changes affected the types of programme on offer to an increasing number of viewers and hence an important element of popular culture.

In February 1989, Rupert Murdoch's Sky Television began to broadcast to the UK from a Luxembourg-owned satellite (the satellite itself was 36,000km above the Congo). The government was apparently powerless to stop individuals buying satellite dishes to receive Sky TV. It was not just Sky that could transmit to the UK from abroad: many immigrants or non-English speakers could often receive channels from their home country. Source B is one media historian's view of the impact of these events on mass media in Britain.

Definitions

Satellite
This can refer to any celestial body that orbits a larger object. The Moon is therefore the largest satellite of the Earth.

Transnational business
A firm with production, distribution, marketing, management and sales operations in more than one country.

Questions

1 Of the four changes listed in the bullet points, which do you think would have had the largest impact on popular culture? Have a group discussion to compare your answers.

2 In what ways does Source B suggest that satellite television impacted upon popular culture in Britain in the 1990s?

Source B

. . . whatever the attitude of governments to the ownership and programming of the companies, satellite TV is essentially a **transnational business** and therefore harder to bring under political control. Its 'footprints' transcend national borders and its operators can ignore the restrictions imposed by some of those countries to which they broadcast. But in Britain this had consequences for terrestrial broadcasting, for the ITV contractors have cited the freedom of satellite operators, with whom they compete for the same audience, to support their own demands for fewer restrictions on ownership and programming.

From Andrew Crisell, *An Introductory History of British Broadcasting*, published in 1997

Question

What do you understand by the term 'globalisation'? Can you think of other ways in which globalisation has affected popular culture and British society? Discuss in class.

Definitions

Convergence

To converge means to approach nearer together as if to meet or join at a point. Digital technology has allowed the convergence of previously separate tools such as computer applications and the Internet, cameras and camcorders, and telephones in a single mobile device. This has further allowed the convergence of mass media, such as radio, television and the press, all available via the Internet on these devices.

Digital

'Digit' originally meant finger or toe, but also came to mean a number from 0 to 9. Digital information is sent in a stream of 0s and 1s (a high voltage and a low voltage) that receivers can read and turn into information such as a sound wave or a pixel colour.

In 1992, at a cost of £191 million, Sky bought the rights to televise all Premiership football matches for five seasons. In 1997 it paid £670 million for a four-season contract and a further £1 billion in 2004 for three seasons. The money injected into the Premier League has had a large impact on the game, with huge salaries attracting more and more talented foreign players. Sky had also bought the rights to televise cricket, rugby union, rugby league, boxing and golf by 1997, removing some key sporting events from terrestrial channels. The number of channels available to British viewers greatly increased after the rise of digital satellite and terrestrial broadcasting in 1998. This further increased the choice of programmes available to British audiences and has contributed to decreased audiences for many prime-time BBC and ITV shows. Like the Internet, this could be seen as a force that fragments *popular* culture into a range of sub-cultures.

Satellite television also meant that news events could be relayed in real time to audiences. Just as radio boosted the immediacy of events for listeners in the 1920s and 1930s, so satellite news channels linked British people to the events as they happened. The 1991 Gulf War is said to be the first 'real-time war'; people began to speak of a 'CNN effect', the impact of seeing events on the other side of the world as they took place. One of the most notable events that unfolded live on televisions across the world was the terrorist attack on the World Trade Center in New York on 11 September 2001. The 'CNN effect' promoted McLuhan's notion of a 'global village' as previously distant parts of the world were instantaneously linked.

What has been the impact of the second wave of new media since 1998?

Of the mass media discussed in this book, it is likely that the most recent wave of new media will have the most profound impact on the way that British people live and experience popular culture. In particular, the rise of the Internet and the **convergence** of a range of digital devices means greater access to information, entertainment and a range of services at all times and in all locations. This has already begun to affect patterns of work and consumption.

Digital television

Digital signals require far less power to generate than **analogue** ones and take up a lot less **bandwidth**; the launch of terrestrial and satellite digital transmitters in 1998 meant many more channels could be broadcast. By 2008, over 12.3 million homes in the UK could receive over 70 channels, including digital radio channels, from **Freeview** terrestrial broadcasters alone. In 2012, the analogue transmissions will be stopped; all UK homes will have the choice of Freeview, pay-tv via cable or satellite, or to go without (and perhaps make do with Internet television!). The number of channels potentially available via satellite runs into thousands. A complete list of the channels would take up several pages, but Source C provides a selection of them.

Source C

From Freeview on terrestrial transmitters:

- BBC1, BBC2, BBC3, BBC4, BBCi, BBC News, BBC Parliament, CBeebies, CBBC
- ITV1, ITV2, ITV3, ITV4, CITV
- Channel 4, 4+1, More 4, E4, E4+1, Film 4, S4C
- Sky News, Sky Sports News, Sky 3
- QVC, Bid TV, Rocks & Co, 1-2-1 Dating, Supercasino
- BBC Asian Network Radio, BBC One Extra
- CNN, Russia Today
- and even . . . Teachers TV!

From a standard Sky mini-dish or via cable: about 800 channels (although some require further payment to decode the signal) including:

- Baby TV
- God TV
- Audi Cars TV
- Thomas Cook TV
- Psychic TV
- Al Jazera
- Punjabi TV
- VH1, VH1 Classic, MTV Dance, MTV Base, MTV Hits
- and most appropriately of all . . . Radio Caroline TV!

With a correctly directed satellite dish (and sometimes the correct decoder):

- Digital channels from Spain, Ukraine, Bulgaria, Sweden, Norway, France, Germany, Denmark, Finland, Slovakia, Turkey, Dubai, Belgium, Poland, Switzerland, Lebanon, Czech Republic and more!

A list of television and radio channels available in the UK in 2009, selected by the author

Out of these channels only 15 had an audience share of more than 1 per cent in 2007. Sources D and E are about the impact of digital broadcasting upon different aspects of television in Britain.

Definitions

Analogue

Analogous means 'similar to'. Analogue information is sent by generating a wave similar to light or sound waves that a receiver can convert into usable information.

Bandwidth

The size of a band of frequencies used to transmit signals. Frequency means the number of times a wave is repeated in a second. For example, many local radio stations transmit on 102 FM; this means your radio must be tuned to receive waves that oscillate 102 million times a second.

Freeview

A **consortium** of the BBC, Sky and Arqiva that has provided free-to-air digital television since 2002.

Consortium

An association of organisations formed for commercial or financial purposes.

Source D

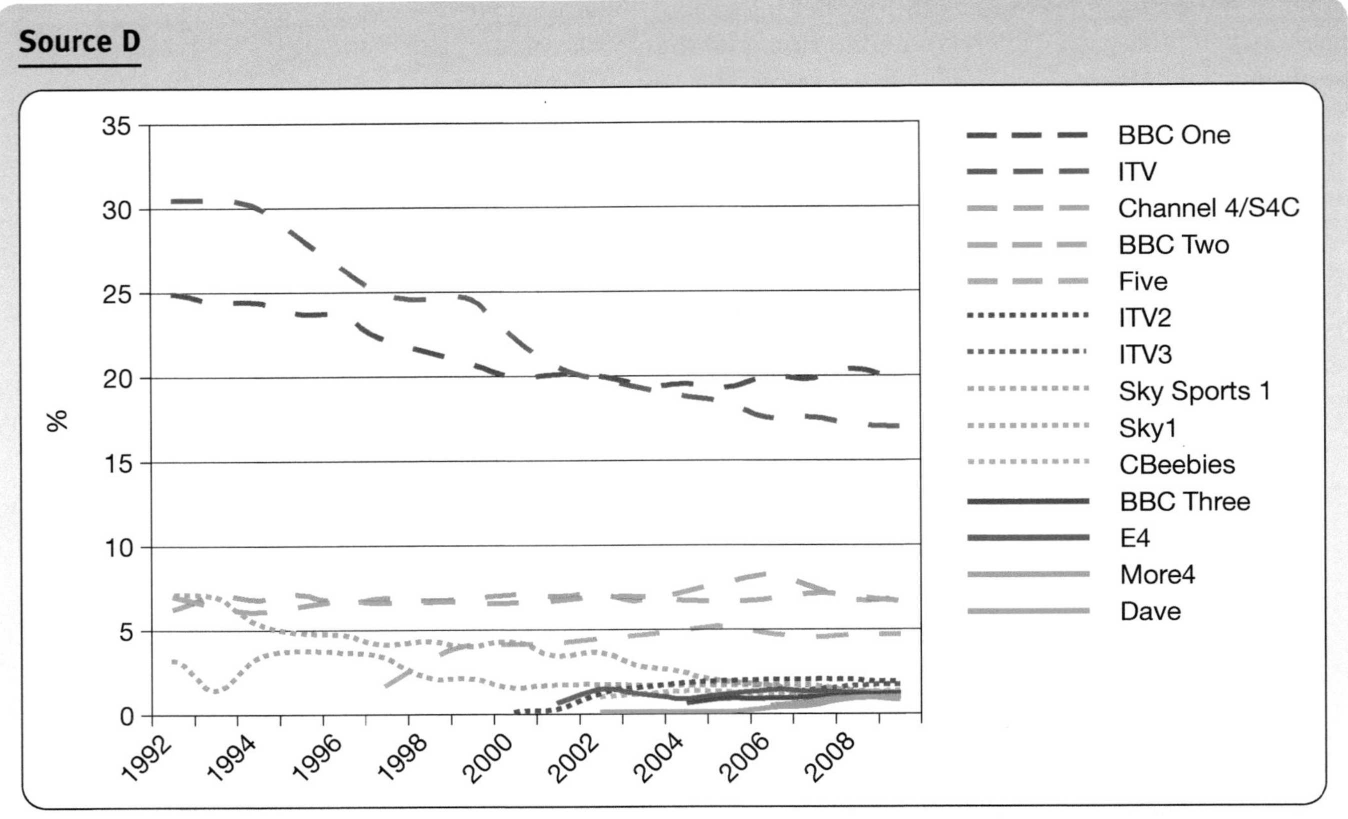

7.2 A chart showing the market share of terrestrial and satellite channels from 1992 to 2009

Source E

Whereas in the 1970s the talent would be concentrated within the schedules of BBC1, BBC2 and ITV, today it is scattered across a far wider area. A predictable consequence of the growth of channels is that there are more hours to be filled. So programme makers of limited skill get commissions now for programmes that, twenty years ago, would have been rejected at the first hurdle. Dovetailing in with that is the fact that the senior executives now in charge of the media industry have a different outlook to their predecessors. No longer do they try to raise the viewers' cultural tastes; rather, they pander to the expectations they believe the bulk of the audience hold. The result is an increase in game shows such as *Who Wants To Be A Millionaire*, 'reality TV' programmes (*Holidays from Hell*, *Airport*), sometimes combining an audience participation element (*Big Brother*), and an obsession with DIY, home and garden makeovers and the like. The BBC's *Panorama* and LWT's *The South Bank Show* get ditched to the graveyard slot and Thames's *This Week* and Granada's *World in Action* are scrapped. For all the technological advances that we have benefited from, the ability of British television to sustain quality programming was always going to be put at risk from the bracing air of true competition.

From Stephen Hopkin, 'Never Mind the Quality', published on the Transdiffusion website on 1 January 2002. Hopkins is a software engineer and media critic based in Cambridge

SKILLS BUILDER

1 In 1988 there were still only four channels available to the vast majority of British people. Just over 20 years later, the vast majority of British people had over 50 channels, and in many cases over 600 channels. What can you infer from Source D about the impact of digital broadcasting on popular culture?

2 Can you infer anything from Source D about the impact of digital broadcasting on British society? Explain your answer.

3 In what ways might Source E alter the inferences you made from Source D in questions 1 and 2? Explain your answer using information from Source E.

4 How far does Source D support Source E?

Mobile phones

Mobile phones have come a long way in a short period of time. Compare and contrast the two phones shown in Source F. How might the differences in technology affect the way they are used?

Source F

7.3 and **7.4** A Motorola DynaTAC 8000X from 1982 and the current Apple iPhone

Mobile phones have had a number of impacts on popular culture and British society. Superficially, many plot lines in films, television shows and novels involve mobile phones. More interestingly, text messaging has taken off in a way that few expected when the Short Message Service (SMS) service was launched in 1992. As mobile phones became cheaper in the late 1990s, more and more teenagers, and even children, had their own handsets; a 'text language' emerged that was sufficiently unintelligible to older Britons that We Are What We Do, a movement that encourages positive social action, released a book for children called *Teach Your Granny to Text*! Many older people, perhaps influenced by media reports like those in Sources G and H, became worried about young peoples' use of mobile phones. Despite these fears, many parents and children have come to regard mobiles as an important aid to personal safety. Some social commentators have become concerned about the way mobile phones have affected parent-children relations and in particular about the rise of 'helicopter parenting': parents who interfere in their children's lives even after they have left home, for example by contacting employers before their child's job interview! The most important impact of mobile phones has resulted from their use as a platform for convergence. An increasing number of people access the Internet (and through this news and live or stored radio and television shows) through mobile devices such as the Apple iPhone. This has had some important consequences for British society and popular culture, as discussed on pages 124–25.

Source G

LAST week *The Sun* columnist Jeremy Clarkson was the victim of a 'happy slap' attack by a gang of teenage thugs which ended in THEM calling the cops, accusing the Top Gear star of being the aggressor. Here is his account of what happened – including his radical solution to the hoodie menace.

ALMOST every day a politician comes onto the news and tells us all that Britain's town centres are being overrun by teenage gangs who drink vast quantities of cider and then run about all night stabbing passers-by, while the event is videoed on mobile phones for the edification of YouTube viewers. It all sounds frightful, but frankly they could be talking about events on the moons of Jupiter because, happily, I live in Chipping Norton, where a lost kitten is front page news. Of course there are teenagers here, and some have hoodies, but mostly they are called Araminta and Harry, and I've never once got the feeling they want to plunge a kitchen knife into my heart. Last week, however, I had to go to Milton Keynes . . . It's a brilliant place, but sadly, because of Mr Blair's smoking ban, you have to go outside for a cigarette – which puts you slap-bang in one of the happy slapping town centres the politicians keep talking about. I wasn't remotely bothered when the swarm of children first approached . . . But they kept coming . . . I grabbed the ringleader by his hoodie, lifted him off the ground and explained it'd be best if he went home. He declined. They all did. In fact they all reached for their mobile phones and began to take pictures of the altercation . . . I therefore put him down, and in a flurry of swearing and hand gestures involving various fingers he was gone. Leaving the entire nation with a very serious problem.

Happily I think I have a solution. Nothing can be done about the parents because they are too thick. It'd be like trying to train a hedgehog to smoke a pipe. There's an equally big problem at school. Children are at liberty to do just about anything because there is absolutely nothing the teacher can do. The police? Oh come on. They are too busy filling in health and safety forms and processing speeding fines. The only place where this issue can be tackled, then, is at school. So you fit airport-style metal detectors at the doors to ensure no pupil is packing heat, you put all the troublemakers in one class and you give the teacher in charge immunity from criminal charges. And a submachine gun.

From 'Jeremy's Happy Slap Ordeal', published in *The Sun* on 7 December 2007

Source H

Children who use mobile phones are five times more likely to develop a type of brain tumour, research has suggested. The Swedish study indicated that under-16s are more at risk of radiation from mobile phones because their brains and nervous systems are still developing. Because their heads are smaller and their skulls are thinner the radiation penetrates deeper into their brains, it is believed. After presenting their findings, the scientists said that children under 12 should only use mobiles for emergencies. They added that teenagers should use hands-free devices and try to restrict themselves to texting. But other researchers have cast doubt on the findings, saying that mobiles have not been on the market long enough to test accurately the risks associated with them.

Around 90 per cent of under-16s in Britain have a mobile phone as do 40 per cent of primary school children.

From Daniel Martin, 'Children who use mobile phones are "five times more likely to develop brain tumours"', published in the *Daily Mail* on 23 September 2008

SKILLS BUILDER

1 What do Sources G and H suggest about the impact of mobile phones on British society?

2 How reliable are Sources G and H as evidence of the impact of mobile phones on British society? Explain your answer with reference to the tone of the content and to the provenance of each source.

3 Sources G and H suggest that mobile phones have had a negative impact on British society, particularly on young Britons. How far do you agree with this view?

4 Compare Source G with Sources E, F, G and K in Unit 3. Have teenagers got worse or is this merely a case of history repeating press exaggeration?

The Internet and the World Wide Web

The Internet is now a global network of computers linked by fibre optic cable and satellite relays. It all began on a much smaller scale: in 1969, an American military system called ARPANET linked just four computers. ARPANET allowed information to be shared instantaneously and the benefits were increasingly realised by the computer scientists who developed the network. By 1980, 213 computers were linked. In 1986, the US National Science Foundation launched NSFNet, a network of five supercomputers that could host information. Internet Service Providers (ISPs) began to provide software that allowed anyone with a computer to join this network via a telephone line. By 1988, 80,000 computers were linked; by 1993, this figure had risen to 1.3 million, by 1996 to 9.5 million and by 1999 to 19.5 million. In 1999, there were 153 million users worldwide, a figure that had increased to 1.5 billion by 2009. In the UK, 65 per cent of all households had broadband Internet connections by 2008. While the decreased cost of computers has facilitated this increase, a major reason for this huge growth in usage was that it became much easier to use. This was thanks to the invention of the World Wide Web by Tim Berners-Lee (see Biography Box below).

Definition

E-commerce

Business that is conducted via the Internet rather than through high street shops or shopping centres. Goods are delivered by post or by a shop's own delivery service.

The Internet and British society

It is already clear that both the 'medium' and the 'message' of the Internet and World Wide Web have the potential to revolutionise popular culture and the way that British people live. Internet usage has already begun to alter the everyday habits of many, from shopping and leisure to work and communication. Potential long-term changes include:

- the end of a predominantly 'face-to-face' society, with the rise of **e-commerce** and social network sites
- the democratisation of society, with universal access to information and education (perhaps making schools and teachers redundant!) and the

Biography

Tim Berners-Lee 1955–

Tim Berners-Lee was born in London where he went to primary and secondary school. Having gained a first-class degree in Physics at Oxford University, he went to work at the European Organisation for Nuclear Research (CERN). It was while he was working at CERN that he developed several crucial ideas that turned the Internet from a tool for scientists into a global portal for education, entertainment and commerce.

The first key idea was hypertext. 'Hyper' is a prefix derived from Greek meaning 'beyond' or 'over'. Hypertext is words (or other symbols) that have an embedded link to other information *beyond* that which is immediately before you. This information (text, pictures, films and so on) is stored on computers across the world linked by the Internet. The links to this information work thanks to two more ideas that he developed: Hypertext Transfer Protocol (HTTP) and Uniform Resource Locator (URL). HTTP is an instruction to a computer to find and display the information requested by clicking on a link; URL is the 'address' where this information may be found.

Tim also created a simple computer language called Hypertext Mark-up Language (HTML) that allowed people to build their own web pages with hypertext links. The ease and usefulness of the web page system has led to the rapid increase in their number since 1991. This could have resulted in chaos had it not been for another of Tim's ideas: a system of domain names, such as .com, .co.uk, .org, to organise web pages. Domain names allow search engines (which Tim originally called 'browsers') to find information in a useful fashion. All of these ideas came together in 1991 to create the 'World Wide Web'. This was initially a very grand name for just one website hosted on a single computer at CERN (you can see the first web page by going to www.pearsonhotlinks.co.uk and entering the express code 5063P). However, the web grew exponentially thanks to the growing sophistication of search engines and the fact that Tim did not copyright his ideas: anyone could use them free of charge. Tim has won many international awards for his work. He was named 'the greatest Briton' of 2004, to which he replied 'I am very proud to be British, it is great fun to be British and this award is just an amazing honour'.

ability of individuals to make their voice heard by uploading information onto the web

- the triumph of cultural globalisation, with the decline of a specifically British identity and the rise of identities based on online communities.

The following discussion, coming as it does only a few years after the real explosion of Internet use in Britain, can offer only tentative conclusions based on recent trends. They are likely to become dated extremely quickly!

The first measurable impacts of the web on British society have been on work and shopping. The charts in Source I are based on data from **British Social Attitudes**. The figures in each were gained by asking questions to a representative sample of British people. Look at the results of the surveys and then answer the questions that follow.

Definition

British Social Attitudes

This is a survey conducted by the National Centre for Social Research. It has been carried out every year since 1983. It asks questions about social, political, economic and moral issues. It is an invaluable tool for modern social historians; see the BritSocAt website for more.

Source I

Year	*People with an Internet connection in their home*	*People who used the Internet for shopping*	*People who used the Internet to keep in touch with groups they belong to*
1999	22	no data	no data
2000	36	no data	no data
2001	44	no data	no data
2002	52	20	6
2003	52	42	15
2005	61	59	19
2007	68	no data	no data

7.5 A table showing the percentage of people in the UK who had the Internet or used it in particular ways between 1999 and 2007, based on data from surveys conducted by British Social Attitudes

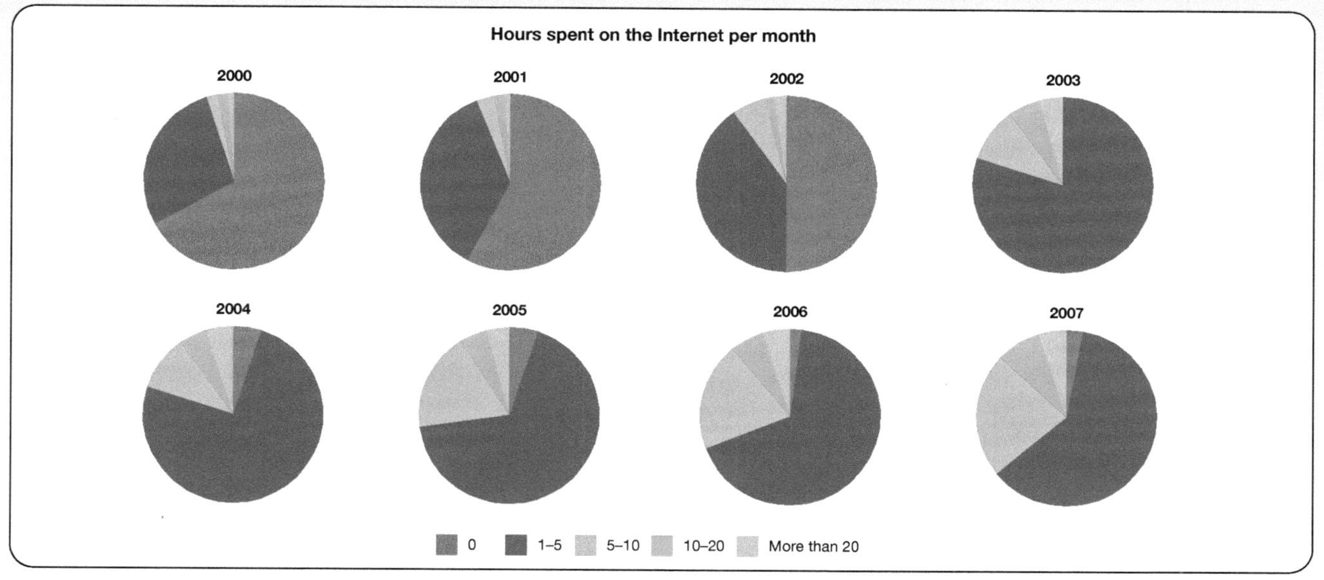

7.6 Pie charts showing Internet usage based on surveys conducted by British Social Attitudes

SKILLS BUILDER

1. Is there anything that surprises you about the results of the surveys in Source I?
2. What can we learn about British people's use of the Internet between 2002 and 2007 from Source I?
3. What can we infer from Source I about the impact of Internet use on:
   - British shopping habits?
   - 'Face-to-face' time?
4. How useful is statistical evidence such as Source I for historians who want to find out about social or cultural change?

The rise of e-commerce has been an important trend and one that is likely to grow in significance as the century progresses. However, at the time of writing, although the value of Internet sales was growing at around 15 per cent a year, it remained only around 3.5 per cent of total retail sales. While almost every major shop has an online presence, it appears as if the shopping centres are safe for the moment. Equally, although a 2008 survey suggested that 57 per cent of British workers use the Internet for work, only for a tiny minority of workers does this mean that they can work from home, rather than commute to work. Some studies have suggested that use of the Internet in the office and home has blurred the boundaries between work and leisure time: people check social networking sites at work and work-related emails at home. It is too early to say whether this is a trend that will significantly affect patterns of work.

How far is it possible to talk of a 'Britain 2.0'?

The largest impacts of the Internet on British society and on popular culture have been the result of recent changes in the way the Internet is used. Many media and social analysts now talk of a 'Web2.0' that grew in the years after 2004. While the technology, in terms of the memory and processing speeds of computers, and the speed of information transfer via fibre optic as opposed to copper wires, has improved, the actual structure of the Internet has not changed. What could therefore be meant by the idea of a 'second generation' Internet?

The key difference between early Internet use and its more recent use has been the *interactivity* of use: rather than merely using the web as a source of information, people are now able to actively participate in what has become known as 'social media': the construction of web content by uploading pictures, videos and blogs, and by editing wiki web pages. As Tim Berners-Lee has pointed out, they *could* have done this from the very start of the web; perhaps it is just the increased number of users and their familiarity with the web that has led to this change in usage.

There are some clear differences between social media and the traditional mass media we have encountered so far:

- Whereas there is some delay between an event happening and its report in mass media, such as radio or newspapers, social media can be produced almost immediately: there is no need to go through an editorial process and to check and polish the way things are presented.
- Whereas mass media have very high start up and running costs, it costs very little to produce and upload social media. This means that it is no longer just governments or private firms that can produce media, but also ordinary citizens.
- Whereas traditional mass media require workers with a good deal of specialist training (for example printers or cameramen), the tools needed to produce and upload social media do not require any specialist training: anyone can do it!

- Whereas mass media products are set in stone once they have been published or broadcast, social media, such as blogs, can be altered at will by their producers.

These differences are already beginning to have some impact on the operation of traditional mass media and the relationship between ordinary people and figures of authority.

Web2.0, newspapers, citizen journalism and blogging

The rise of the Internet and social media has had a large impact on newspapers and television news reporting. The traditional mass media have had to adapt to the new media in order to survive and try to retain their prominent position in society. Source J helps to explain a major cause of newspaper publishers' concerns.

Source J

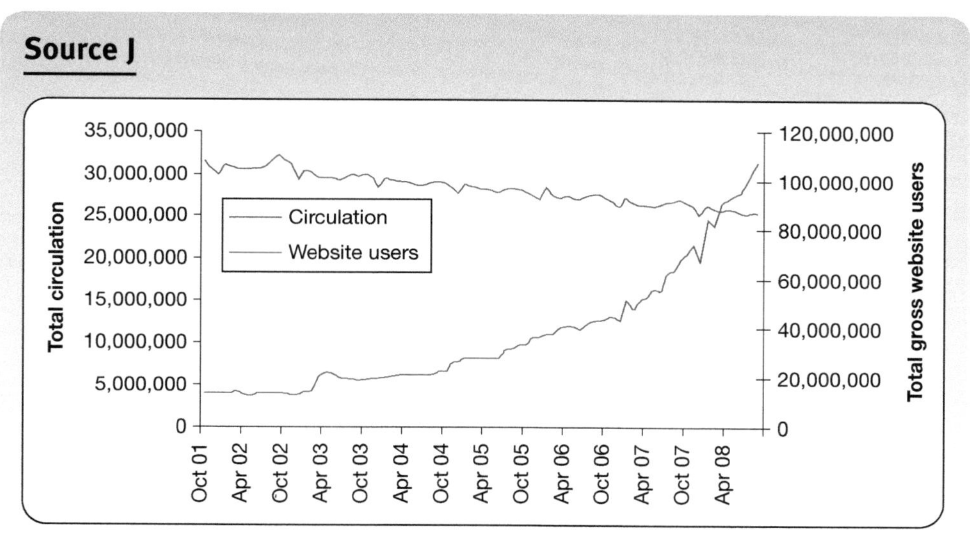

7.7 A chart showing a comparison between newspaper circulation and Internet usage in the UK from 2001 to 2009

Whereas in 1983 only 22 per cent of British people did not read a newspaper, by 2007 more than half never read a newspaper. However, even in 1984, only 20 per cent of people saw papers as their main source of news; over 60 per cent saw the television in this capacity. In addition to falling sales and loss of advertising revenue to websites, the cost of producing computers has fallen much faster than printing costs; it is now cheaper to make a transistor for a circuit board than to print a single letter! Free newspapers, entirely reliant on advertising revenue, have struggled: in September 2009, Rupert Murdoch's *thelondonpaper* was closed after making losses of almost £13 million that year. The fall in revenue has forced many major daily newspapers to sack journalists; this has led to even greater reliance on 'wire-copy' for stories: early in 2009, *Private Eye* exposed *The Daily Telegraph* for using made-up journalist names in their sports report by-lines to make it look as if they still had a full team of reporters! Many newspapers have launched online editions to adapt to the trend for British people to search for news on the Internet, but even the most popular online paper, *The Guardian*, only gains slightly more hits in a month (16.7 million) than the BBC News website gets in a week (14 million). The problem is that the vast majority of people are not prepared to pay to view online newspapers. However, it is too early to predict the end of printed news: in addition to huge sales of magazines, 45 per cent of Britons still buy and read a daily newspaper; while the average online news reader looks at only 1 per cent of the stories, people on average look at 79 per cent of a printed paper. It is clear that many people are still prepared to pay for their news; it is difficult to estimate how long this will continue to be the case when people can get the news for free online.

Question

Which is a greater cause for concern in your opinion: the growth of cross-media ownership or the recent decline of newspaper circulation?

Citizen journalism and **blogs**

The 'CNN effect' had an impact on the way news was reported because it left little scope for editing images before they were broadcast. However, many armies learned from the way the British military handled the media during the Falklands war to limit this effect: the American and British armies in Iraq (2003–10) and Afghanistan (2001–) 'embedded' journalists with troops to control where they conducted their live reports; in this way they 'sanitised' reports and ensured that they did not give away strategic information. The Internet has undermined this arrangement because of the rise of 'citizen reporters' who are able to blog from war zones (notable examples included 'Riverbend', the online name of an anonymous young woman in Baghdad), and to capture images and video on their mobile phones and upload them onto sites such as YouTube; even soldiers have uploaded videos of their experiences to this website. Many news programmes on television now use such clips and encourage viewers to send in their photos and clips. In November 2009, the BBC appointed its first Social Media editor; this is clearly a reflection of the growing importance of citizen journalism. As with blogs and music downloads, citizen reporting has reduced the ability of a few powerful individuals or organisations to control the information available to a wide audience. It is unclear what the impact of citizen journalist war reports have been on the way the British public have viewed recent conflicts: as Daniel Bennett (author of Enquiry source 5D, page 126) has concluded, 'they provide a fascinating taste of the experience of modern conflict but usually offer no tactical or strategic explanation of what is happening'.

Definition

Blog

Short for weblog, an online diary of comments usually displayed in reverse chronological order. Blogs usually contain a mixture of text, images and video and have an area for people to post comments.

One of the most important examples of social media are blogs. By 2008, it was estimated that almost 200 million blogs had been created, although many of these had fallen into disuse (giving rise to the rather nice phrase 'dotsam and netsam'!). In that year there were estimated to be over 3 million active blogs in the UK. The key question is the extent to which they are a positive force for democratisation. The vast majority of blogs are personal diaries; whereas in the past you might have needed an expensive printing press or radio transmitter to spread your ideas, now all you need is a computer and an ISP. This means that there is now far more 'bottom up' information and organisation than in the past. Such blogs can also serve as virtual communities where people with similar interests can pool their ideas and observations. These are clearly an important new arena of free speech. Many blogs provide a range of information that people might not otherwise have easy access to, from the best goods and services available to the workings of the government in Westminster. Lastly, blogs offer a direct link between the public sphere (for example politicians) and the private sphere. These are all examples of how blogs, and the Internet in general, can be seen as a democratising force in Britain as it levels the differences between the 'haves' and the 'have nots' in society.

However, most of the 'influential' political blogs are written by professional journalists or by people connected with the political establishment. In addition, some commentators are worried about the lack of professionalism, accuracy and accountability in news-related blogs. Lastly, it is estimated that only 20 per cent of Internet users in Britain (or 15 per cent of the population) read any blogs at all! For these reasons, some would dispute the extent to which blogs should be thought of as a source for democratisation. Read the enquiry sources below and then discuss the questions that they raise.

Questions

1 How would mobile phones and the Internet have changed the reporting of the Falklands war?
2 How might the fact that almost all British people have the potential to be 'citizen journalists' affect relations between figures of authority and ordinary citizens?

Enquiry 5: What has been the impact of blogging on authority and news reporting?

Enquiry source 5A

Today, self-publication on the Internet is dispensing with editors . . . Thanks to the blogging revolution the power of publicity is in everyone's hands. Every minute of every day thousands of fingertips are reporting the actions of the high and mighty straight onto the web. Everyone will soon be held accountable. Everything will soon be revealed. 'Watch it buddy, I'm blogging this!'

From Erik Ringmar, *A Blogger's Manifesto*, published in 2007. Ringmar is a professor of Social and Cultural Studies; he wrote his book having been told to 'take down and destroy' his blog by the Director of the London School of Economics who was unhappy about criticism of the standard of teaching at the university

Enquiry source 5B

Journalistic integrity, you know, fact-based reporting, serious investigative reporting, how to retain those ethics in all these different new media and how to make sure that it's paid for, is really a challenge. But it's something that I think is absolutely critical to the health of our democracy . . . I am concerned that if the direction of the news is all blogosphere, all opinions, with no serious fact-checking, no serious attempts to put stories in context, that what you will end up getting is people shouting at each other across the void but not a lot of mutual understanding.

From an interview with US President Barack Obama, published in the *Pittsburgh Post-Gazette* in September 2009

Enquiry source 5C

Blog name	*Author*
Iain Dale's Diary	Iain Dale: a journalist who writes for *The Daily Telegraph* and *GQ Magazine*. He stood as a Conservative candidate in the 2003 General Election
Guy Fawkes' blog	Paul Staines: an Irish Conservative Liberal. He has helped to expose government spin
Liberal Conspiracy	Many: mainly *The Guardian* journalists who want to promote left-liberal debate
ConservativeHome's ToryDiary	Tim Montgomerie: has worked in a number of capacities for the Conservative Party; contributes articles to *The Guardian*, *The Independent*
politicalbetting.com	Mike Smithsom: former Liberal Democrat councillor, stood as a Liberal candidate in the 2003 General Election
Labourlist	Many: openly partisan in favour of the Labour Party
Dizzy Thinks	Phil Hendren: stood as a Conservative councillor in 2007
Liberal Democrat Voice	Many: all Liberal Party members
The Devil's Kitchen	Chris Mounsey: a former UKIP member
Harry's Place	Anonymous group of left-wing commentators

A list of the top ten influential blogs according to the Wikio website, posted in June 2009

Question

How far do you agree with the following statements:

- 'Blogs are a menace to serious news-gathering and distribution.'
- 'Blogs have the capacity to be an effective tool of democratisation in Britain.'

You could do some more research on the Internet, especially on blogs about the wars in Iraq and Afghanistan and the July 2005 London bombings, before discussing this question.

Enquiry source 5D

The rise of blogging in the last decade of the twentieth century was perceived to be a threat by traditional media journalists. Bloggers did not always conform to the norms and practices of professional media standards. Operating on exceptionally minimal budgets, sometimes no more than the cost of a computer and an Internet connection, they often published, reproduced and distributed content for free. Some journalists regarded them as a menace to serious newsgathering and distribution undermining the business model of journalism which charged for news content. They were also worried that blogging would lead to the domination of uninformed commentary and opinion on the Web at the expense of serious news. But journalists' attitudes to blogs gradually began to change. They recognised that some bloggers were producing valuable news content particularly after their contribution to the coverage of the London bombings in 2005. They also began experimenting with the blogging format themselves, leading to the widespread adoption of blogs by traditional media organisations. Today, most journalists accept that blogs will co-exist with the traditional media both co-operating and competing in a new media landscape.

From a letter to the author, written in December 2009 by Daniel Bennett. Bennett is completing a PhD on the impact of blogging and new media on the way the BBC has reported the war in Afghanistan

Web2.0, popular music, radio and Internet piracy

In addition to newspaper publishers, the Internet is a source of concern for big record labels, partly because it removes the need for their existence and partly because of the damage it has done to their profits. In 2005, four big record labels dominated global album and single sales (of which the UK made up 11 and 29 per cent respectively). Their advantage over competitors was the size of their production, advertising and distribution structures, which allowed them to cash in on album sales and merchandising. Source K discusses ways in which the Internet has undermined these advantages.

Source K

On 17 October 2005, a group from Sheffield called Arctic Monkeys released a single entitled 'I Bet You Look Good on the Dancefloor'. It went straight to number one in the charts and was included on their first album *Whatever People Say I Am, That's What I'm Not* [which you may now know to be a line from the film *Saturday Night and Sunday Morning!*, see page 25] released in January 2006, which sold more than 120,000 copies on the first day and 363,000 copies (all that were available) in the first week . . . What made this episode special was the way the Arctic Monkeys made their music and found an audience. When they were ready to record, they did not go to an established multinational such as EMI or Warner, but to a small, independent company called Domino, founded as a one-man, one-woman enterprise in a South London flat in 1993. Next, they studiously avoided the usual route of demonstration disc, manager and record company, in favour of the Internet. They made their first music downloads available for free and encouraged their fans to exchange tracks. Whatever they may have foregone in royalties they made up many times over by creating a very large and loyal following who flocked to their concerts.

From Tim Blanning, *The Triumph of Music*, published in 2008. Blanning is Professor of Modern European History at the University of Cambridge

Questions

1 In what ways does Source K suggest that the Internet has undermined the control of big record labels over the music industry?
2 How might the rise of musical social media (as opposed to industrially produced and distributed music) affect popular culture in Britain?

The most common way of listening to downloaded music is the Apple iPod, which commands around 90 per cent of the MP3 player market. Just as the jukebox allowed black Americans to listen to the type of music they wanted in the 1930s and 1940s, so digital music players such as iPods allow the user to customise their listening. Source L discusses the impact of iPods on their owners and on society more generally.

Source L

The iPod immerses the listener in a private world, cut away from the community-building nature of popular music that has been a characteristic through much of its history. So much of rock 'n' roll was fired by a shared experience of rhythm, dancing, sweating and singing. The iPod is different, slicing the geography and history away from sound. Even albums are lost as the single finds new life in innovative mixes, excised from the original running order. It is a personal soundtrack, not a collective sonic experience . . . The immersion of these students in their pods has created a fascinating social effect. We have a whole generation that looks down at their digital platform, rather than up to hear and see the analogue environment. This is a downward-facing digispace when personal connectivity means more than concentration . . . What will be the consequences in building communities and consciousness, let alone knowledge and social justice, by living in an individualised, atomised, customised, consumerist world?

From Tara Brabazon, 'The Isolation of the iPod People', published in *The Times Higher Education Supplement* on 3 April 2008. Brabazon is Professor of Media Studies at the University of Brighton

Questions

1 On what grounds does Source L conclude that the iPod is having a negative impact on society?
2 How far do you agree with the author's judgements?
3 How far does the continued success of radio undermine Source L's view of young Britons 'living in an individualised, atomised, customised, consumerist world'?

Definition

Digital native

Someone who cannot remember a time before the Internet; people born after the mid-1990s in developed countries such as the UK are members of this group. They are also sometimes referred to as the 'iGeneration' or 'Millenials'.

The rise of MP3 players and downloads has not damaged the popularity of radio. Radio has been forced to adapt, for example with the release of 'podcasts', and the provision of programmes on 'listen again' sites such as BBC iPlayer, but seems set to thrive in the Internet era in a format recognisable to listeners in the 1970s. Radio 1 plays the latest pop music, a good deal of this from America, Radio 2 plays 'classic' pop tracks for older listeners, Radio 3 plays real classical music (although with more 'world' music in the evenings), while Radio 4 remains the home of the spoken word. A 2009 report by Radio Joint Audience Research Limited (Rajar) confirmed that listening figures at home and on mobile phones continue to rise.

Enquiry 6: Should 'Internet piracy' be illegal?

Since the late 1990s it has been possible to download music for free by installing file-sharing software on your computer. While Napster, one of the most famous early peer-to-peer file sharing sites was shut down after a range of copyright lawsuits in 2001, other sites such as Limewire continue to flourish. Source K mentioned 'downloads' and 'exchange tracks'; as '**digital natives**' someone in your class is likely to have done one, or both, of these things. If you have used a peer-to-peer network site, or a music download site that is not owned by a big record label, you are not alone: according to the 2009 report *Digital Britain*, 7 million people in the UK downloaded music illegally in the previous 12 months with a total value of £120 billion! The report says that many young people now see free music, like other free services on the Internet, as a right. At the time of writing, the government was unsure what to do about this 'Internet piracy': on the one hand it would be impossible to criminalise 7 million people, but on the other hand there are concerns that the music industry could collapse due to plummeting sales if nothing is done. The Digital Economy Bill of November 2009 suggested that the government intends to reform copyright law so that big record labels will be able to force ISPs to disconnect people who make illegal downloads. However, these proposals are being fought by a wide range of organisations including Google, Facebook, Yahoo, and eBay. What will you think?

Question

Should 'Internet piracy' be illegal? You could conduct some further research on this controversial topic on the Internet before holding a class debate.

Enquiry source 6A

In recent years we have seen an unprecedented onslaught on the rights of the individual. We are treated like criminals when we share entertainment digitally, even though this is just the modern equivalent of lending a book or a DVD to a friend. We look on helpless as our culture and heritage, so important for binding our society together, is eroded and privatised. Now there is a democratic alternative. We, the people, can take back our rights. We, the people, can overturn the fat cats and the corrupt MPs who hold our nation's cultural treasures to ransom, ignore our democratic wishes and undermine our civil liberties. The Internet has turned our world into a global village. Ideas can be shared at incredible speed, and at negligible cost. The benefits are plain to see, but as a result, many vested interests are threatened. The old guard works hard to preserve their power and their privilege, so we must work hard for our freedom . . . Outdated laws must change, and will change. The only question is when we will change them. Join our cause, and help make this change happen now!

From the website of the Pirate Party UK. The Pirate Party are an international Internet-based political party that campaigns for copyright reform, reduced surveillance and increased freedom of speech. The party was founded in Sweden in 2006 where it is now the third largest party in terms of membership

Enquiry source 6B

Internet piracy is a despicable crime . . . but try telling that to the Jolly Roger crew I've fathered! My wild guess is that roughly half of Britain's teenagers and young adults walk around every day with stolen property worth more than £100 on their persons . . . All four of my boys own iPods, stocked with . . . literally thousands of recordings – enough between them to stock an entire floor of HMV's flagship Oxford Street shop in the days of vinyl. If they'd downloaded them legally, at 79p a track or £7.99 an album, they would have had to pay well into four figures. But did they? I very much doubt it. The sad truth is that among many or even most of my sons' circle, it's thought downright eccentric to pay for a download . . . As a journalist, with nothing but words to sell, I have a strong vested interest in the principle of protecting intellectual property. My employers, who own the copyright to my columns in return for my salary, have every reason to be annoyed when the work in which they've invested pops up on other people's websites without permission or payment.

From an article in the *Daily Mail* by journalist Tom Uttley, published on 28 August 2009

Enquiry source 6C

Companies face significant security risks when employees file-share on corporate networks. Research conducted by Ipsos-MORI for IFPI in the UK in November 2007 indicates that one in ten office employees are using the workplace to download music, two thirds of them illegally, exposing their employers not only to computer network risks, but to legal risks too. Nearly half of those who download music illegally in the workplace (43%) know that their employers have a policy on copying, sharing and downloading music – suggesting they disregard rules set by their bosses. The problem appears to be concentrated among younger workers. The survey indicated that one in five under 25s illegally download music at work. It only takes one person to download an infected file and expose the company to huge risks.

From 'The hidden dangers of illegal downloading', part of the International Federation of the Phonographic Industry's *Digital Music Report*, published in 2008. The infected files contain malware, short for malicious software. An increasingly common type of malware is spyware, a program that can send personal information from your computer about your web-browsing habits to other people without your knowledge

Web2.0 and television

Television on the Internet looks set to further the trend that began with videos, and was accelerated with satellite and digital television, towards the fragmentation of televisual popular culture. All the major terrestrial channels now offer a 'watch again' facility so viewers are not constrained by schedules. These channels have also made available large selections of old programmes to download and watch on services such as iPlayer, 4oD and ITV Player, further enhancing viewers' choice. Perhaps a sign of greater change to come has been the rise of YouTube as a source of entertainment. In 2009, it was estimated that 20 hours of footage were uploaded to the site every minute. Instead of whole shows, clips related to a particular theme are generally watched on YouTube. These changes could greatly accelerate the changes discussed in connection with video recorders and cable: rather than audiences of millions tuning in to watch popular programmes, discussing them the next day and being influenced by them, Internet television looks set to promote individual as opposed to mass viewing habits. It is likely that this will further promote the growth and co-existence of a range of sub-cultures rather than reflect or mould a single, monolithic culture as was more the case before the rise of new media.

However, the most famous 'YouTube celebrities' to date owe their fame principally to exposure on terrestrial television: the clip of Scottish singer Susan Boyle was seen 103 million times in just nine days after she sang on the ITV show *Britain's Got Talent*; Charlie and Harry Davies-Carr (the stars of 'Charlie bit me, again!', the fifth most watched YouTube clip of all time with 105 million hits) rose to fame after their appearance on daytime TV show *Richard and Judy*. There has already been a good deal of convergence between 'old media' television and the new media, but this has not had a dramatic impact on the content of terrestrial television. Significant changes, such as the growth of lifestyle shows and reality television, for example *Big Brother* (Channel 4 2000–), *I'm A Celebrity, Get Me Out of Here!* (ITV 2000–), took place after the 1990 Broadcasting Act yet before the explosion of Internet usage after 2002. It is worth noting that popular shows such as *Strictly Come Dancing* (BBC1 2004–) and *Britain's Got Talent* were able to attract audiences of 13 million and 19.2 million respectively, while around 9 million people still watch *EastEnders* and *Coronation Street* every week.

Web2.0 and British society

While it is still very early to gauge the overall impact of Web2.0 on British society, a lot of research is being conducted by researchers in a number of fields. Oxford University launched the Oxford Internet Institute in 2001 and now runs a Masters Degree course in 'The Social Science of the Internet'. They have begun to research the impact of the Internet on things as diverse as meeting, dating and marriage, ideas about privacy and the British sense of humour. All of this research is at a very preliminary stage and it is too early for a textbook such as this to report any firm conclusions. However, some changes are already very apparent: Source M is an example of some recent research into the impact of the Internet.

Source M

One of the most pronounced changes in the daily habits of British citizens is a reduction in the number of minutes per day that they interact with another human being. In less than two decades, the number of people saying there is no one with whom they discuss important matters nearly tripled. Parents spend less time with their children than they did only a decade ago. Britain's disinclination for togetherness is only equaled by her love of communicating through new technologies. This is now the most significant contributing factor to society's growing physical estrangement. Whether in or out of the home, more people of all ages in the UK are physically and socially disengaged from the people around them because they are wearing earphones, talking or texting on a mobile phone, or using a laptop or Blackberry. Eye and ear contact between people of all ages and relationships is declining . . . Children now spend more time in the family home alone in front of TV/computer screens than doing anything else: twenty five per cent of British five-year olds own a computer or laptop of their own. There is an enormous increase in 'social networking' among younger and younger children, which is now their main reason for using the Internet. UK social networking usage is now the highest in Europe.

From Dr Aric Sigman, 'Well Connected?: The Biological Implications of "Social Networking"', published in *Biologist* on 1 February 2009

SKILLS BUILDER

1 What conclusions does Dr Sigman reach about the impact of the Internet on British society in Source M? Is the Internet the only factor for change referred to?

2 Source M is from the journal *Biologist*. Does this mean it is only of limited use to historians who wish to explore the impact of the Internet on British society?

The Internet has not affected everyone equally in Britain and many commentators predict that the 'digital divide' (between those who have access to information and services on the Internet and those who do not) will have negative consequences for British society. By the end of 2009, Swindon was the only town in the UK to offer free wi-fi access to all residents. Although the government has pledged to help fund broadband access for every home by 2012, even then not everyone will use it. A survey in 2008 suggested that 70 per cent of Britons over the age of 65 have never used the Internet. In a 2006 report, Internet researcher Davide Di Gennaro found that while the Internet promoted more widespread active participation in politics (most commonly through **e-petitions** to government on issues such as road tax), those who participated tended to be male, middle-aged and highly educated, precisely those people who were already active in politics anyway. As he put it 'inequalities in offline political participation tend to be reproduced and magnified in online participation'. Source N discusses the impact of the age-related 'digital divide', while Source O explores an income- and class-related divide.

Definition

E-petition

A petition is a demand sent to a figure or body of authority with a number of signatures that indicate people's support.
An e-petition is an Internet version of this.

Source N

Despite a rise in the number of 'silver surfers', people aged over 65 emerged as the least likely to use the web . . . The findings were attacked by groups representing the elderly as evidence that the government was not doing enough to bridge the so-called 'digital divide'. David Sinclair, the head of policy at Help the Aged, said it was vital that elderly people were connected to the Internet, especially during the current credit crisis when the best deals for electricity, gas and food are available on the web.

'Exclusion from modern society is increasingly less about being able to get to the library and more about being able to access the rivers of information flowing in and out of British homes each day,' he said. 'If you cannot access these rivers you cannot take part.'

'This is not only about getting cheap car insurance online. It is about equality in the marketplace. We know Internet access can mean a difference of hundreds of pounds over the year from deals on utility bills, food to all other manner of other goods. In a time when costs are rising should we not allow the poorest among us a chance to keep afloat?'

From Nicole Martin, 'Record Number of Homes Have Broadband', published in *The Daily Telegraph* on 26 August 2008

Source O

While the majority of people in the UK have access to the Internet, there are still 10 million people who do not. Of these people, 4 million are the most socially and economically disadvantaged in the country. 15 per cent of people living in deprived areas have used a government online service or website in the last year, compared to 55 per cent nationally; 49 per cent of people without access are in the lowest socio-economic groups; 70 per cent of people who live in social housing aren't online; 80 per cent of government interactions with the public take place with the bottom 25 per cent of society, so failing to encourage everyone online keeps government costs high.

Information from the 21st Century Challenges website, compiled by Martha Lane Fox, an early e-commerce entrepreneur appointed as Britain's first 'Digital Inclusion Champion' in June 2009

Source P

I despise Facebook . . . [It is] a heavily funded program to create an arid global virtual republic where your own self and your relationship with your friends are converted into commodities on sale to giant global brands.

From Tom Hodgkinson, 'Why You Should Beware Facebook', published in Australian newspaper *The Age* on 19 January 2008

Questions

1 What can you infer from Sources N and O about the impact of unequal access to the Internet on sections of British society?

2 Which source is more useful to an historian who wants to find out about the digital divide in Britain in the first decade of the twenty-first century?

For all the reasons mentioned above, it would appear that new media is inherently a democratising force. However, there are a number of reasons why this might not be the case. Firstly, old media still has a large degree of influence on the popular awareness of Internet-based media: in addition to the *Richard and Judy* example above, television news editors select the citizen journalist clips they use; the biggest e-petitions have had widespread old media coverage. Secondly, big commercial interests have already begun to dominate Web2.0 and use it as a platform to advertise their products in a more effective manner. In July 2005, Rupert Murdoch's News Corporation bought MySpace for $580 million; Facebook, its value estimated at $8–15 billion, has been linked with possible sales to Microsoft and Google. The reason why Facebook is worth so much is because of the profitability from advertising revenue: by the end of 2009 there were 350 million Facebook users worldwide who each provide information about themselves (age, gender and so on) that helps companies to target their marketing through a program called 'Facebook Social Ads'. Source P is how one critic has described Facebook.

Unit summary

What have you learned in this unit?

There have been two waves of new media since the 1980s. Both waves have affected mass media, but their impact on popular culture and British society are less clear. New media have led to greater choice and forced old media to compete for audience share. Overall, old media producers have done well to adapt to the challenge of new rivals and have used convergence with new media to their advantage. While the Internet is now a feature of a majority of British people's lives, this has not been to the exclusion of old media.

The Internet has affected the way that many people communicate and shop. Again, this has not led to a wholesale revolution in British society; rather, British people have adapted and used new technology to make aspects of their lives more convenient. However, there are already signs that the Internet could have a more profound impact on social and family relations as people spend more and more time at their computer screens.

The Internet has the potential to undermine the dominance of mass media by a few large organisations. However, similar to the increased concentration in the ownership of newspapers since 1945, and to the take-overs of ITV franchises and local radio since 1990, large media firms have already begun to spend huge sums of money to ensure new media promotes their interests and views.

What skills have you used in this unit?

You have analysed and interpreted a range of statistical sources. You have compared and contrasted these sources with textual information. You have weighed up the relative usefulness of academic or statistical market research with headlines and opinion columns from newspapers. This has helped to further refine your evaluative skills. You have also tested your comprehension skills with a number of the sources in this unit.

SKILLS BUILDER

1 Which new media do you think had the greatest impact on British society and popular culture since the 1980s: video, satellite television, digital television or the Internet?

2 On pages 120–22 there were a number of possible changes that the Internet might make to British society in future. Look again at Sources I to P and decide how far recent trends support the likelihood of these changes. Once you have done this, rank the possible changes in order of likelihood.

Exam tips

This is the sort of question you will find appearing on the examination paper as a (b) question.

Study Sources I, L and M and use your own knowledge.

Do you agree with the view, expressed in Source L, that new media have promoted an 'individualised, atomised, customised, consumerist world'?

You tackled a (b) style question in Units 4 and 6. Build upon the earlier tips with the advice below.

As with your previous (b) style answers, you want to avoid basing paragraphs on particular sources. Rather, you want to use (and ideally cross-reference) information from more than one source in a paragraph based on a theme that directly helps to answer the question. With a question such as the one here, a number of themes for paragraphs have been suggested for you: what are they? It is good practice to 'question the question', to make sure you directly tackle the question set, rather than regurgitating a similar essay you might have completed in the past! Armed with your paragraph themes you are ready to tackle the source content and provenance in the way suggested in the previous exam tips section.

RESEARCH TOPIC

Choose one of the websites below and conduct research to find out the following things:

- Who created the website?
- What is the 'mission statement' or motto of the website?
- Who now owns (or who wants to own) the website?
- How much money do the websites make for their owners?
- What has been the impact of the website on British people?

Google, Wikipedia, Facebook, MySpace, YouTube, Amazon. You may, after consultation with your teacher, conduct research on a website you think is socially and culturally significant other than those listed here (for example Second Life or World of Warcraft).

UNIT

8 How far have mass media undermined figures of authority in Britain?

What is this unit about?

Units 2 to 7 have been in chronological order to give you a good feel for the cultural, social and media developments in each decade. The next two units are synoptic: they give a general view of some important trends across the whole period. You will need to look back at relevant sections from earlier units to refresh your memory of some of the things referred to here. As you go through the next two units, keep in mind a central question: during what period did the greatest rate of change occur, and why?

This unit considers the extent to which mass media have changed the relationship of traditional figures of authority with the British people since 1945. In particular, the extent to which newspapers, television and new media have undermined popular respect for authority figures will be discussed.

Key questions

- How far have mass media undermined respect for the government?
- How far have mass media undermined respect for the monarchy?
- How far have mass media undermined respect for the police?
- How far has the rise of 'celebrities' undermined respect for authority figures?

Timeline

1953	Coronation of Queen Elizabeth II is televised
1957	Elizabeth II makes the first televised Christmas Day broadcast. It becomes an annual tradition; by 1961 over half the British population either watch or listen to the broadcast
1969	An audience of around 500 million watch Prince Charles' investiture
1977	Elizabeth II's Silver Jubilee celebrations
1978	Parliamentary proceedings broadcast on radio on a regular basis
1979	Police Complaints Board is established. It is replaced in 1984 by the Police Complaints Authority and the Independent Police Complaints Commission in 2004
1981	Marriage of Prince Charles and Lady Diana Spencer
1986	Marriage of Prince Andrew and Sarah Ferguson
1989	Parliamentary proceedings are televised for the first time; regular television broadcasts are made after 1990

1990	Press Complaints Commission is set up as a self-regulatory body with a code of conduct for journalists
1992	Charles and Diana announce that they are to divorce. Prince Andrew and Sarah Ferguson separate
	The Sun publishes the 'Squidgygate' tape transcriptions, recorded in 1989
1995	Princess Diana features in a BBC *Panorama* documentary about her life
	Criminal Justice and Public Order Act increases the police powers to arrest, imprison and fine people
1996	Charles and Diana, and Prince Andrew and Sarah Ferguson, are divorced
1997	Death of Princess Diana in a car crash in Paris
2000	Start of Channel 4 reality TV show *Big Brother*
2001	Anti-Terrorism, Crime and Security Act allows the government to lock up suspected terrorists for up to 28 days without trial
2002	Elizabeth II's Golden Jubilee celebrations

Source A

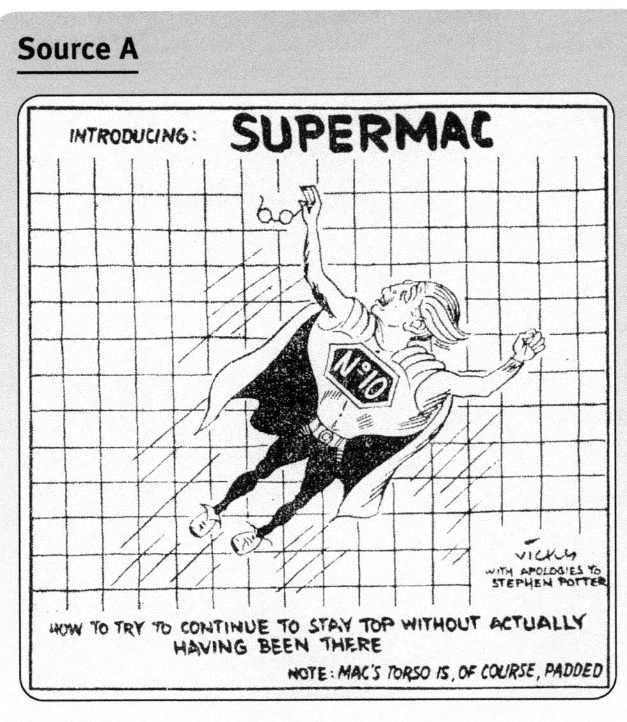

8.1 A cartoon by Victor Weisz ('Vicky') of Harold Macmillan, Conservative Prime Minister (1957–63), published in the *Evening Standard* on 6 November 1958

Source B

8.2 A cartoon by Steve Bell of John Major, the Conservative Prime Minister (1990–97), published in *The Guardian* in 1992 shortly after the release of the Conservative manifesto 'The Best Future for Britain'

SKILLS BUILDER

1 In what ways do Sources A and B poke fun at the prime ministers?
2 Are there more similarities or differences in the way the cartoonists make fun of the prime ministers?
3 What can we infer from the differences between Source A and Source B about how the media's representation of authority figures has changed since 1945?

We have already seen how the 'satire boom' of the early 1960s paved the way for more critical attacks by mass media on figures of authority in Britain. The Profumo scandal hinted at the way in which the private lives of authority figures would increasingly fall under the spotlight of media coverage. This coverage has increasingly blurred the boundary between traditional authority figures and '**celebrity** role models' (and even 'reality TV stars'). The key question is the extent to which such coverage has led to a loss of trust and respect for authority figures.

> **Definition**
>
> **Celebrity**
>
> From the Latin for 'renowned', it means to be a widely known popular figure. Increasingly, celebrities appear in gossip magazines with revelations about their intimate private lives. Whereas in the past, people had to be exceptional in their field to be a celebrity, now the label applies to anyone who can attract media attention for long enough.

How far have mass media undermined respect for the government?

Apart from a few exceptionally popular individuals, most politicians have been seen as self-seeking and untrustworthy since 1945. In Unit 2 we saw that most people did not trust politicians' promises of post-war improvements. However, increased coverage of parliamentary proceedings, the legacy of the 1960s satire boom, and greater press intrusion into politicians' private lives have all changed public perceptions of government.

Mass media access to parliament

News reports on television and by the press have shifted from a broadly deferential tone to a questioning one. Some legal changes help to account for this shift. In 1944, the BBC agreed that it would not discuss an issue for 14 days before it was due to be debated in parliament. Winston Churchill defended the '14-Day Rule' as it stopped the 'expressions of opinion by persons who had not the status or responsibility of Members of Parliament' influencing parliamentary debates. However, by 1956, BBC and ITV journalists had grown frustrated with the rule; a government report concluded that contemporary coverage of debates would increase interest in parliament and greatly relaxed the rule. In 1958, Harold MacMillan became the first prime minister to be interviewed by a journalist on television. Source C is the journalist's view of the significance of the interview. Use the Internet to research the interviews of politicians by political interviewers such as David Frost, Jeremy Paxman, Andrew Marr and Jon Snow.

Questions

1 Why does Robin Day think his interview of Harold Macmillan was 'historic'?
2 In what ways could Source C be seen as a less than totally objective account?
3 How far do you agree that this was an 'historic' moment in the relationship between politicians, mass media and the public?

Source C

My interview with Macmillan lasted 13 minutes . . . The interview was historic and unprecedented. The significance of my ITN interview with Macmillan is difficult to convey today. Here was the nation's leader, the most powerful and important politician of his time, coming to terms with the new medium of television. He was questioned on TV as vigorously as in parliament. His TV performance that Sunday evening was an early recognition that television was not merely for entertainment or party propagandists, but was now a serious part of the democratic process.

From Robin Day, *Grand Inquisitor: Memoirs*, published in 1989

Definition

Sound bite

The phrase was coined by American author Mark Twain to mean 'a minimum of sound to a maximum of sense'. They are short, memorable quotes that sum things up neatly, clearly intended by politicians for use in news bulletins.

Question

Is increased mass media access to parliamentary proceedings good for democracy?

Debates over the '14-Day Rule' were mirrored by those over the broadcasting of debates in parliament: those in favour stressed the increased popular involvement with democracy, while those against mistrusted broadcasters and feared that media debate would become more important than parliamentary debate. Before 1975, the only way to find out what was actually said in parliament was to read the relevant detailed section in the broadsheets. In June 1975, debates in the House of Commons were broadcast for the first time on BBC Radio 4. Listeners were shocked by the level of heckling, something not reported in newspapers. A letter to *The Times* said it was 'an affront to the British electorate, destructive of any lingering respect it might have had for parliamentary procedure'. Nevertheless, radio broadcasts of parliamentary business remained a regular feature from 1978 onwards. After much debate by politicians, television footage from parliament was also broadcast on a regular basis from 1990. This has led to increased mass media scrutiny of parliamentary business and the growth of simplistic '**sound bite**' politics. With the launch of The Parliamentary Channel in 1992 (called BBC Parliament after 1998) there was no need for in-depth sections on parliamentary debates in the broadsheets; as some critics feared, opinion and discussion of sound bites has replaced such detailed reporting.

Satire and politicians

The satire boom of the 1960s also contributed to the decline of media deference to politicians. Publications like *Private Eye* and television shows such as *TW3* paved the way for investigative journalism and more mainstream reporting of political scandals. Harold Wilson, Labour Prime Minister (1964–70, 1974–76), welcomed press attention on his way to power, but became hostile towards the press once in power as they criticised his failings and characterised him as a liar. Later satire, both in the press and on television, became even more biting and personal: on the puppet show *Spitting Image* (ITV 1984–96) David Mellor (see page 140) always had green gas coming from his mouth as a sign of his halitosis, while Labour MP Roy Hattersley spat everywhere at all times. You might like to watch shows such as *Spitting Image, Have I Got News For You* (BBC2 1990–) and *Bremner, Bird and Fortune* (Channel 4 1999–).

Investigative journalism has exposed a number of scandals involving corruption that might have gone unnoticed in the past. Some of these have concerned bribes used to secure lucrative arms sales, such as the 1985 Al Yamamah affair. Bribes of millions of pounds were suspected to have been paid to members of the Saudi Royal Family in return for an arms deal worth over £43 billion to the UK arms trade. A 1992 National Audit Office report into the deal has not been published (the only such report not to be published); a 2003 Serious Fraud Office investigation was suspended by the Attorney General Lord Goldsmith in 2006, shortly after another round of deals with the Saudis. In 1995, *World in Action* and *The Guardian* both reported that Jonathan Aitken, then Minister of State for Defence Procurement, had allowed Saudi businessmen to pay for his recent stay at the Paris Ritz Hotel. Aitken called a press conference where he delivered the speech in Source D. Aitken was later found to have committed perjury: he had knowingly lied about important information under oath in court. This is a serious offence as it can lead to miscarriages of justice; in 1999 Aitken was sentenced to 18 months in prison.

Politicians and political parties have also been exposed for receiving personal bribes to do various things. In 1994, Conservative MPs Neil Hamilton and Tim Smith were accused by *The Guardian* of accepting £2000 for each question they asked in parliament on behalf of businessman Mohammed Al-Fayed. This was part of allegations of Tory 'sleaze' in the press. Hamilton lost his seat in the 1997 General Election to journalist Martin Bell, who stood as an independent 'anti-corruption' candidate. In 1997, the Labour Party returned a £1 million donation from Formula One boss Bernie Ecclestone after press coverage of their decision to reverse a pledge to ban tobacco advertising for F1. In 2006, the Labour Party was accused of awarding peerages in return for donations. In 2009, four Labour peers were recorded by *The Sunday Times* journalists accepting bribes of up to £120,000 to amend legislation in the House of Lords. Politicians have also been exposed as using their positions for personal financial gain. In 2009, *The Daily Telegraph* published MPs' expenses claims, which exposed widespread abuse of taxpayers' money for personal gain. However, very few politicians have had their careers ruined by such scandals. Most notably, Peter Mandelson has survived two resignations over press-exposed scandals yet has gone on to become a Lord and amass considerable power in Gordon Brown's Labour government.

Press intrusion into politicians' private lives

The British media, unlike their counterparts in many other countries, are not bound by sweeping privacy laws in what they can report. Journalists have self-regulated what they print, a situation that was formalised in 1990

Source D

If it falls to me to start a fight to cut out the cancer of bent and twisted journalism in our country with the simple sword of truth and the trusty shield of British fair play, so be it. I am ready for the fight. The fight against falsehood and those who peddle it. My fight begins today.

From Jonathan Aitken's press conference speech on 10 April 1995

Question

Politicians have been regarded as untrustworthy for a long time. In what ways might statements such as Source D further undermine public respect for politicians?

with the establishment of the Press Complaints Commission (PCC). However, disputes over what 'privacy' actually means, or which stories are deemed to be 'in the public interest', combined with the profit incentive for sensational scoops, have led to increased press intrusion into the private lives of public figures. The extent of this intrusion was highlighted by the part the media played in the death of Diana, Princess of Wales in 1997 (see pages 150–54). While this led to the tightening of the PCC Code of Conduct, it has not substantially altered the behaviour of journalists or **paparazzi**. Such intrusion has contributed to a blurring of the divide between politicians and celebrities. Stories of a scandalous sexual nature that would once have been hushed up, have been turned into national scandals by mass media, the tabloid press in particular, since the 1980s. Examples of these include:

- 1983 – Cecil Parkinson was forced to resign as Secretary of State for Trade and Industry after the press revealed he had an affair with his secretary.
- 1992 – David Mellor claimed he had been hounded out of his job as Secretary of State for National Heritage by the press after they published a series of **embellished** stories about his affair with an actress.
- 1994 – Tim Yeo resigned as Minister for the Environment and Countryside after newspapers ran a story about his 'love child' with a mistress. This also contributed to the general allegations of 'sleaze' in the Conservative Party.
- 2006 – Liberal Democrat Mark Oaten resigned as Home Affairs Spokesman after the *News of the World* reported that he had paid male prostitutes for sex in 2003. Oaten said in 2009 that the papers had this story for 3 years, yet only published it when he was more famous so it would sell more copies.

The changing relationship between politicians and mass media has had a number of results. We have seen that politicians have become ever more media conscious in their use of spin doctors to release information. Political parties have also increasingly used **focus groups** and surveys to avoid unpopular policies that could result in press criticism. Politicians have also courted newspaper owners: in 2001 *The Sun* was told the date of the General Election before the Queen!

While respect for most politicians was never particularly high, the number of scandalous stories may have contributed to a rise in public apathy in general elections. Sources E and F provide information about the decline in voter turn-out since the 1980s.

Definitions

Paparazzi

From the Italian for the irritating buzzing sound of mosquitoes, they are freelance photographers who pursue celebrities in order to take their pictures.

Embellish

To spice up a story with fictitious additions.

Focus group

A group of people, representative of particular parts of society, who are questioned about political issues so that their opinions can be studied and used to inform policy.

Source E

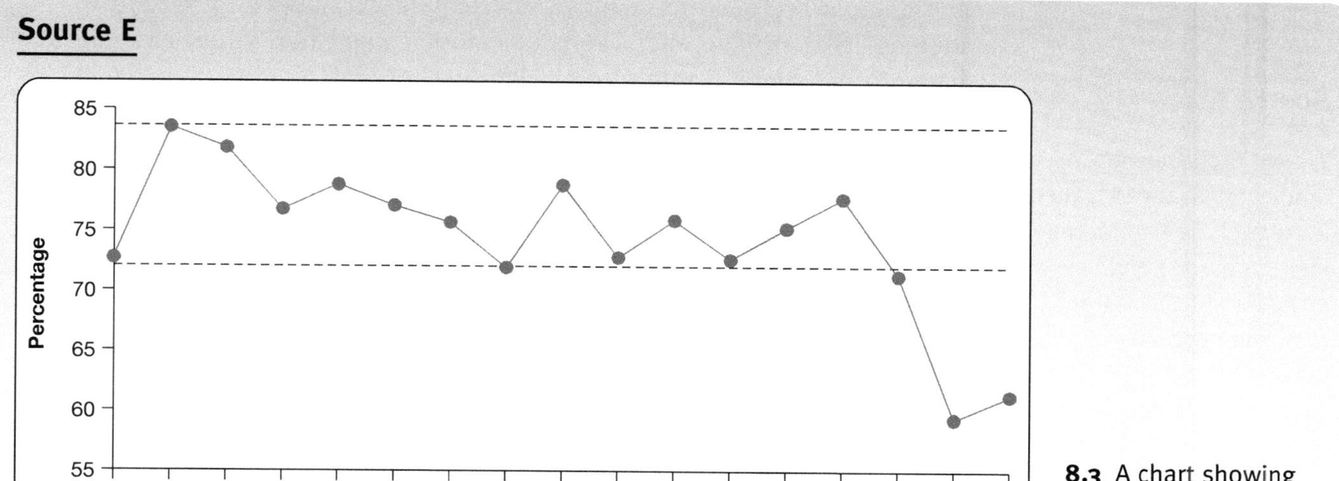

8.3 A chart showing voter turn-out at general elections from 1945–2005

Source F

- Not voting was something most participants had consciously chosen to do. '*Not voting is like a vote in itself.*' (Many)
- Many younger voters were concerned that they did not know enough to make an informed choice. '*I haven't got a clue who to vote for. I don't know what is going on in politics. So I have never voted because I don't know what is going on. I can't see the point in voting.*' (Female, 18–24, non-voter, Stockport)
- The media – especially television – plays a key role in creating or transmitting the images which gave our group their negative perceptions. Although politics is seen as familiar (often on radio/TV and in the newspapers) it is also perceived as distant and out of touch. '*. . . when I flicked on the telly and see them in parliament, they stand up and sit down and address each other. You see people arguing and laughing, you think "I don't want to listen to this".*' (Female, 18–24, non-voter, Stockport)

From an Ipsos-Mori report, *None of the Above: Non-Voters and the 2001 Election*, published on 10 September 2001

SKILLS BUILDER

1 How far do Sources E and F suggest that mass media have undermined respect for politicians in Britain since 1945?

2 Out of Sources E and F, which provides the better evidence of a link between greater media pressure on politicians and a loss of public respect for these authority figures?

How far have mass media undermined respect for the monarchy?

Stories about the monarchy have always been newsworthy. It is no surprise therefore that it is newspapers and television that have had the most impact on attitudes towards the monarchy. The only film about a contemporary monarch since 1945 was the highly popular *The Queen* (2006), which presented Queen Elizabeth II, dealing with the aftermath of the death of Diana, Princess of Wales in 1997, in a sympathetic, favourable light. While television has brought images of royalty to a vastly wider audience, it has been the tabloid newspapers that have uncovered the increasingly intimate and scandalous stories about the Windsor family that have turned some of them into 'celebrities'.

The royal family could no longer entirely remain detached, mysterious and aloof in an age of mass communication. In order to remain a relevant part of British society, the Windsors have had to accept, and to a degree invite, mass media attention. Queen Elizabeth II recognised this fact from the outset and insisted that BBC cameras be allowed to broadcast live images of her Coronation on 2 June 1953 (you can use the Internet to research the event). 'Coronation fever' led to a surge in sales of 500,000 televisions (television licences were slower to catch up!) in the weeks before the event, a clear sign of the popularity of the monarchy in the years after the Second World War. Despite the fact that there were only 2 million television sets in June 1953, an estimated 20 million people gathered around them to watch the ceremony. A total of 227 million are estimated to have seen the Coronation around the world in the days after the event. Source G is one contemporary account of watching the Coronation on television.

Mass media clearly boosted loyalty and affection for the monarchy in 1953. However, the royal family were not 'celebrities' in the 1940s and 1950s as they became in the 1980s and 1990s through tabloid press coverage of their private lives: BBC cameras at the Coronation were not allowed close-ups as this was deemed to be too intrusive. Compare the discussion of popular reaction to royal births in 1948 and 1982 in Sources H and I and to royal relationships in Sources J and K.

Source G

We got the sandwiches ready and arranged chairs in front of the set. I went into the garden and picked a bunch of large red, white and blue flowers for the sitting room mantelpiece. Then I put our flag up – we have fixed a tall pole to the garage . . . We were all ready and sitting in front of the set when the broadcast began . . . When the Queen appeared on the balcony we stood and drank her health, and then settled down to watch the fireworks.

From the diary entry of a London housewife on 2 June 1953

Source H

Thinking of Mrs Howson's words made me keener to notice what people said of the new Royal baby. [Mrs Howson doubted that the birth of Prince Charles would cause much excitement] . . . It poured as we came home and I realise I'd heard snatches of conversation of local gossip, Xmas preparations, Mrs Horne's lovely new evening dress, prospects of snow after Christmas, coal shortages and fuel cuts, odd scraps of shopping gossip – but not one word of the Royal baby, though they are a kindly lot up there, and many are grandmothers!

From Barrow-in-Furness housewife Nella Last's diary entry on 16 November 1948

Source I

Diana, Princess of Wales, has given birth to a boy sixteen hours after checking in to St Mary's Hospital, in London. The boy, who has been named William, was born at 9:03pm, weighing 7lb 1½oz. He is second in line to the British throne after his father the Prince of Wales, who accompanied Princess Diana to the hospital at 5am this morning and stayed with her throughout the day. Outside the hospital crowds had gathered to wait for news of the birth, with some saying they would wait through the night if necessary. Flowers arrived all day long and were taken into the hospital. Thousands also gathered outside Buckingham Palace, where the birth was formally announced.

From a BBC news report on 21 June 1982

Source J

Daily Mirror

FRI NOV. 21 1947

ONE PENNY

FORWARD WITH THE PEOPLE

No. 13,698

Registered at G.P.O. as a Newspaper.

A DAY OF SMILES

And this one is unforgettable

Princess Elizabeth, hand in hand with her husband, walks from the pomp of the Westminster Abbey ceremony through the guard of honour in the West Porch.

As she nears the end of the canopy, where an expectant world waits to see the bride, she flashes a quick smile at Rover Sea Scout L. F. Cartwright (extreme left)—a member of the mixed Army, Navy and ATS guard, chosen for their associations with the bride and groom's military service.

Philip ushers his Princess into Honeymoon House

From JOAN REEDER and ROBERT GLENTON

ROMSEY (Hants), Thursday Night.

A TALL young man in naval uniform sprang out of a limousine that crunched up the gravelled drive to the south-west wing of the country mansion of Broadlands, near Romsey, at 6.37 tonight.

He raced the chauffeur, opened the car door himself, and helped a pale slender girl, wearing a two-piece suit in love-in-the-mist blue, on to the wet path and up the steps.

The royal bride and bridegroom—Princess Elizabeth, Duchess of Edinburgh, and Prince Philip, Duke of Edinburgh—were arriving at their honeymoon home.

The butler, Mr. Frank Randall, opened french windows to let the hall light shine down the six stone steps.

The restful quietness of the old mansion, owned by Earl and Countess Mountbatten, embraced the young couple as they walked slowly through the hall to the foot of the shallow stairway leading to their suite on the first floor.

His Arm Went Round Her

On a table in the hall was a bowl of lilies. Prince Philip threw his cap on to a chair as he passed to the inner door, with the Princess's Corgi dog Crackers bounding ahead.

The Princess's grey-blue eyes were misty, and her smile for the staff, standing hesitantly, was a little tremulous.

Then, for the first time, she relaxed. Her proud slim shoulders drooped a little as Philip's arm went round her at the bend of the stairway.

She leaned against him looking up with a grateful, shy smile.

Banking the iron balustraded stairway were groups of white hydrangea and fern.

And in the bedroom overlooking the swift-flowing

Continued on Back Page

PHILIP: "I AM PROUD—OF MY COUNTRY AND MY WIFE"

THE King raised his glass in Buckingham Palace yesterday afternoon and said, "Our daughter is marrying the man she loves."

Only two remained seated. They held hands, looked at each other and smiled.

For the toast was "Elizabeth and Philip"—the moment was theirs.

Before the 150 guests sat down again with their champagne, the young bridegroom had jumped to his feet. There was no shyness. His speech was short, sincere.

"I am proud," he said. "Proud of my country and my wife."

And when the Princess rose after him pride was in his eyes.

The Princess spoke only a few sentences. She thanked her father and mother and her guests. She told how pleased she was to have her grandmother, Queen Mary, at the wedding table.

Of her marriage, she said just this: "I ask nothing more than that Philip and I should be as happy as my father and mother have been, and Queen Mary and King George before them."

There were fifteen tables in the mirrored Ball Supper room. The Kings of Norway, Denmark, and Rumania sat with the King and Queen. Queen Mary, Princess Andrew of Greece (mother of the bridegroom), Princess Margaret, and the Princess and Philip.

Every table bore a gold vase of white and pink carnations. Plates, knives and forks were gold. The wine was champagne.

But the meal was austerity—just three courses.

Ronald Aubrey, the King's chef, honoured the couple with two of them—the sweet was Bombe Glacee Princess Elizabeth, and the fish Filet de Sole Mountbatten.

The last word should have been "Edinburgh," but the menus were printed last week, before announcement of the bridegroom's dukedom.

The King noticed it, laughed, and apologised to his son-in-law. "But we had to keep it a secret," he said.

The main dish—partridge in casserole—had been chosen by the King because it is unrationed.

All the waiters went out before the speeches were made.

Coffee was served in the Blue Room.

The Princess cut the cake with the bridegroom's sword. Mr. Ainsley, the Palace steward, cut the cake into small pieces, and handed them to the guests.

For the first time at a Palace wedding, none of the upper tiers of the cake was removed. But there WAS a spotlight for it.

8.4 The front cover of the *Daily Mirror* published on 21 November 1947, the day after the marriage of the then Princess Elizabeth and Philip, Duke of Edinburgh

Source K

THE Sun 30p

BLAIR TO SORT MIGRANT MESS

WORLD EXCLUSIVE

FINALLY.. Wills gets a girl

PRINCE & KATE SO CLOSE IN KLOSTERS

SENSATIONAL PICTURES: PAGES 2, 3, 4 & 5

8.5 Front page of *The Sun*, published on 1 April 2004. Other *Sun* headlines since then have included 'Wills and Kate split', 'Wills flies in to Kate's garden', 'Wills takes Kate on family hols'

The relationship between the royal family and the British public (or at least the relationship the public expected) had shifted by 1982. One reason for this was a 1969 documentary called *The Royal Family*, screened on both the BBC and ITV. This was the first glimpse of the royal family in a domestic setting, away from the formality of occasions such as Charles' investiture as the Prince of Wales in the same year. Another reason was the huge media interest after 1981 in the glamorous Diana, Princess of Wales. The increased appearances of royalty on television reduced the mystique of the family. This alone might not have eroded respect for royalty, but the way in which some members of the royal family sought to modernise their relationship with the people via television certainly did. In 1987, three of the Queen's grown-up children, Prince Edward, Princess Anne and Prince Andrew took part in a slapstick game show called *It's A Royal Knockout* on BBC1. The show involved running around obstacle courses in giant foam costumes. Although the event raised £1 million for charity, it was deemed a public relations disaster. The Queen did not want the event to go ahead, but Prince Edward, who wanted a career in television, was determined for it to happen. The press and the public were bemused and the event harmed the dignity of the royal family.

SKILLS BUILDER

1 What can we learn about changing media coverage of the monarchy from Sources H, I, J and K?

2 How far could you base conclusions about the popularity of the monarchy in 1947, 1948, 1982 and 2004 on these sources?

3 How far do the sources suggest that the media has fuelled greater interest in the personal lives of the royals?

Sensational stories about royal marital problems made things even worse for the Windsors in the 1990s. The Queen called 1992 her 'annus horribilis', and with good reason. Three of her children were involved in high profile divorce stories: Princess Anne divorced Mark Philips, Prince Charles and Diana, Princess of Wales announced they were to be divorced, as did Prince Andrew and Sarah, Duchess of York. Even more damaging were a series of embarrassing stories and photos published by the press and discussed on television. In August 1992, the *Daily Mirror* published a photograph of Sarah Ferguson, then Duchess of York, apparently having her toes sucked by an American businessman while sunbathing in St Tropez. Sales of the *Daily Mirror* rose by 500,000 on the days when it ran the story and the pictures. In 1992, the press ran the '**Squidgygate**' and 'Camillagate' stories. Both stories concerned taped telephone conversations which provided evidence of extra-marital affairs. The, at times bizarrely graphic, Camillagate conversation between Charles and his long-term friend and sweetheart Camilla Parker-Bowles was recorded by an amateur radio enthusiast on 18 December 1989. As with Squidgygate the conversation was almost certainly recorded from a tapped telephone line and then broadcast from a small, private transmitter in the hope it would be picked up by radio amateurs. Although newspapers acquired copies of the tapes soon after they were recorded, extracts from the 'Camillagate' tape were not released by the tabloid press until 1992; by this time, journalist Andrew Morton's book *Princess Diana: Her True Story in her Own Words*, had made public the extent of marital problems. Charles and Diana finally divorced in 1996, after Diana, referring to Charles' relationship with Camilla Parker-Bowels, had said things such as 'Well there were three of us in this marriage, so it was a bit crowded' in a 1995 *Panorama* documentary. They had both used the media to put across their

Definition

Squidgygate

James Gilbey referred to Diana as 'Squidge' or 'Squidgy' 53 times during the conversation. 'Gate' is frequently added to any scandal by the press after the scandal at the Watergate Hotel in 1972 where President Nixon ordered secret agents to steal information about political enemies.

side of the story; in doing so, they had bridged the divide between royalty and other media celebrities. The monarchy slumped to their lowest level of popularity in late 1997 when they failed to publicly display their grief for the loss of Diana, Princess of Wales (see Enquiry Source 7F on page 153) many people thought the royal family were uncaring and out of touch with the feelings of the people.

A number of documentaries since 2000 have possibly helped to restore the dignity of the Windsors. In 2007, a BBC documentary that followed the Queen and her husband the Duke of Edinburgh, called *Monarchy: The Royal Family At Work*, was generally well received; a few critics said that it was overly flattering and deferential. In 2008, newsreader Trevor MacDonald followed the Duke of Edinburgh for a week; the Duke has always been popular for his inappropriate comments; the show confirmed his place in the public affection. However, even before these programmes were broadcast, there is clear evidence that the monarchy had successfully modernised its relationship with mass media and managed to remain popular, despite the problems in the 1990s. Despite predictions that the 2002 Golden Jubilee would be a non-event, popular celebrations were held across the country. A clear sign of the monarchy's successful embrace of mass media was the 'Party at the Palace', a rock concert held to celebrate the Jubilee in the gardens of Buckingham Palace. One million people watched on screens outside the palace, while an estimated 200 million watched on television around the world. Source L is a table that shows people's attitudes towards the monarchy.

Questions

1. What can we learn form Source L about popular attitudes to the monarchy since 1983?
2. Which mass media has had the greater impact on the relationship between the royal family and the British public since 1945: television or the press?
3. How far did mass media undermine respect for the monarchy after 1945?

Source L

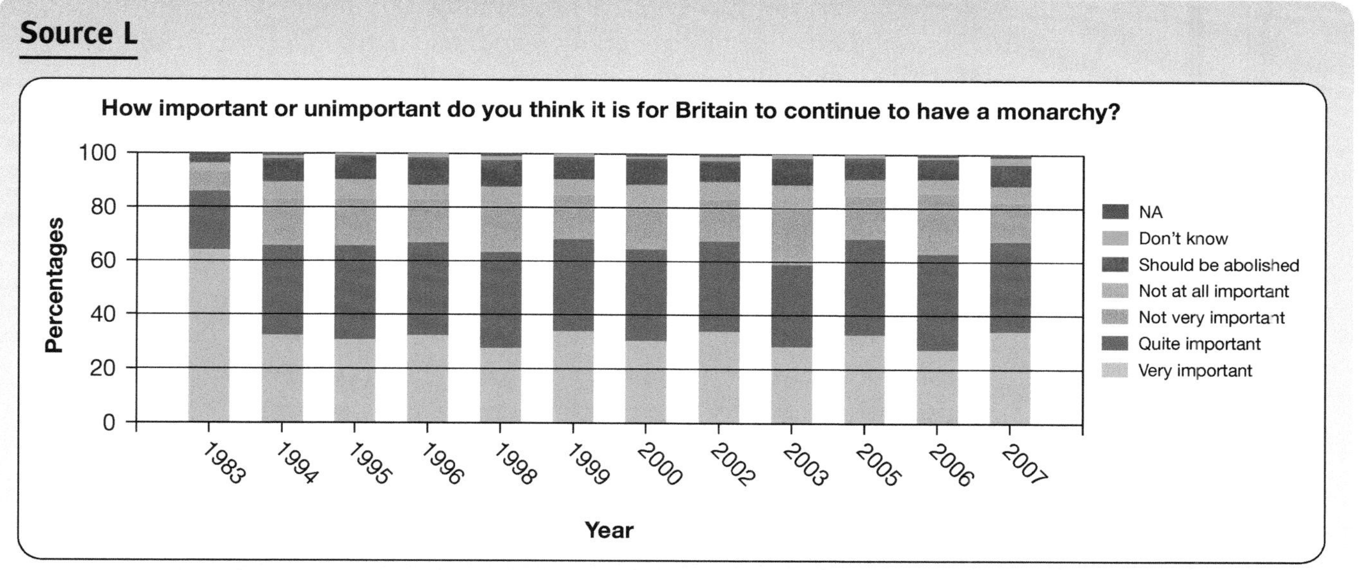

8.6 A graph showing people's attitudes towards the monarchy between 1983 and 2007. Compiled from data from the British Social Attitudes surveys conducted by the National Centre for Social Research. The data is available on the BritSocAt website, developed by the Centre for Comparative European Survey Data

Definition

Maverick

Samuel Maverick (1803–70) was a Texan cattle-owner who did not brand his cattle. His unbranded cattle became known as mavericks; it now means an unorthodox or independent-minded person.

How far have mass media undermined respect for the police?

In general, the image of the police has fared rather worse in the press than it has done in the cinema or on television. A few New Wave films, such as *Beyond This Place*, *Hell is a City* and *Never Let Go* (all 1959–63), did depict a grimier image of police work than that presented on television, and there have been a few American films about police corruption, such as *The Departed* (2006). However, these films are not typical of the depiction of policemen on film. A series of escapist American 'cop' movies in the 1980s and 1990s presented policemen as either good-hearted but strange (*Police Academy* series, *The Naked Gun*) or **maverick**, all-action heroes (*K9*, *Lethal Weapon*, *Die Hard*, *24 Hours*, *Beverly Hills Cop*, *Bad Boys*). The two most notable British films since the early 1960s that focus on policemen, *The Wicker Man* (1973) and *Hot Fuzz* (2007), both show the police in a mainly positive light: the central characters of both films are highly professional, courageous policemen.

On television, we saw in Unit 5 that *Dixon of Dock Green* (BBC 1955–76), with an audience of over 13 million into the 1970s, was the personification of 'continuity, tradition and service' and that *Z-Cars* (BBC 1962–78) and *The Sweeney* (ITV 1975–78) both portrayed an edgier, though essentially respectable police force. The Lancashire Constabulary had initially received thanks for its advice for *Z-Cars* in the credits, but asked that this be removed after a plot line about an officer's marital problems; they wrote a letter that complained the show was 'making us look like fools'. The comedy programme *Monty Python's Flying Circus* (BBC 1969–74) certainly *did* make the police look like fools: Constable Pan Am and Harry 'Snapper' Organs were frequent characters who were clearly stupid, and, at times, corrupt. Into the 1980s and 1990s, a number of drama programmes again showed the police in a generally favourable light. *Juliet Bravo* (BBC 1980–85) was significant in that it was the first such programme to star a female police officer; the main character was resourceful and professional. This was built upon by *Prime Suspect* (ITV 1991–2006), in which actress Helen Mirren's tough character Jane Tennison starts as a Detective Chief Inspector and finishes as a powerful Superintendent. A number of dramas about detectives, such as *Inspector Morse*, *Inspector Wexford* (both ITV 1987–2000), *Taggart* (ITV 1983–), all showed the police as intelligent and highly successful at solving crimes. *The Bill* (ITV 1984–) is the most successful police series of all time; while the **Police Federation** have criticised some story lines, such as one that dealt with the issue of racism in the force, the series does depict the force in a positive fashion. In the interests of a satisfying storyline, the criminal almost always gets caught on TV. However, by the early 2000s, only 23 out of every 100 recorded crimes were cleared up; of these, only six led to a conviction.

Definition

Police Federation

A staff association for police officers (they are not allowed to join a trade union).

Aside from dramas, there have been more programmes about real crime and police work on television since the 1980s, and especially since the rise of satellite television. *Crimewatch* (BBC 1984–) was a pioneering show that sought to use the power of mass media to bring forward new leads to help solve real crimes. A spate of more sensationalist programmes, such as *Police, Camera Action!* (ITV 1994–2008), *Traffic Cops* (BBC 2003–) *Street Crime UK* (Bravo 2002–05), have shown police actually at work, generally dealing with motoring offences and drunken, disorderly behaviour. The police always appear professional and reasonable in the way they deal with drunken, aggressive behaviour. One programme that did expose problems with the police was a 2006 Channel 4 documentary called *Dispatches: Undercover Copper*. Source M is a report about the documentary.

Source M

The film aired in April 2006 and revealed alleged apathy, sexism and bullying in the Leicestershire police force. In one scene, officers were shown playing poker and indoor cricket. In another, one member of the force pretended he had not seen someone lying injured in the road because he had a football match to watch. The undercover film by police officer Nina Hobson also revealed that reports of sexual assault and rape are not being taken seriously, to the extent that one of her colleagues said that if she was ever raped, she would not report it to the police. Ms Hobson rejoined the Leicestershire police force in order to film undercover for four months for the *Dispatches* documentary, five years after she had left the force, disillusioned.

Following the *Dispatches* programme, the IPCC carried out an investigation into the allegations made in the documentary, interviewing 26 officers. As a result of the IPCC inquiry, five officers were given formal written warnings and 14 were given 'words of advice/guidance'.

From Tara Conian, 'Channel 4 backs Dispatches in police row', published in *The Guardian* on 10 May 2007

It is unlikely that these programmes were the main reason for shift in popular respect for the police. In his 1950 study on English attitudes, Geoffrey Gorer found that 75 per cent expressed 'an enthusiastic appreciation for English police', especially compared with the reputation of the police on the continent. By 1963, when PC Dixon was still the media embodiment of the police, a poll found that 40 per cent believed that policemen took bribes, 33 per cent that they used unfair means to get their information, 30 per cent that they distorted information in court. While TV dramas have shown the police in a positive light since the 1970s, source N suggests that the police have gone down in public estimation.

One explanation might be the sensational way in which the tabloid press have reported crime and problems with the police. Police activities only become newsworthy when they have been incompetent or done something wrong; in addition to the cases mentioned on page 74, there have been further examples of this since the 1990s.

Source N

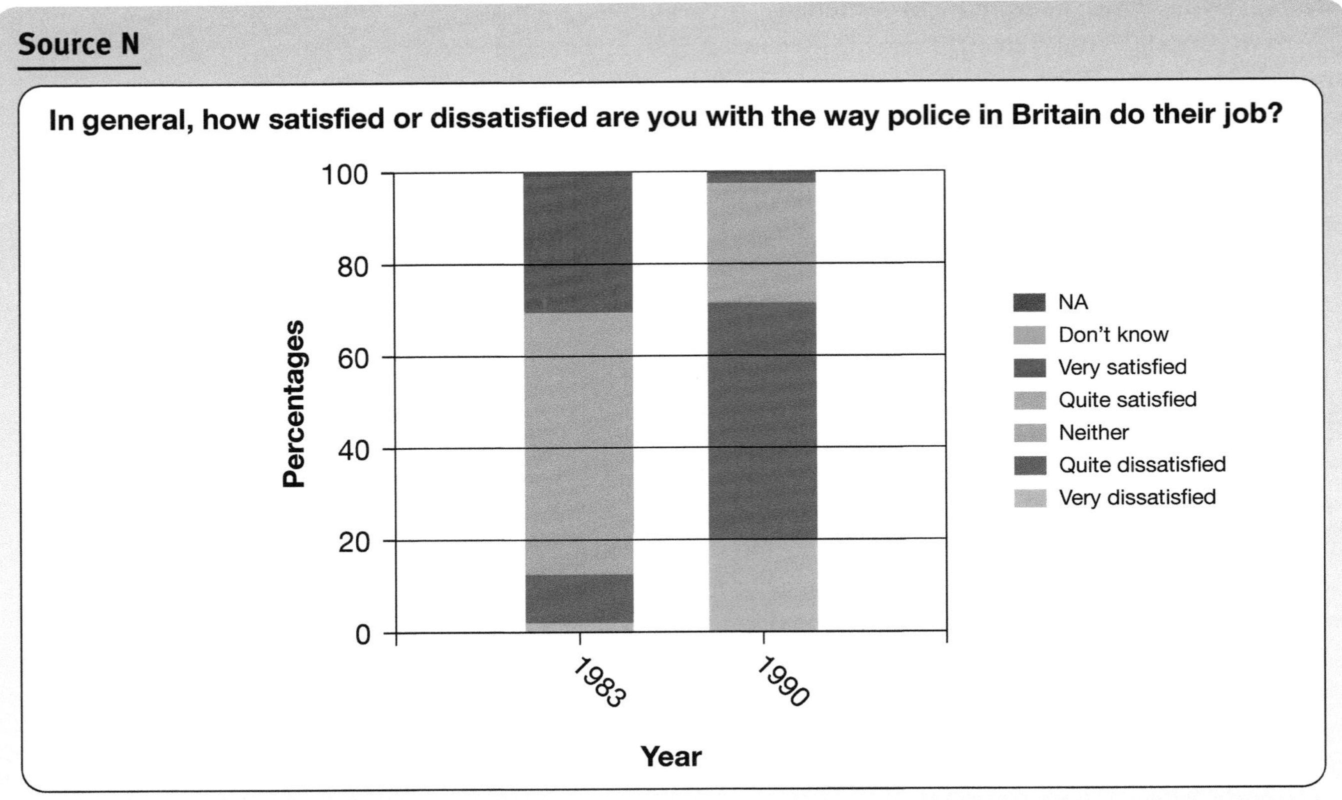

8.7 A graph showing levels of satisfaction with the police in 1983 and 1990. Compiled from data from the British Social Attitudes surveys conducted by the National Centre for Social Research. The data is available on the BritSocAt website, developed by the Centre for Comparative European Survey Data

Question

If television or cinema cannot explain the trend highlighted in Source N, what can? Discuss this question before reading further!

SKILLS BUILDER

1 Which out of Sources M and N is more useful to an historian who wants to find out how far respect for the police has been undermined in Britain since the 1980s?

2 How typical is Source M of the media portrayal of the police since 1945?

- In 1999, the MacPherson Report into the way the Metropolitan Police handled the enquiry into the murder of black London teenager Stephen Lawrence in 1993 concluded that the force was 'institutionally racist'. The police failed to provide adequate first aid at the scene of the attack and failed to follow up some obvious leads that could have led to the successful prosecution of five murder suspects.
- In 2005, members of the Metropolitan Police shot in the head a 27-year-old Brazilian, Jean Charles de Menezes, in the mistaken belief that he was about to carry out a suicide bomb attack on an underground station.

An Independent Police Complaints Commission report cleared the individual officers of any blame, but criticised the way Commissioner Sir Ian Blair tried to present the story to the media.

However, while television and the press do dwell on crime, there is no doubt that actual levels of crime have increased dramatically in Britain since 1945. It is almost certainly the increased number of Britons who have been a victim of crime that have led to a perceived worsening of police performance. The number of recorded offences rose from 500,000 in 1957 to 1.7 million in 1972, 3 million in 1981, 5 million in 1996 and 5.8 million in 2002. Some blame the liberalisation of laws in the 1960s for the increase while others blame social dislocation, especially family breakdown, for the dramatic increase in crime since the 1970s. Since 2000, the majority of criticism about the police has been that there are not enough of them, and that they have too much paperwork to do, rather than more serious allegations of corruption or racism.

How far has the rise of 'celebrities' undermined respect for those in the public eye?

Celebrities have been mentioned throughout this unit as a possible reason for the changing way in which the British public have perceived authority figures. Who are these celebrities, and how fair is it to blame them for the undermining of authority? Until the late 1990s, most celebrities were either stars of film, television, music or sports. In the 1975 referendum on whether Britain should remain inside the EEC, the 'yes' campaigners were successful largely because they gathered more celebrity backers; many people did not have a clear idea about the issues involved, many simply voted for the views of people they liked and trusted. These included Jack Warner (P.C. Dixon), *Carry On* actor Kenneth Williams, popular boxer Henry Cooper and football manager Sir Matt Busby. Politicians such as Harold Wilson and Tony Blair have tried to win popularity by associating with popular celebrities (The Beatles and Britpop band Oasis respectively). As popular celebrities are not authority figures in the same way as politicians or royalty, and because most depend upon media exposure for their continued success, the tabloid press and gossip magazines have felt justified in the publication of intrusive stories. Women's magazines such as *Hello!*, *OK*, *Closer*, *Now*, *Heat*, *Glamour* (and many more) publish photos of the most trivial aspects of celebrity lives. Since the rise of reality TV, celebrities do not even have to have a particular talent, other than being famous. Jade Goody (1981–2009), who rose to fame on *Big Brother*, is perhaps the most notable example of an ordinary person who was made and used by the tabloid journalists to boost sales.

There has increasingly been less of a distinction in the way mass media treats celebrities and figures of authority. Authority figures' lives have been held up for public scrutiny in a way that only film or TV stars had had to endure: one only has to think of the scandalous stories about the private lives of politicians such as David Blunkett, John Prescott and Mark Oaten, or the tragic story of the death of David Cameron's disabled son in February 2009. At the same time, the deeds of entertainment celebrities, and even reality TV stars, have become the subject of 'news' items in (even quality) newspapers and on television: a clear example of this was the coverage of Jade Goody's battle with cancer in the first 3 months of 2009. This has contributed to a shift in the relationship between authority figures and the public: some politicians have clearly courted the mass media in a bid to promote their public persona while the public demands greater scrutiny of formally private matters such as expense claims. To a greater degree than in the past, figures of authority must assume that a good deal of their private lives is likely to feature in the public arena via mass media.

Enquiry 7: How far did mass media's relationship with Diana Spencer affect popular attitudes to the monarchy?

Mass media, especially newspaper paparazzi, followed Lady Diana Spencer from the moment she was known to be Prince Charles' girlfriend, through their wedding in 1981, the birth of two sons in 1982 and 1984, throughout the events that ended in their divorce in 1996 and right up until her last moments of her life on 31 August 1997, as she sat mortally injured in the back of a car that had just crashed in a Parisian tunnel. While many blame mass media for this gross intrusion, others see Diana herself as guilty of changing the relationship between the media and the royal family. Use the following sources to draw your own conclusions about the relationship between Diana and the mass media.

Enquiry source 7A

8.8 A photograph of Lady Diana Spencer taken in 1981, shortly before the announcement of her engagement to Prince Charles

Enquiry source 7B

8.9 One of the last photos taken of Princess Diana, shortly after midnight on 30 August 1997

Enquiry source 7C

DAILY Mirror

Wednesday, August 26, 1992 NEWSPAPER FOR THE NINETIES 27p

THE ONLY QUESTION THAT REALLY MATTERS

LOVE TAPES AFFAIR

DIANA

Gilbey named as the love tapes man

By GEOFF SUTTON and ROD CHAYTOR

TAPES of an intimate phone call between Princess Diana and a male friend are almost certainly genuine, it emerged last night.

Handsome bachelor James Gilbey was named as the pal most likely to have been the lovey-dovey caller.

It was also disclosed that newspapers which printed transcripts of the conversation, and snooper Cyril Reenan who taped the call, could be prosecuted.

Last night, Buckingham Palace made NO move to end the controversy.

FRIEND: Gilbey

Its silence fuelled belief that the tapes, which include details only close friends could have known, ARE genuine.

Scotland Yard also confirmed they had received no complaint about the tape.

And without a complaint it cannot investigate the case.

In the 23-minute recording – taped 2½ years ago – the man comforts the woman, who says her husband "makes my life a torture".

He calls her "Darling," says "Love you, love you" and the con-

● Turn to Page 2

Do YOU still want her to be our Queen?

DAILY Mirror ROYAL CRISIS POLL

VOTE NOW! LET THE PEOPLE SPEAK

● Pages 2, 3, 4 and 5

DAILY Mirror

Thursday, August 27, 1992 NEWSPAPER FOR THE NINETIES 27p

YES You want Queen Di

Yesterday's Mirror

LONG TO REIGN OVER US!

ROW: Allan Lamb

'Cheat' bowlers start racism rumpus

By COLIN PRICE

THE furious Pakistani cricket team started a racism row last night after England batsman Allan Lamb accused them of cheating by tampering with the ball.

In a Mirror exclusive headlined 'How Pakistan Cheat At Cricket', Lamb said the tourists had got away with murder all summer.

But pace bowlers Wasim Akram and Waqar Younis said in a statement: "We are amazed that a fellow professional has stooped so low as to make such unfounded comments.

"We can only guess at Allan Lamb's motives in the Daily Mirror, but we hope they are nothing so base as money or, even worse, our nationality."

"TAMPERED": Ball

Team manager Intikhab Alam described Lamb's remarks as "a cowardly attack".

Northampton captain Lamb was yesterday banned for two matches by his club and fined heavily – not for his comments, but for failing to clear them with the county.

Last night defiant Lamb said: "I stand by what I said. The truth is the truth."

● Full story: Pages 38, 39 and Back Page

● Griffin's Eye – Page 6

BY APPOINTMENT: The Royal coat of arms

Your landslide vote of confidence for love tape Princess

THOUSANDS of Mirror readers yesterday voted a massive 7-1 in favour of Diana becoming our next Queen.

The astonishing show of support came on the day it was revealed that tapes of an intimate phone call between Di and a male friend are almost certainly genuine.

In one of the biggest-ever Mirror phone-ins, 51,136 of you said a resounding YES to our question: Do you still want Diana to be Queen?

Only 7,065 said No. And hundreds of callers said Charles should never be King.

By GEOFF SUTTON

Furious

They blamed the Prince for the "torture" his wife is suffering.

Last night there was more evidence of the couple's unhappiness when it was disclosed that they had a furious row at Balmoral shortly before the "love tapes" were published.

Their late-night shouting match was so noisy it kept staff awake.

In the 2½-year-old tapes, a man believed

● Turn to Page 2

READERS' VERDICT YES:51,136 NO:7,065

8.10 and **8.11** Front covers of the *Daily Mirror* on 26 and 27 August 1992

Enquiry source 7D

Diana went for a swim in the pool at the British Ambassador's official residence in Cairo, where she was staying. Swimming helped her clear her head, and in May 1992 she had a lot on her mind . . . I spotted a glint of reflected light from the building opposite.

Camera lens, I thought. I told the Princess and she climbed from the pool, wrapped a towel over her one-piece swimsuit and went back inside. I followed her, and found that from the residence we could see men on the roof of the building where I had seen the flash. As they continued to take picture after picture, even though there was now nothing of interest to photograph, Diana spoke of her feeling of total isolation. 'Ken,' she said calmly, 'I want out of this once and for all.' I could not help but agree with her, at least where this intrusion into her privacy was concerned. I walked across and entered the building, playing the policeman to the limit. When I got to the roof some of the photographers were still there with their cameras trained on the pool. An ITN cameraman, a freelance named Mike Lloyd, was also there, although he was just preparing to leave. When I confronted them all they admitted that they had bribed the guard to let them on to the roof. Although hardly welcome, such longlens photography was to be expected on private holidays, but most of these photographers had official accreditation passes from the Palace to cover the royal tour – an official tour, during which they would attend scores of photo sessions – and I told them that their behaviour was a blatant intrusion into the Princess's privacy. They agreed to leave immediately, although whether swayed by my anger, or by their fear of losing their accreditation, I do not know. Next morning, inevitably, the pictures appeared in most of the British newspapers, and ITN even ran the intrusive footage on the news. Diana, determined that her trip should not be trivialised, was concerned in case the pictures shown on British TV should offend Muslim sensitivities, given that they showed her in a swimsuit, and feared that they might create a false impression of her attitude to her official tour, following so closely on the row over the Duchess of York's island-hopping holiday in the Far East. Diana's press aide, Dickie Arbiter, sprang into action, issuing briefings and threatening action against those who had snatched the pictures. He told one newspaper, 'If the first thing people see of her in Egypt is her swimming around in a pool, it puts her in a frivolous light.' Not for the first time, Fleet Street totally missed the real story and **traduced** the Princess, printing the swimming-pool shots rather than following her as she set about a full program of engagements.

From Ken Wharfe, *Diana: Closely Guarded Secret*, published in 2002. Wharfe was Diana's bodyguard from 1987–93

Definition

Traduce

From the Latin for 'to lead', it means to misrepresent or speak ill of someone.

Enquiry source 7E

I woke up at about ten minutes to eight this morning to discover that the Princess of Wales had died in a car crash in Paris . . . I don't think I've ever really had much time for the Princess of Wales ever since *that* interview for Panorama, where she came across as a rather superficial person, who thought herself far more important than I thought her . . . It's no good, I can't pretend that I feel any more grief at her death than I would at the death of anybody, so I won't be going on a pilgrimage to Buckingham Palace with flowers and a card. In fact, if anything I feel *less* grief because Diana was such an unreal figure; a character in a soap opera. Part of my mind keeps wondering what the actress has done to get herself written out, and expecting her to crop up heading her own sitcom or police series in a couple of months. This is ridiculous of course, and a little horrifying. She was a real person, and she died tragically last night after being chased like a fox by a pack of hounds with cameras.

The responsibility for her death filtered steadily upwards yesterday . . . The paparazzi who chased her were the first to be blamed – and certainly the French Police agreed, arresting seven of them. But several people then pointed out that the paparazzi were only obeying orders, and that if newspaper editors didn't pay vast sums of money for the photos they took, they wouldn't do it. Newspaper proprietors were similarly accused, for pushing their editors to publish these photographs to boost circulation. Finally it was realised that circulation wouldn't actually *be* boosted if the public didn't buy the papers, and the public was ultimately responsible for creating a demand . . .

Already, pictures of Diana dying in her car are being hawked around the world's press. So far, the world's press has huffed and puffed and refused to buy the pictures. I doubt they'll be hidden forever, though. At some point, someone will buy them, or they'll find their way onto the Internet – they're possibly already there. How popular will they be? Very, is my guess, and if you can't believe that, consider how often the footage of the death of JFK is shown.

From David Matthewman, diary entry for 31 August 1997. Matthewman is a web manager from Cambridge and an early blogger

Enquiry source 7F

Her silent, mourning army of people marched with their chrysanthemums and dahlias. The pavements and the parks of West London were a moving river of colour. A cult was starting around the Princess who died because of fame . . . The ropes of empty flagpoles slapped against the wood in the wind. No tribute was raised there for the People's Princess. It was not understood by the crowd, who knew nothing of the protocol and said it was a shame. The great flag on the Parliament building flew straight out at half-mast. Flags on the other buildings were lowered. But nothing flew over the Queen's home because it was not in the ancient books that it should . . .

The flowers led you to the People's Princess in London yesterday. They were in the hands of children and the ordinary people she said she loved. The park is incredibly quiet. Yet close by, thousands of people from all over the country stand shoulder to shoulder.

By midday the carpet of roses, carnations and chrysanthemums stretched 10ft from the gates, twining round railings until it was almost impossible to see Diana's home. A few hours later, as darkness fell, it was more than 50ft deep.

From John Edward, 'I never knew there were so many flowers in the whole world', published in the *Daily Mail* on 2 September 1997

SKILLS BUILDER

1 Study Sources 7C, 7D and 7E. How far are the views expressed in Source 7E supported by Sources 7C and 7E?

2 Study Sources 7A, 7B, 7E and 7F and use your own knowledge. To what extent do you agree with the view expressed in Source 7E that Diana was like 'a character in a soap opera'?

Practice source evaluation

1 Rank these sources in order of their use to an historian who wants to find out about the impact of mass media on Diana Spencer, with 1 for the most useful and 7 for the least useful. You may rank some sources equally if you wish. Remember to consider the content and provenance of each source when you make your decisions.
2 Now repeat the exercise, but this time from the point of view of an historian who wants to find out about how mass media representations of Diana Spencer affected the public perception of her.
3 Lastly, rank the sources in order of their use to an historian who wants to find out about the impact of Diana Spencer on the way mass media present the royal family to the public.

Is there a difference in the rank order of sources for each question? If so, how do you account for this?

Use the analysed and evaluated sources as evidence to help answer the following question:

'It was Diana, rather than the mass media, who was more to blame for the increased view of the royal family as mere celebrities 1981–97'. How far do you agree with this statement?

Unit summary

What have you learned in this unit?

Figures of authority have not been able to avoid mass media; many have had to welcome a degree of media attention as a part of their public role. The cost of this has been the intrusion of the media into personal or sensitive areas of their lives in a way that was once reserved for celebrities. Some authority figures have done a better job at preserving their popularity or respect than others. This suggests that there are other, underlying reasons for the loss or maintenance of respect other than mass media attention.

What skills have you used in this unit?

You have carried out comparative evaluations of sources to determine a hierarchy of usefulness. This has helped you to prioritise information from sources when answering a question. You have also considered the usefulness of a source depending upon the question that is being asked; in doing so, you have carefully considered what a particular question is asking for from a source.

SKILLS BUILDER

1 Look back at Sources A, B, H, I, J and K. Now that you have completed this unit, use your knowledge of the changing relationship between authority figures and mass media to contextualise each source. In what ways does your background knowledge help to explain the content and tone of each source?

2 Look back over the information in this unit to help answer the following questions.

- Which figures of authority discussed in this unit have fared the best or worst in terms of their authority being undermined by mass media?
- Which aspect of mass media attention do you consider to have had the greatest impact on authority figures' standing with the British public: news reports, satire or gossip columns?

Exam tips

This is the sort of question you will find appearing on the examination paper as an (a) question.

Read Sources C, D and F.

How far do Sources C and D support the opinion in Source F that television has played the key role in creating negative perceptions of politicians?

You tackled (a) style questions at the end of Units 2, 3 and 5. Look back at the exam tips you were given there. In addition, consider the further tips below.

It is all too easy to offer a generalised evaluation of a source by merely describing its nature, origin, purpose. You will get far more credit if you are able to *specifically* evaluate the source. In order to do this you need to use your own knowledge to contextualise the source:

- What events in popular culture were unfolding at the time the source was created?
- What was the state of mass media at the time?
- What relationship did the author have with the events that are being described?

A specific source evaluation will allow you to more accurately determine how far an opinion expressed in the source reliably supports or contradicts the views of another source.

RESEARCH TOPIC

One group of authority figures not discussed in this unit are the clergy. Use the Internet to research the extent to which news reports, satire and gossip columns have undermined popular respect for the Church of England and the Catholic Church (there is more on popular attitudes to faith and religion in the next unit). Have clergy become celebrities in Britain? If not, why not?

UNIT

9 How far have mass media moulded or mirrored British attitudes?

What is this unit about?

This unit builds upon information on women, racial minorities and homosexuals in previous units. It considers the extent to which mass media have changed British people's views about these different groups within society. The representation of such groups on film, television and in the press have shaped the way people think about and interact with them. However, the impact of mass media must be weighed against the impact of legislation and **demographic** changes.

Key questions

- How far have mass media changed attitudes to women?
- How far have mass media moulded or mirrored attitudes to sexuality?
- How far have mass media moulded or mirrored attitudes to racial minorities?
- How far have mass media moulded or mirrored attitudes to faith and religious minorities?

Definition

Demographic

The study of human populations: births, deaths marriages, migration, etc.

Timeline

1948		Nationality Act
		SS Windrush arrives at Tilbury Docks in London
1958		Nottingham and Notting Hill race riots
1962		Commonwealth Immigrants Act
		First Hindu temple opens in UK
1965		First Race Relations Act establishes the Race Relations Board
1967		Sexual Offences Act (see Unit 4)
		The National Front is formed
1968		Second Race Relations Act establishes the Community Relations Commission
		Enoch Powell makes 'rivers of blood' speech
1969		Divorce Reform Act (see page 49)
1970		Matrimonial Property Act – the work that women do in the home is now taken into account to ensure that they get a fair division of wealth in divorce
		Equal Pay Act (see page 66)
	February	First National Women's Conference is held at Ruskin College, Oxford

Year	Month	Event
	October	Germain Greer's *The Female Eunuch* is published
1975		Sex Discrimination Act (see Unit 5)
1976		Third Race Relations Act leads to the establishment of the Commission for Racial Equality
		Formation of the Anti-Nazi League and Rock Against Racism
1978		BBC drops *The Black and White Minstrel Show* from television schedules
1979		BBC drops *Miss World* from television schedules
		Margaret Thatcher becomes first woman Prime Minister
		Viv Anderson becomes the first black person to play for the England football team
1981		Race riots take place in Brixton, London and Toxteth, Liverpool
		Scarman Report on causes of race riots is published
1988		Section 28 of the Local Government Act outlaws the promotion of homosexuality and the acceptability of homosexual relationships in schools. It was repealed in Scotland in 2000 and the rest of the UK in 2003
1992		Foundation of the Muslim Parliament of Great Britain
1997		Labour government appoints a Minister for Women
1999		Macphearson Report declares the Metropolitan Police 'institutionally racist'
2001		Race riots occur in Oldham, Bradford and Burnley
2002		Paul Boteng becomes the first black man in Cabinet as Chief Secretary to the Treasury
2003		An EU directive means it is against the law to discriminate on grounds of sexuality
2004		Civil Partnership Act allows homosexual couples to form civil partnerships and to enjoy all the legal benefits of being married

Questions

1 What can you see in Source A that would probably have been familiar to viewers of the original *Come Dancing* in the 1950s?

2 What can you see in Source A that would probably have surprised someone in 1950s Britain shown the 2007 final of *Strictly Come Dancing*?

Source A

9.1 A photo of the *Strictly Come Dancing* judges. The judge on the far right, Bruno Tonioli, is openly homosexual. 12 million viewers saw the show

How far have mass media moulded or mirrored attitudes to women?

As you have already seen, there have been a number of important changes since 1945 in the way that women are perceived and in the way they see their role in life. Mass media may have contributed to this change, but this must be weighed against the impact of changes in work, legislation and education that have affected the way women live.

Women and the context of work

Women are far more likely to work in the twenty-first century than they were in late 1940s; this is especially true if they are married or have children. In 1951, a quarter of married women worked; by 1961, this had risen to a third, in 1971 a half, and by 1990, two-thirds. In the 1950s, the majority of women who had a child did not return to work for 10 years; by the 1970s this period had fallen to 4 years. Between 1981 and 1997, the proportion of women who returned to work within a year of giving birth trebled to 60 per cent. The changing way in which women saw their roles was a major reason for this shift. By the late 1950s, a *Manchester Guardian* survey revealed that while 40 per cent of housewives were content in this role, 50 per cent were bored a lot of the time. There was already a desire to work, not out of financial necessity, but simply to get out of the house, make new friends and find fulfilment outside of the family context. As highlighted by Source B this was at a time before the prominence of independent female role models in mass media, suggesting that other factors drove aspirations to work. Source C provides a few clues as to what these other factors might have been.

Source B

[Women are] born to love, born to be partners to the opposite sex . . . and that is the most important thing they can do in life . . . to be wives and mothers, to fix their hearts on one man to love and care for him with all the bounteous unselfishness that love can inspire.

From Monica Dickens, published in *Woman's Own* magazine on 21 January 1961

Source C

The emphasis has now shifted from the discussion of 'what *can* women do?' to one of: 'What *should* women do?' . . . At this juncture in our social history women are guided by two apparently conflicting aims. On the one hand, they want, like everybody else, to develop their personalities to the full and to take an active part in adult social and economic life within the limits of their individual interests and abilities. On the other hand, most women want a home and a family of their own . . . In the old days, women knew where they stood and their lives were spent in the care of their families. Their world was bounded by the walls of their homes . . . The technical and social developments of the last few decades have given women the opportunity to combine and to integrate their two interests in Home and Work . . . No longer need women forgo the pleasures of one sphere in order to enjoy the satisfactions of the other. The best of both worlds has come within their grasp, if only they reach out for it.

From Viola Klein and Alva Myrdal, *Women's Two Roles*, published in 1956

SKILLS BUILDER

1 How far do Sources B and C agree about the role of women in the late 1950s and early 1960s?

2 In what ways does Source C argue that things had changed for women by 1956? What might be inferred by the references to changes?

3 Source C was thought to be quite radical in 1956, yet appears conservative to modern readers. Find statements from the source that would probably divide readers from the time and modern opinion.

A range of things have allowed, or in some cases forced, women into the workplace. Firstly, as sociologist Anthony Heath has commented, 'the reduction in the gender inequalities in attainment is one of the more striking education changes in the second half of the century'. The percentage of girls who have gained the equivalent of GCSEs or higher has risen faster than that for boys; by the 1960s there was gender equality at this level. Education has opened opportunities for women to work in an economy that has become far more service-based. Many of these opportunities were found in the expanded **welfare state** with jobs in schools or healthcare, a clear continuity of the traditional female role of carer. Secondly, legislation may have boosted female participation in the workplace. The 1970 Equal Pay Act and the 1975 Sex Discrimination Act have gradually removed pay differences for men and women who do the same job. However, neither of these factors are likely to have been the main cause of increased female employment: the number of women in full-time employment remained fairly constant between the 1950s and 1990, while the percentage employed in generally low-paid, low-status part-time work increased from 11 per cent to 44 per cent. Such work does not require high levels of education, while the high level of part-time employment still means that women are on average paid less than men.

Technological and financial reasons also help to explain the rise in female employment. As you saw in Source E in Unit 4, the ownership of domestic labour-saving devices has greatly increased since 1951; this, together with the fact that men have contributed more to housework since the 1970s, has given women more time and energy to work outside the home. Increased materialism has meant that many male incomes are not enough to afford all the goods that are now deemed to be 'essential'. More significantly, the rise of cohabitation, lower rates of marriage and higher rates of divorce mean that there are more single women and single mothers who must take on work to supplement other forms of income.

Definition

Welfare state

A system where the government provides a range of services to promote the health and well-being of the people.

Question

How far do you agree that more women work in twenty-first century Britain than the 1950s simply because they want to?

Mass media may have inspired more women to work through female role models and enabled more women to work by helping to overcome the stigma that used to be attached to working wives and mothers. Not only was there thought to be shame attached to men who could not provide for their wives and families, but such working women were felt to be 'taking men's jobs' and making life difficult for other families.

Women in the twenty-first century fulfil many roles on radio and television that were once the preserve of men. This was a slow, gradual process, spearheaded by some exceptional women in the 1950s and 1960s and accelerated after the 1980s. Arguably, by the 2000s, women had achieved parity with men on radio and television. Barbara Mandell (ITV 1955) and Nan Winton (BBC 1960) were early television newsreaders, but Angela Ripon became the first permanent female news anchor in 1974. She was joined in the early 1980s by Moira Stewart and Sue Lawley. Today almost every news programme has a male and female presenter. Kate Adie led the entry of women into 'dangerous' reporting from 1980 to 2003, covering such stories as the Lockerbie bombing of 1988, protests in Beijing's Tiananmen Square in 1989 and the Rwandan genocide of 1994. Women also broke into mainstream comedy in the 1980s after the success of a few early comediennes. Joyce Grenfell and Jill Day were early comedy writers and performers on radio and television with shows in the 1950s. A few female-dominated sit-coms were broadcast from the 1960s, including *The Rag Trade* (BBC 1962–63), *The Liver Birds* (BBC 1969–79) and *Butterflies* (BBC 1978–83), the last two written by a woman, Carla Lane. Since the 1980s, comediennes Dawn French and Jennifer Saunders have inspired other female comics including Jo Brand, the *Smack the Pony* team (Channel 4 1999–2003), Caroline Aherne and Catherine Tate. As Source A showed, women now act as judges on several television competitions, including successful female **entrepreneurs** on *Dragon's Den* (BBC2 2005–). More recently, women have also become sports presenters, with Hazel Irvine, Clare Balding and Gabby Logan hosting snooker, horse racing and football programmes respectively. While there are still glamorous female assistants on game shows and battling housewives on soaps, there is a far greater diversity of female role models on television in the twenty-first century.

> **Definition**
>
> **Entrepreneur**
> A person who takes risks by investing money in new businesses.

Both film and popular music have provided female icons who may have inspired women to aspire to seek greater personal fulfilment. While there have been popular female singers since 1945, there are now more examples of women who write and perform their own songs, such as KT Tunstall, Katie Melua and Amy Winehouse – perhaps a more genuine form of 'girl power' than that hyped-up by the Spice Girls who were formed, packaged and marketed by men. Another form of popular culture, soap operas, have also offered strong role models for women, as discussed in Source D.

Source D

... as regards gender, the conventions of soap opera, developed for a largely female audience, require strong, active women, in direct contradiction to conventional gender roles, as shown in most other television programmes. Indeed soap operas have been thought of as countering or undermining the 'masculine' ethos of most popular culture, especially prime-time television with its certainties, consistencies and plot linearity, by providing a female voice and a feminine form ... Women's pleasure in soap operas derives in part from the centrality of images of the powerful mother and also from the dominant role of the villainess, an expression of that part of themselves which women must usually suppress.

From Sonia M. Livingstone, *Making Sense of Television*, published in 1998

It is difficult to estimate the overall impact of mass media and popular culture on attitudes to female employment. The collapse of the 'marriage bar', the expectation that women would give up work as soon as they were married, was possibly the largest change in attitudes. In 1943, 58 per cent of people opposed married women working; by 1965, this had fallen to 11 per cent if there were no children. British people also became more comfortable with the idea of mothers, even of pre-school children, as workers: in 1980, 11 per cent opposed mothers of school children going to work, while 60 per cent opposed work for mothers of pre-school children; by 2008, an equal number (40 per cent) supported and opposed part-time work for mothers with pre-school children. The first change took place when only a few women challenged male dominance in mass media; the second occurred without any notable mass media role models. This suggests that mass media *responded* to social changes caused by other factors, more than they led or inspired such changes.

Question

How far does Source D suggest that the popularity of soap operas has altered gender relations in Britain?

Women and family context

The traditional role of women as mothers, wives and homemakers is still a key part of many women's identities in twenty-first century Britain, but to a far less degree than in the 1950s or 1960s. From a peak of marital rates for women in the early 1970s, the total number of marriages had dropped by a third by the 2000s. Rates of divorce trebled between the 1970s and 2000s. Levels of cohabitation before marriage rose from 6 per cent of couples in the 1960s to 70 per cent in the 1990s; whereas in 1970, 7 per cent of babies were born to cohabiting couples, this figure had risen to a quarter by 2008. Higher rates of divorce, and the fact that relationships based on cohabitation are less stable than those based on marriage, have led to an increase in the percentage of single-parent families from 7.5 per cent of all families in 1971 to 17.5 per cent in 1991; of these 90 per cent were single-mother families. A number of factors have led to this decoupling of sex and child-rearing from marriage since the 1970s.

Definition

Shotgun wedding

An enforced or hurried wedding.

The changes were partly driven by the liberal legislation of the 1960s. The 1967 Abortion Act meant more pregnancies ended in abortion rather than a **shotgun wedding**. In 1969, 54 per cent of pre-marital conceptions resulted in marriage, while only 11 per cent resulted in abortion. Since 1967, the rate of abortion for women in general, but especially those between the ages of 18 and 20, has risen steadily from eight abortions per 1000 women in 1969 to 19 per 1000 in 2008. The Divorce Reform Act and Matrimonial Property Acts of 1969 and 1970 also led to a decline in marriage due to the increased rate of divorce, demonstrated in Source E. The second of these Acts in particular meant it was more viable for women to seek a divorce as it guaranteed them a fair division of the couples' wealth. The huge growth in cohabitation since 1970 is largely a result of couples not seeing the point of marriage. Levels of divorce have fallen slightly since the mid-1990s, and this could partly to be due to the implementation of the 1996 Family Act, which encouraged **mediation** before divorce was granted.

Definition

An attempt to reach an agreement through negotiation.

Question

What can we infer from Source E about the main causes of changes in the rate of divorce since 1945? Explain your answer with details from the source.

Source E

Year	*Total number of divorces*	*Divorce granted on petition of husband*	*Divorce granted on petition of wife*	*Divorce granted on petition of both*
1945	15,634			
1955	26,816	12,034	14,782	
1965	37,785	15,993	21,633	159
1975	120,522	38,477	81,693	352
1985	160,300	44,574	115,144	582
1995	155,499	45,985	109,023	491
2003	153,490	47,009	106,310	171

9.2 A table showing numbers of divorces in the UK and which party requested the divorce from 1945 to 2003. Source: Office for National Statistics

A number of financial changes have also contributed to the rise of divorce and the number of single parent families. Firstly, the increased ability of mothers to find work has allowed more to divorce as they do not have to rely on the father's income. Secondly, critics, such as former Conservative MP Norman Tebbit, have blamed overly-generous welfare payments to mothers for the breakdown of the link between marriage and child-rearing: the percentage of single mothers who received government benefits rose from 30 per cent in 1970 to almost 90 per cent by 1990. Single mothers also get higher priority for council houses. Lastly, in order to reduce government costs, the Child Support Agency was established in 1993 to help force absent parents to pay for the upkeep of children cared for by the lone parent.

In the 2000s, *EastEnders* had a higher proportion of single-parent families on the show than there was in the real world. This being a soap opera, the mothers were generally tough characters who did a good job with the support of the community. There were also far more cohabiting couples on a range of soaps and dramas. Other than this, mass media, and the press especially, condemn rather than condone high levels of divorce and the growth of single-parent families. The portrayal of ideal couples on television and on film, and more recently real couples on shows such as *Wife Swap* (Channel 4 2003–), will almost certainly have led more men and women to compare their relationships with those on screen. Whether such comparisons have contributed to greater rates of divorce and separation, or whether they have promoted greater communication and openness between couples is difficult to say. Either way, the impact of mass media in this context appears marginal when compared with the other factors discussed above. Once again, mass media have reflected rather than brought about these significant changes in family life.

Women and the female image in mass media

The fact that mass media have reflected rather than caused changes to women's lives since 1945 does not mean that they are without any significance whatsoever. The link between mass media and sexuality is discussed on pages 165–68, but images conveyed by mass media, principally in advertising, have shaped the way in which women think of themselves and in the way that men see women. The key question is whether mass media have empowered women and promoted gender equality, or whether they have marginalised women as mere housewives or sex objects. As discussed in Source F, women have become huge consumers of magazines, and hence advertising.

Source F

Between 1957 and 1967, annual spending on weekly and monthly publications went up from £46 million to over £80 million . . . By far the most successful were the so called 'women's magazines' . . . In 1957 *Woman* was being read by one in every two women in Britain between the ages of sixteen and forty-four. Newspapers, struggling to prop up their advertising revenue after the launch of commercial television and eager to attract female readers, scurried to employ journalists giving the 'woman's angle', and even *The Times* launched a 'women's page' dispensing advice on fashion, cookery and childcare. By the beginning of the sixties, five out of every six women read at least one magazine a week. Women's magazines concentrated more on the woman as a consumer rather than a housewife, and advertisers played a central role in determining the look and appeal of the magazine.

From Dominic Sandbrook, *White Heat*, published in 2006

Question

According to Source F, what has been the impact of female demand for magazines on the British press as a whole?

The impact of this, aside from boosting advertising revenue for publishers, has been the growing influence of mass-media generated ideals in terms of looks, dress, lifestyle and relationships for both women and men. Sources G and H compare two images from the 1950s and 2000s.

Source G

9.3 An advertisement from 1951

Source H

9.4 An image from the 2000s

SKILLS BUILDER

1 How far would you agree that the portrayal of women in Source H is more negative than in Source G? Explain your answer.

2 How far do you think differences in the depiction of women in advertisements might have influenced the way women see themselves and the way they are seen by men?

Critics are quick to blame adverts with perfect skinny women for the increase in depression and eating disorders such as anorexia and bulimia. Women are nine times more likely than men to suffer from such disorders, and they affect more teenagers, who are perhaps more image conscious, than older women. However, the numbers of women who are affected by these disorders is very small with around 10–20 per 100,000 of the population. This suggests that other traumas and psychological issues are more significant. Use the research task on page 177 to investigate the portrayal of women in advertising further.

How far have mass media changed attitudes to sexuality?

The growth of a 'permissive' society has already been discussed in the context of the 1960s and 1970s. Since then, there have been a number of important changes, especially with regard to sex before marriage and homosexuality.

Sex before marriage

It is difficult to generalise about how far attitudes to sex have become 'liberated'. On the one hand, sex before marriage became far more acceptable in the last quarter of the twentieth century: whereas in 1983, over 40 per cent of people thought sex before marriage was 'sometimes wrong, mostly wrong or always wrong', by 2003 this had dropped to just over 20 per cent. The growth in teenage pregnancy in the 1970s and 1980s may have been partly due to this shift in attitude. On the other hand, throughout the same period around 90 per cent thought sex with someone other than your partner was 'mostly wrong' or 'totally wrong'.

Girls' magazines have increasingly promoted the idea that sex before marriage is a desirable and normal experience. 'Romantic' magazines such as *Mirabelle*, *Valentine* and *Boyfriend* fell out of favour in the early 1960s with the rise of more sexually orientated magazines such as *Jackie* and *Honey*. In the 1980s and 1990s, magazines such as *Sugar* and *More!* became even more explicit with sexual advice and even tips. The mid-1990s also saw the rise of sexually charged men's magazines such as *Loaded* and *FHM*. However, sexual health experts generally conclude that such magazines, together with sexualised advertising and television shows such as *Celebrity Love Island* (ITV 2005–06) or *Skins* (Channel 4 2007–), are only one cause of the rise in teenage pregnancies since the 1970s.

Source I

There are three major factors for the UK's failure to reduce its teenage conception rates alongside those of other European countries [in 1998, the UK rate was double that of Germany, three times that of France and five times the birth rate of the Netherlands].

- Low expectations. Teenage pregnancy is more common among young people who have been disadvantaged and have poor expectations of education or the job market . . . As the report said 'put simply, they see no reason not to get pregnant'.
- Ignorance. Young people in the UK lack accurate knowledge about contraception and sexually transmitted infections, they are uncertain of what to expect from a relationship and have an unrealistic picture of parenthood.
- Mixed messages. Young people are surrounded by sexual images and messages which imply that sexual activity is the norm. Yet some parents and many public institutions are at best embarrassed about dealing with young people's sexuality or try to ignore it completely.

From the Social Exclusion Unit, *Teenage Pregnancy*, published in 1999. The Social Exclusion Office was a government task force that sought to reduce social exclusion. It was replaced in 2008 by the Social Exclusion Task Force

Questions

1 To what extent does Source I suggest that mass media and popular culture are the cause of high levels of teenage pregnancy in the UK?

2 How useful is this source to an historian who wants to find out about changes in sexual behaviour in the UK since the 1970s?

Definitions

Civil partnership

A legally joining contract like marriage but without the religious ceremony.

Camp

Exaggerated, theatrical, effeminate behaviour.

Homosexuality

There has been a huge shift in favour of homosexual rights and the acceptability of homosexual relationships, as shown in Source J.

The 1967 Sexual Offences Act made a big difference to gay men in England and Wales as it decriminalised homosexual relationships. Apart from the lowering of the age of consent to 18 in 1994, there were no further legal advances for homosexuals until a raft of changes in the 2000s. Between 2000 and 2009 homosexuals were no longer allowed to be discriminated against in speech, employment or services they received; were allowed to form **civil partnerships**, adopt children and serve in the armed forces. This official legitimisation of homosexual relationships must have had an impact on public perceptions. However, Source J shows that popular acceptance of homosexual relationships rose steadily in the 1990s despite the lack of legislation in those years. Mass media and popular culture go a long way to explaining this shift.

In the 1950s and 1960s, homosexuals were associated with espionage due to media stories surrounding the Cambridge Spy Ring after 1951 and John Vassall in 1962. A poll in 1963 revealed that 93 per cent thought that homosexuals were ill and needed medical treatment rather than punishment. They were openly persecuted by mass media, as shown in Source K.

As with women in popular culture, a number of pioneering men began to make **camp** behaviour, if not homosexual relationships, acceptable in the 1970s. TV stars such as Larry Grayson, presenter of popular shows *Shut That Door!* (ITV 1975–77) and *The Generation Game* (BBC 1978–81) and John Inman, who played the popular character Mr Humphries in the sit-com *Are You Being Served?* (BBC 1972–85), were camp but publicly denied being gay. Although Grayson had catchphrases such as 'What a gay day'

Source J

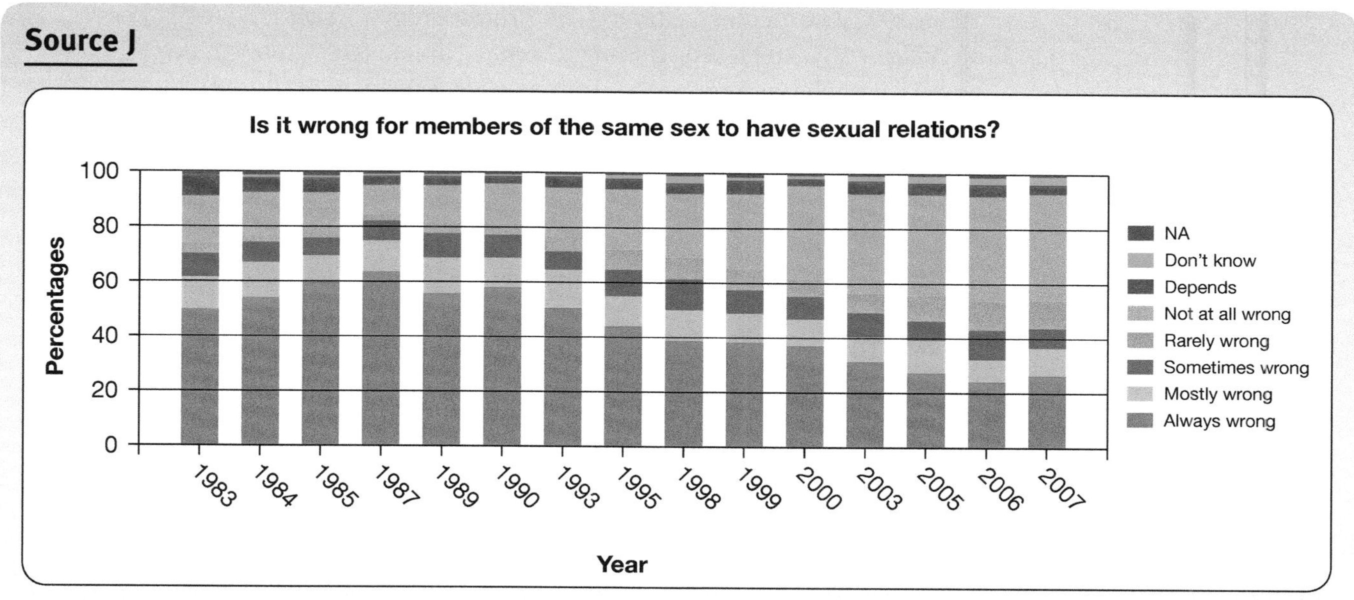

9.5 A graph showing attitudes to homosexual relationships between 1983 and 2007. Compiled from data from the British Social Attitudes surveys conducted by the National Centre for Social Research. The data is available on the BritSocAt website, developed by the Centre for Comparative European Survey Data

and 'Seems like a nice boy', he told the *Daily Mirror* in 1972 that 'I'm not really a queer or a homosexual. I'm just behaving like one. That's the big difference'. *The Naked Civil Servant* (ITV in 1975), was a highly successful TV film about the life and times of Quentin Crisp, a flamboyant homosexual writer and life-class model who became a gay icon after he published his memoirs of his early life in 1968. Also in the 1970s, some leading pop stars such as David Bowie and Elton John publicly admitted to being bi-sexual; Elton John finally admitted he was gay in the early 1990s.

The 1990s saw a breakthrough of open homosexuals into mainstream popular culture, boosting their 'cultural visibility': the increased appearance of openly gay celebrities and characters in mass media has made homosexuality generally more acceptable to British people. Although lesbianism was never illegal, homosexual women had also faced a large degree of discrimination in public and in the media before this decade. *Emmerdale*'s character Zoe Tate (in the show from 1989–2005) was the first major character to 'come out' as a lesbian. The first pre-watershed lesbian kiss was shown on *Brookside* in 1993. The popular American TV show *Buffy the Vampire Slayer* (BBC2 1997–2003) included a long lesbian romance involving Willow, one of the main characters. In the real world, several female celebrities also 'came out', including American actress Ellen DeGeneres and tennis player Martina Navratilova. Boy George, George Michael and other pop stars 'came out' as gay. Films such as *Four Weddings and a Funeral* (1994) had popular gay characters. Actors such as Sir Ian McKellan and Simon Callow were openly gay. A number of television shows were hosted by gay entertainers such as Dale Winton (*Supermarket Sweep* ITV 1993–2001), who came out in 2003 and Graham Norton (*So . . .* Channel 4

Source K

Evil Men: Most people know there are such things – 'pansies' – mincing, effeminate, young men who call themselves queers. But simple, decent folk regard them as freaks and rarities. [Homosexuality is] a spreading fungus.

From the *Sunday Pictorial* newspaper, published on 25 May 1952

1998–2002); comedies, such as *The Brittas Empire* (BBC 1991–97), *The Vicar of Dibley* (BBC 1994–99), *Gimme, Gimme, Gimme* (BBC 1999–2001) all had openly gay characters, as did dramas such as *This Life* (BBC 1996–97) and *Queer as Folk* (Channel 4 1999), which also contained explicit sexual scenes and references. *Brookside's* first gay main character's appearance was in 1982; *EastEnders* (1987), *Emmerdale* (1989), radio soap *The Archers* (2003), *Coronation Street* (2004) and *Hollyoaks* (2006) followed. The degree of change in public perception of homosexuals is perhaps best shown by the winners of mass popularity contest *Big Brother* in 2002 and 2004: Brian Dowling, an openly gay man and Nadia Almada, a Portuguese transsexual respectively. Since 1982, a Gay Pride carnival has been held in London; in the 2000s many other cities across the UK began to host their own version of the event. Source L is a snapshot from 1998 of how far homosexuals had progressed in terms of their acceptance in British society.

SKILLS BUILDER

1 How far does Source L support Source J about the increased acceptance of homosexuality in British society in the 1990s?

2 Which out of Sources J and L is more useful to an historian who wants to find out how far gay people became accepted by British society in the 1990s? Explain your answer with reference to the content and provenance.

3 How far do Sources J, K and L suggest that mass media and popular culture have contributed to the increased acceptance of homosexuality in British society?

Source L

Compared to a decade ago, the cultural visibility of homosexuality has grown by leaps and bounds. When even *The Archers* has a gay character, you know that lesbian and gay people really *are* making serious inroads into the mainstream. Further proof that we are winning over Middle England came last September when an out gay man, Elton John, accompanied by his male lover, was invited to sing in front of the Queen in Westminster Abbey at the funeral of the mother of the future King. Yet despite these gains, there remain many homo-free zones. No major High Street company uses gay couples to advertise its products . . . the number of out British sports stars is zero . . . The same mixed fortunes are evident when it comes to press coverage of gay issues. Nowadays you rarely see anything as vicious as *The Sun*'s 1986 feature: 'Perverts To Blame For The Killer Plague', which denounced gay people with AIDS as 'terrorists holding the decent members of society to ransom'. Today's newspaper homophobia tends to be more subtle, and the quality broadsheets are often just as guilty as the tabloids. *The Times* obituary of Sir Michael Tippett insultingly said he never married, ignoring his 30-year openly gay relationship with Meirion Bowen . . .

The trend towards gay people coming out in soaps merely reflects real life, where ever increasing numbers are declaring their sexuality. Celebrities, too, are flinging open the closet doors. That means more gay role-models for young kids which, together with often gay-sympathetic television and teen magazines, is making it easier for many to accept their homosexuality . . . The last decade has seen a strong cultural shift towards greater acceptance of lesbians and gay men, but attitudes nevertheless remain contradictory. This is confirmed by *The People*'s 1997 survey, in which 93 per cent of respondents classified themselves as more tolerant of homosexuals than they used to be; yet a mere 36 per cent endorse fostering by gay couples and only 45 per cent back gay marriage. We may have come a long way baby, but we've still got a mighty long way to go.

From Peter Tatchell, 'Ads – A gay-free zone', published in *Campaign* magazine on 30 January 1998. Tatchell is a leading gay rights activist who co-founded the pressure group OutRage! in 1990

How far have mass media changed attitudes to racial minorities?

The key difference between immigration into the UK before 1945 and after 1945 can be summed up in one word: colour. Whereas most immigrants in the nineteenth century had come from Ireland, and from Eastern Europe in the first half of the twentieth century (a pattern repeated for very different reasons at the start of the twenty-first century), most immigrants after 1945 came from the West Indies, former British colonies in Africa and the Indian subcontinent. Initial waves of Irish and Jewish immigrants from Eastern Europe experienced hostility upon arrival in Britain for cultural and economic reasons. Immigrants after 1945 faced the additional problem of racism. The key question is how far the British population became more racially tolerant and inclusive since 1945.

The demographic context

Even before the *SS Empire Windrush* docked on 22 June 1948, there were already 75,000 black and Asian people living in England, most of them born in Britain.

Source M

Year	*Total ethnic minority population of UK*	*As a percentage of total population of UK*
1951	80,000	0.2
1961	500,000	0.8
1971	1,500,000	3.3
1981	2,200,000	4.1
1991	3,000,000	6.4
2001	4,600,000	7.9

9.6 A table showing the rise in numbers and percentage of the **ethnic minority** population in the UK between 1951 and 2001. Source: Office for National Statistics

Definition

Ethnic minority

A group with physical or cultural differences from the majority of people in society.

We saw in Unit 2 that black and Asian immigrants mostly settled in areas where their labour was required: London, Birmingham and south-east Lancashire. A good deal of the subsequent increase in the ethnic minority population was a result of families coming to join the original economic migrants, and the birth of first, second and third generation black-British and Asian-British people. Most of these minorities were initially concentrated in cheap housing in inner-city areas, such as Southall and Brixton in London, or Toxteth in Liverpool. They also did mainly low-paid work. One notable exception to this was the settlement of 27,000 Ugandan Asians who were expelled by dictator Idi Amin in 1972. Many of these entrepreneurial people opened 'corner shops' in towns across Britain in the 1970s and 1980s. The prospects of second and third generation children have varied from group to group, with those of Indian descent far more likely to gain better qualifications, higher incomes and houses in 'white' suburbs than those of African or West Indian origin. As all these immigrants had to face similar white reactions and laws, cultural differences must go a long way towards explaining such varied rates of success. While large swathes of the UK remained ethnically homogenous, the huge changes in many urban areas provoked anger but also led to a good deal of cultural exchange.

The legal and political context

Successive governments since 1945 have had a confused stance towards immigration and racial minorities. On the one hand, they have sought to make minorities welcome (especially when their labour was required in the early 1950s) and promote racial harmony through a series of Race Relations Acts in 1965, 1968, 1976 and 2000 that have banned discrimination in employment, housing, public institutions and services, and through bodies designed to enforce these laws such as the Commission for Racial Equality, set up in 1976. When racial problems have been exposed, such as with the riots of 1981 and the handling of Stephen Lawrence's murder in 1993, the government has ordered Commissions of Enquiry, in these cases the Scarman and MacPherson Reports respectively. The MacPherson Report has led to a large increase in the proportion of ethnic minority officers in the Metropolitan Police, from only 384 out of 28,000 in 1994. On the other hand, governments have sought to limit subsequent immigration (until accession to the European Union (EU)) through a series of Immigration Acts in 1962, 1968, 1971 and 2008. These were mainly passed in response to the unexpectedly high number of black and Asian immigrants between 1948 and 1962, and Eastern European immigrants after many their countries joined the EU in 2004. Politicians in the main political parties feared that white British alienation and anger would lead to votes for fascist parties such as the National Front (1967–) and the British National Party (1982–). Such fears were justified to a large extent as the following list of racist events and sources suggest.

- August 1958 – St. Ann's district of Nottingham: violence escalated after a fight outside a pub.
- September 1958 – Notting Hill: an attack by Teddy Boys on a white woman with a black partner, escalated into violence involving hundreds of youths. The Notting Hill Carnival was founded the following year to promote racial harmony.
- 1964 – Smethwick: Conservative Party candidate Peter Griffiths won his seat with the slogan, 'For more Nigger-type neighbours, vote Labour'.
- April 1968 – Birmingham: Conservative MP Enoch Powell gave a speech in which he called for the repatriation of Commonwealth immigrants to avoid future violence and bloodshed. A Gallup Poll reported that 74 per cent of Britons agreed with what he said.

- August 1976 – Notting Hill, London: the Carnival descended into violence after the police began to arrest black people they suspected of being petty criminals. 450 people were injured and 56 were arrested.
- April 1981 – Brixton, London: riots exploded after the police had stopped and searched thousands of mainly black locals as part of 'Operation Swamp'.
- July 1981 – Toxteth, Liverpool: black unemployment was 60 per cent and frustration led to violence. It took four days to bring the violence under control. 100 buildings were destroyed and 800 police were injured.
- July–August 1981 – less serious violence was reported in London, Birmingham, Leeds, Leicester, Ellesmere Port, Luton, Sheffield, Portsmouth, Preston, Newcastle-upon-Tyne, Derby, Southampton, Cirencester, Nottingham, Hull, Slough, Keswick, High Wycome, Bedford, Edinburgh, Wolverhampton, Stockport, Blackburn, Bolton, Huddersfield, Halifax, Reading, Chester, Cardiff and Aldershot.
- May 2001 – Oldham: violence escalated after a fight between white and Asian gangs. This triggered similar violence in Bradford and Burnley in June.

Source N

9.7 A photo of a window of a house offering bed and breakfast accommodation in the early 1960s. Such signs were common in B&Bs in many British cities in the 1950s and 1960s

Source O

The reports of conditions at Notting Hill continue to be the cause of great concern. The Commission has received reports of a persistent feeling on the part of West Indians that the police are not impartial (for instance moving on a group of West Indians and leaving a group of others across the street), and have shown partiality in making arrests where West Indians are involved.

Another source of growing concern are reports of increased activity in vice of some West Indians. Here we are concerned only for those who become the victims of poor housing conditions and the absence of proper meeting places to satisfy the normal impulses to meet each other in healthy social intercourse. These impulses tend to drive decent citizens towards and into these undesirable clubs, cafés and practices.

The situation is further aggravated by the unrelated activities of movements like Mosely's which are reported to distribute their propaganda sheets from door to door and incessantly stimulate ill feeling against the West Indian.

Extracts from a letter from the West Indies High Commission to the Secretary of State for the Colonies, written on 1 September 1959. Oswald Mosely had been leader of the British Union of Fascists before the Second World War. In 1948 he formed the Union Movement, which among other things called for an end to coloured immigration

Source P

This huge addition to our population, consisting of multi-racial, largely unskilled, illiterate immigrants, who for the most part have not our language, was . . . never planned or called for: it was just allowed to happen, as if it were a chastisement which we *had* to suffer. No one really knows how many of these resented and resentful people are already in our midst, but the evidence suggests there can be no less than *a million*. And the ineradicable social problems created by the introduction of this huge alien population into our midst are only beginning to develop. But already the day is gone when a Briton returned from a foreign land can walk our streets feeling that he is again among his 'ain folk' [sic].

From John Sanders, *The Incredible Folly*, a pamphlet printed and distributed in Birmingham in 1965. Sanders was the chairman of the Birmingham Immigration Control Association, founded in 1960

SKILLS BUILDER

1 To what extent do Sources N, O and P suggest that British society was racist in the 1960s?

2 In what ways do Sources O and P disagree about the causes of racial tension in the 1960s?

3 How reliable are the views presented in Sources O and P? Refer to the content and provenance of each source in your answer.

Mass media, popular culture and racial tolerance

The key question is whether the media promoted and facilitated integration and tolerance between different ethic groups or whether it provoked and sustained white anger, especially in areas with high levels of black or Asian immigration.

Many critics have suggested that the British press has exacerbated racial tension. The reports of the 1958 Nottingham race riots are thought to have triggered copycat acts of violence in other areas. Source Q is an extract from a press report on the Notting Hill riots.

Source Q

. . . I saw a mob of over 700 men, women and children stretching 200 yards along the road. Young children of ten were treating the whole affair as a great joke and shouting 'Come on, let's get the blacks and the coppers. Let's get on with it.' In the middle of the screaming, jeering youths and adults, a speaker from the Union Movement was urging his excited audience to 'get rid of them' (the coloured people) . . .

Within half an hour the mob which had now swelled to uncontrollable numbers had broken scores of windows and set upon two negroes who were lucky to escape with cuts and bruises. Women from the top floor windows laughed as they called down to the thousand strong crowd, 'Go on boys, get yourself some blacks.'

From the *Kensington News and West London Times*, published on 5 September 1958

Members of the press perhaps learnt their lesson as the Brixton riots were, according to historian Mark Garrett, ' . . . barely reported by the media. This was a rare example of responsibility, taking into account the danger of "copycat" riots might spread further'. More recently, media critics have expressed concerns about the way that Muslims, asylum-seekers and economic migrants from Eastern Europe have been portrayed in the press. Shortly after the July 7 bombings in London in 2005, the *Daily Express* led with the bold headline 'BOMBERS ARE ALL SPONGING ASYLUM SEEKERS'. It later emerged that none of the bombers involved were asylum seekers.

At the cinema, British films throughout the 1950s, 1960s and 1970s gave confrontational or patronising views of black people, even when the overall aim was to present them in a sympathetic light. The 1959 film *Sapphire*, is about a murder investigation of a Notting Hill girl thought to be white until her black brother turns up. The film shows a successful black barrister and doctor as well as criminals, but there is a lot of casual racism. In one scene, a white observer notes that another apparently white girl is of mixed blood when she starts to dance, saying 'you can always tell . . . once they hear the beat of the bongo'. Other films which portray blacks in a similar fashion include *Flame in the Streets* (1961), about a mixed-race relationship, and *Winds of Change* (1961), about a Teddy Boy obsessed with mixed couples and violence. Later films, such as *My Beautiful Laundrette* (1985), *East is East* (1999), *Dirty Pretty Things* (2002) and *Bend It Like Beckham* (2002), do present racial minorities in a far more positive light. Since the 1990s there have been far more (American) films with black and Asian actors where race is not a key part of the film, including many of actor Will Smith's films such as *Independence Day* (1996), *Wild Wild West* (1999) and *I Am Legend* (2007).

On television, ethnic minorities, like homosexuals and women, have had an increasingly high profile on many non-fiction shows, and a less stereotyped portrayal in soaps and dramas since the 1970s. Presenters such as newsreaders Trevor MacDonald, Moira Stewart, Zeinab Badawi and Krishnan Guru Murphy, reporter Rageh Omaar, children's television anchor Andy Peters and Reggie Yates, comedians Charlie Williams and

Jos White in the 1970s, Gary Wilmot and Lenny Henry in the 1980s, sports pundits Garth Crooks and Robbie Earle, have all helped to show racial minorities in an empowered and professional light.

We have already come across two popular sit-coms with strong racial elements: *Till Death Do Us Part* and *Rising Damp*. While writer Jonny Speight wanted to expose the stupidity of Alf Garnett's racist and **bigoted** views, the audience more often laughed along with Garnett's outbursts than they did at his final comeuppance. Source R is an example of one contemporary review of the show.

In *Rising Damp*, Philip was a sophisticated black character but he did play up to primitive, sexually threatening stereotypes to annoy Rigsby. There was even more racial stereotyping in the ITV sit-com *Love Thy Neighbour* (1972–77). However, a number of soaps and dramas began to include black and Asian characters in a more representative fashion in the 1970s and 1980s (see Source D in Unit 5). In February 2009, *EastEnders* had its first 'all-black' episode that focused on the experiences of Patrick Trueman, a character since 2001, who had come to London from Trinidad in the 1950s. Source S discusses the significance of the way in which racial minorities have been presented on television.

Definition

Bigotry

Intolerant and narrow-minded views based on a range of prejudices.

Source R

[Alf Garnett's views] can be seen and heard most days in most pubs, factories and boardrooms in the land . . . Fortunately, there are few of us who possess all of Alf's . . . hates and prejudices. But it is only a saint among us who does not share at least one.

From Milton Shulman, published in the *Evening Standard* 21 February 1968

Source S

[Enoch] Powell claimed that there was a 'gulf between the overwhelming majority of the country on the one side, and on the other side a tiny minority, with almost a monopoly hold upon the channels of communication', and there was much truth in this assertion . . . From the perspective of the white population, the depiction of ethnic minorities in the media was particularly crucial in the 1970s, since for many people, the only black faces they were likely to encounter came on the television screen. Britain was becoming multi-racial, but it was a patchy phenomenon . . .

From Alwyn Turner, *Crisis? What Crisis?*, published in 2008

SKILLS BUILDER

1 How far do Sources Q, R and S support the idea that mass media promoted racism in the UK?

2 Of Sources Q, R and S, which is the most representative of the relationship between mass media and attitudes to racial minorities in Britain since 1945? Use the content of each source and your own knowledge in your answer.

Other areas of culture have seen a huge rise in tolerance and integration. In sport, the Kick Racism Out of Football campaign, launched in 1993, has helped in this respect, but probably not as much as the rise of talented black players. By 1979, 50 out of 2000 professional footballers were black. In November that year, Nottingham Forest defender Viv Anderson became the first black man to play for England. Fans who had made monkey noises and thrown bananas on to the pitch when he played in league matches cheered him in his England strip! In 2008, English fans at an away leg were shocked by such behaviour from Spanish supporters. In 1999, Lennox Lewis became world heavyweight boxing champion, a feat never accomplished by the hugely popular Frank Bruno in the 1980s. Black athletes such as Kris Akabusi, Linford Christie and Colin Jackson were highly successful in the 1980s and 1990s. In 1958, Butlin's put Chinese food into every camp. This helped to launch the popularity of ethnic minority foods; by the 1990s, chicken tikka masala was considered a national dish alongside fish and chips. While black and Asian communities have their own musical subcultures, many ethnic minority performers have become part of mainstream pop culture, from The Specials in the 1980s, to Seal in the 1990s and countless hip hop artists since 2000.

For all the racist events outlined above, the vast majority of British people have rejected political racism. The National Front was a failure and almost went bankrupt in the 1970s; the rise of the British National Party at the end of the 2000s was limited to a few local councils and a couple of seats in the European parliament. The varied success of different ethnic groups suggests that racism, or the portrayal of minorities in the mass media, have not been the most significant problems such groups have had to face. Rather, some groups, such as those of West Indian or Bangladeshi descent, have struggled with poverty and all the problems and disadvantages that this brings regardless of ethnicity.

How far have mass media changed attitudes to faith and religious minorities?

Although Britain is often said to have been '**secularised**' in the twentieth century, it is perhaps more useful to think of the British being 'de-churched'. Numbers attending church once a week had already fallen before 1945, from 35 to 13 per cent of the population. *Puzzled People*, a Mass Observation report in 1947, concluded that 'most people nowadays don't think much about religion, don't set much conscious store by it and have decidedly confused ideas about it'. By 2007, synagogue attendance had fallen dramatically and church attendance had fallen to just 6 per cent. Since the 1970s, only Hindus, Muslims and Sikhs and a few small Christian denominations have increased attendance figures. Belief in God fell from 70 to 40 per cent of the population from 1950 to 2007. Yet at the same time, the 2001 Census revealed that almost 72 per cent considered themselves Christian, while only 15 per cent said they had no religious beliefs (including the 0.7 per cent who claimed to be 'Jedi'). Mass media and popular culture are just two factors out of many that help explain these trends.

Definition

Secularisation

The process whereby religious thinking, practices and institutions lose their social significance.

In his book *The Death of Christian Britain*, Callum Brown sees the growth in permissive values after the 1960s as the key factor. He particularly notes the impact of girls' and women's magazines on female attendance. However, many historians have criticised this view as it ignores the pre-1960s decline. James Obelkevich, among others, sees the rise of urbanisation and industry as far more significant: the traditional rural calendar and holidays were strongly linked to Christian festivals; the introduction of bank holidays in 1871 and the commercialisation of the remaining festivals of Easter and Christmas have severed this link. The process was perhaps completed in 1994 when the Keep Sundays Special campaign failed to stop supermarkets opening on 'the Lord's day'.

The Anglican Church has often 'played catch-up' with popular morality in a bid to maintain relevance. The ordination of women after 1994, and the acceptance of openly gay clergy by the Anglican Church in the UK, came after the huge strides made by these groups in other social spheres. Attempts to modernise have failed to attract more people and divisions between reformers and traditionalists have alienated many former church-goers.

Mass media and popular culture have reflected more than inspired de-churching. There was no scandal when anthropologist Desmond Morris said in his book *The Naked Ape* (1967) that 'Religion has given rise to a great deal of unnecessary suffering and misery'; indeed, it boosted sales of the *Daily Mirror* when it serialised the book. The Monty Python film *The Life of Brian* (1979) did cause some outrage because of its blasphemy: it was banned in Surrey, east Devon, Harrogate and in Swansea. Many people living in those areas visited cinemas elsewhere where they could see the film. In soaps and dramas, with the exception of the *Vicar of Dibley* (BBC 1994–2007), clergy have not featured highly. While religious controversies still get wide coverage on radio and in the press, the time allocated to religious programming on television has been cut: in 2005 ITV cut such coverage from 104 to 52 hours per year.

SKILLS BUILDER

1. Out of cinema, television and the press, which mass media has had the greatest impact on popular attitudes towards women, homosexuals and ethnic minorities?
2. Out of women, homosexuals and ethnic minorities, which group's experiences since 1945 have been most affected by mass media and popular culture?
3. Hold a class debate: 'This class believes mass media and popular culture to have reflected more than provoked changes in attitudes to women, homosexuals and ethnic minorities'.

Unit summary

What have you learned in this unit?

While some popular culture has perhaps empowered or inspired British women, some forms of pop culture, especially advertising, have exaggerated gender stereotypes and encouraged women to live up to an unrealistic ideal of beauty.

Mass media and popular culture have generally moved away from stereotyping minorities towards a more realistic and representational portrayal. They have increasingly provided positive role models for members of ethnic minority groups and promoted inclusive views among the vast majority of white Britons.

Mass media and popular culture were not the only factors that have affected the experiences of different minorities; changes in laws, education and employment have also been major causes of shifting popular perspectives.

What skills have you used in this unit?

You have brought together the skills of close analysis, detailed evaluation and cross-referencing of sources to use them in a highly sophisticated manner when answering historical questions. You have used a good deal of background knowledge from this unit and earlier in the book to specifically contextualise sources.

Exam tips

This is the sort of question you will find appearing on the examination paper as a (b) question.

Study Sources Q, R and S and use your own knowledge.

Do you agree with the view that 'the depiction of ethnic minorities in the media was crucial' in changing popular attitudes towards ethnic minorities in Britain since 1945?

Explain your answer using Sources Q, R and S and your own knowledge.

You tackled (b) style questions at the end of Units 4, 6 and 7. Look back at the previous exam tips and then plan an answer to this question.

Now test yourself! Look back at your plan and make sure you have:

- structured paragraphs in your answer according to points or themes not sources
- analysed the content of each source for points in favour and against the statement
- cross-referenced points of agreement and disagreement between different sources
- used your own knowledge to specifically evaluate sources and to reinforce or challenge what they say
- decided upon a balanced, measured conclusion.

RESEARCH TOPIC

Adverts and social change

Adverts depict people in a way that is most likely to appeal to people in order to sell goods. In doing so, they give an insight into what people thought of particular groups within society, or what was thought to be acceptable. Divide into groups to study the 1960s, 1970s, 1980s, 1990s and 2000s; in your group consider the depiction of gender, sexuality and ethnicity shown by adverts. Use the Internet to help you with your research. The following words are a good place to start.

- British Ads from the 1950s 1960s 1970s, uk itv adverts, nike adverts, oxo adverts, tv advertising – sexist?, tv adverts – racist?

RESEARCH TOPIC

Popular perceptions of British social change

- Ask one or more older relatives what they think about how life has changed for the British since 1945. Record their answer.
- Focus their answers by asking them to say the first things that come into their heads when you say 1940s, 1950s, 1960s, 1970s, 1980s, 1990s. Again, record their answers.
- Now compare your research with others' in class. How similar are all your relatives' memories?
- Have your relatives looked back through 'rose-tinted glasses'? Compare their memories with your knowledge of mass media, popular culture and social change since 1945.

Thematic review: source-based debate and evaluation

It is important, especially when dealing with a topic that addresses change over time, to stand back and review the period you have been studying. You need to ask yourself not only what happened, but why it happened and why it happened then and not, say, 100 years earlier or 20 years later. What had driven change? Which factors were significant and which were not? Were there any events that were critical turning points? The majority of this book has worked through changes in mass media, popular culture and British society since 1945 in chronological order to help you make sense of the pace and nature of changes in each decade. The following thematic summary, together with the thematic review questions that follow, are designed to focus your thinking on the thematic changes that span the whole period.

The role of newspapers, radio, cinema and television in society since 1945

The comparative significance of the different mass media mentioned above has changed since 1945. In the late 1940s radio, newspapers and cinema were all highly popular while television was still in its infancy. In the 1950s, television ownership increased rapidly, especially after the coronation of Elizabeth II in 1953, while cinema attendance began a decline that was only halted in the mid-1980s. In addition to increased ownership, the growth of commercial television after 1955, and radio after 1973, meant that these mass media became key sources of popular culture. The end of the BBC monopoly arguably meant that mass media increasingly reflected and reinforced important changes that were taking place in British attitudes and values rather than merely promoted the values of those who controlled public service broadcasting.

The 1980s and 1990s saw the gradual growth of competition in mass media with the rise of cable and satellite television and the deregulation of commercial broadcasting. While far more programmes are now produced, some would argue that there has been a general 'dumbing down' of output. Together with the rise of the Internet, the rise of digital television and radio in the 2000s meant that people in Britain could receive news and entertainment from all over the world; this could potentially fragment British identities in the twenty-first century that had been reflected and reinforced by mass media in the last quarter of the twentieth century. Newspaper circulation went into decline in the 1980s, a trend that accelerated after the late 1990s due to the rise of the Internet as a source of news. Despite the growth of competition, the BBC continues to serve as a very important public service broadcaster in radio, television and online. For more on the impact of technology and ownership of mass media on popular culture and British society see pages 3–6, 18–24, 34, 39–42, 54–56, 60–61, 71–72, 74–81, 87–98, 112–32.

The relationship between mass media and changes in attitudes and values in British society

The key debate is whether mass media have served more as a mirror or moulder of British attitudes and values. While mass media have never been the root source of important changes, they have helped to promote and reinforce changes in attitudes and values that perhaps would have taken far longer to come about, or perhaps not have happened so pervasively. Important examples include:

- The growth of consumerism and materialism in British society has perhaps been fuelled by images of luxury and 'lifestyle' programmes on television, and by advertising in all commercial mass media, but it is unlikely that this change could have happened without the general increase in disposable income and range of goods available that has taken place since the 1940s. Indeed, arguably the greatest growth in materialism took place during periods of strong economic growth, in the late 1950s and in the 1980s. For more on mass media, popular culture and consumerism see pages 17, 24, 51–53, 87, 94–96, 120–22.

- The blurring of class identities has been a gradual process in which mass media have played some role. Youth culture from the 1960s onwards blurred class barriers by popularising similar styles of dress and the 'classlessness' of rock or pop icons. The rise of commercial television and radio meant that more regional accents were heard rather than the received pronunciation of earlier BBC broadcasters. The satire boom of the 1960s also undermined remaining class deference. However, a good deal of the rigid class identities and a sense of deference had been broken down before 1945, especially as a result of the World Wars. Class barriers were also blurred by the general growth in disposable income and by de-industrialisation in the 1980s and 1990s: at the start of the twenty-first century there was a far larger middle class and smaller working class than in 1945. It would be inaccurate to suggest that class has disappeared as it still makes up an important part of British identities; however, it is fair to say that it became less easy to determine a person's class by appearance or accent than in 1945. For more on mass media, popular culture and class see pages 13, 15, 52, 73, 78, 87.
- The growth of more liberal attitudes towards the status of women workers and as individuals, was promoted by some mass media more than others (and by television in particular). However, it is clear that mass media reflected changes that had already begun due to other factors. Whereas in 1945 it was uncommon for married women, and especially mothers, to work, it had become far more common and acceptable by the start of the twenty-first century. This was a gradual process largely driven by women's desire to work, to support their independence or to top up family income. Approval of the 'marriage bar' had dropped significantly before the 1970s while there were very few female media role models; this suggests media mirrored changes more than it moulded them in this instance. Women were also far more likely to be unmarried at the start of the twenty-first century than in 1945. This was partly due to the huge increase in divorce rates since legislation reform in 1969 and 1970; it was also due to the increased acceptability of cohabitation without marriage since the early 1970s. Mass media may have contributed slightly through the presentation of 'ideal relationships' that real ones failed to live up to. However, with the exception of soap operas in the 1990s and 2000s, mass media have generally condemned these changes. This again suggests that mass media have served more as a mirror of underlying change. For more on mass media, popular culture and women see pages 16, 70, 73, 158–63.
- Mass media have had little to do with the rise of single parent families and the increased isolation of the nuclear family. Greater technology and wealth has generally led to increased geographical and occupational mobility; this has allowed a greater proportion of people to move away from their parents and weakened inter-generational relations. Changes in housing in the 1960s, with slum clearance and the construction of flats also meant extended families lived further apart in working-class areas. This has led to greater reliance on the state or private institutions to provide certain services, such as childcare or care for elderly relatives that would have been provided by the extended family in 1945.
- The growth of more liberal attitudes towards sex before marriage was a gradual process but one which accelerated after the 1980s. Teenage boys and girls magazines have promoted this change in attitudes, but there is also a strong link between a lack of education and social deprivation with teenage pregnancy. In general, it would be unfair to suggest that adults are far more liberal about sex and relationships at the

start of the twenty-first century than they were in 1945; the largest change has been the openness with which such things have been discussed in mass media since the 1960s and especially the 1970s.

- The growth of more tolerant attitudes towards homosexuals took place largely in the 1990s and 2000s. Positive media role models, especially on television, go a long way towards explaining this change in attitude as significant legal reforms (especially the decriminalisation of homosexuality in 1967) took place before and after this growth of tolerance. For more on mass media, popular culture and attitudes to sex and sexuality see pages 17, 35, 50, 54, 62, 78–80, 165–68.
- The growth of generally more tolerant attitudes towards racial minorities has again been a gradual process in which mass media have had a mixed role. In the 1950s and 1960s several films contained casual racism while newspapers may even have fanned racial violence at times. By the 1990s there were far more positive depictions of racial minorities in all mass media which helped to promote more harmonious relations. However, Race Relations legislation since 1965, and the fact that second and third generation racial minorities are generally wealthier and live in suburbs as well as inner cities, have also helped to promote integration and tolerance since the 1980s. For more on mass media, popular culture and attitudes towards racial minorities see pages 13, 17, 71, 169–75.

The impact of mass media on British society: challenges to authority and figures of authority

Mass media have altered the relationship between the public and figures of authority: it is no longer possible for such individuals to ignore the media and operate behind closed doors. The royal family, politicians, police chiefs and religious leaders must be media savvy to a much greater degree than in 1945. They must also be prepared to have their private lives scrutinised by the public to an extent unthinkable in 1945. Both of these developments have been driven to a large extent by the growth of investigative journalism and the impact of the 'satire boom' since the 1960s. However, it is not the case that figures of authority have been the victims of this process: many have sought to use the increased reach and pervasiveness of mass media for their own ends. Although it is commonly thought that this process has undermined respect for authority since 1945, it is not entirely clear that this is the case. Politicians have always been mistrusted by the British public; with the exception of those groups who feel threatened or persecuted by them, the police have been generally respected; the popularity of the royals has fluctuated more with their family fortunes than the growth of the media, reaching a low point in the mid-1990s before resurging since the death of Princess Diana in 1997. For more on mass media, popular culture and authority see pages 16, 54–62, 73–75, 109, 124–25, 137–50.

Youth culture from the mid-1950s

While mass media cannot be said to have invented youth culture, it increasingly played a large part in its growth and pervasiveness. All mass media reflected the emergence of a distinct 'teenage' youth culture in the 1950s, with cinema and pirate radio in particular popularising rock and roll. The rise of independent television and the competition of pirate radio led to increased broadcast time for programmes dedicated to a youth audience in the late 1950s and especially in the 1960s. Youth fashion promoted materialism in the baby boomer and subsequent generations while the 'subversive' youth music of one decade had a large impact on the popular music of the next. Every generation of adults has felt that some elements of youth culture have been a threat to decency and that to a degree mass media has been to blame. In part this is a reflection of the different tastes and priorities of adults and youth, but it is also the case that the levels of youth crime, violence, drug and alcohol abuse have increased since the early 1980s. While there are some legitimate concerns about the impact of violent films and computer games, such trends clearly have more to do with the increased incidence of unstable family life and the greater gap between rich and poor in Britain since the rule of Margaret Thatcher. For more on mass media, popular culture and youth culture see pages 32–39, 76–77, 127–29.

The significance of the US in changing leisure patterns

At a superficial level, American films, popular music and, increasingly, television programmes have been popular with the British people since 1945. However, it is unclear whether these have had any major impact on British society, particularly when compared to the impact of domestic productions. Possibly the largest impact has been on British youth culture with the import of rock and roll, disco, punk and hip hop. In general, what many might refer to as the 'Americanisation' of British society is in reality the growth of materialism and a shift towards the free market across the political spectrum since the 1980s. These in turn have been influenced by American financial and political muscle, via increased wealth and globalisation, rather than American media products. For more on mass media, popular culture and Americanisation see pages 22, 24–25, 38–39, 90, 94–95.

The relationship between 'elite' and 'popular' culture

The links between 'elite' and 'popular' culture have not been strong in Britain in the twentieth century; this reflects the different spheres in which the audiences for the respective cultures operate: wealthier, educated, upper or middle class people have tended to visit the opera, ballet, classical music concerts and the theatre far more than working-class people, who favoured the pub, dance halls and clubs, cinema and popular sports. However, there have been a few important examples of the links between elite and popular culture since 1945. In particular, there have been educated elites who have been prepared to challenge the status quo in public: John Osborne and the 'Angry Young Men' of literature in the late 1950s who inspired the 'New Wave' in British cinema; journalists, broadcasters and satirists who challenged 'the establishment' in the 1960s; a raft of rock stars such as Mick Jagger who formed bands at universities and art colleges; and intellectuals such as Germaine Greer who gave a media voice to feminism in the 1970s. Television and radio broadcasts have also made opera, ballet and classical music performances more accessible to those who previously may not have had the opportunity to enjoy such entertainment, either due to cost, lack of local performances or social inhibition. However, although this elite culture has become more accessible since 1945, it has struggled to win a wider audience. This is partly because so few broadcast hours are devoted to elite culture and partly because the division between elite and popular culture has been reinforced by broadcasting or publishing for one or the other audience: for example, Radios 1 and 3 since 1967, tabloids and broadsheet newspapers, Sky Arts and BBC 4 in the digital era for 'elite' television audiences. For more on the relationship between popular culture and 'elite culture' see pages 6–7, 43, 56.

The impact of the Internet and the World Wide Web on individuals and society

It is still too early to conclude with any confidence about the overall impact that the Internet and the World Wide Web will have on British people and British society. The Internet has already begun to affect leisure habits with more people shopping online rather than going into towns and outlet centres. British people have increasingly used the Internet for communication, entertainment and news since the late 1990s, a trend that looks set to continue despite the persistence of a 'digital divide' at the end of the 2000s. The increased interactivity of Web2.0 has begun to alter the relationship between producers and consumers of news and popular culture. Uploading and downloading of information has undermined the ability of big record labels to dominate the music industry while 'citizen journalism' could undermine the ability of media moguls and corporations to determine the news agenda. Such interactivity also looks set to alter the relationship between the public and the political classes, with some commentators talking of the potential rise of an 'e-democracy', removing the need for much traditional party activity such as door-to-door canvassing and fundraising, and promoting a much wider discussion of political goals and initiatives. It is likely that the acceleration in computing power and other related technologies will have a huge impact on all aspects of life in Britain in the twenty-first and twenty-second centuries. For more on the impact of the Internet and World Wide Web see pages 119–132.

Thematic review questions

The following thematic questions will require you to take information on a particular topic from across the entire period. Use the page references above to put together the information you need about the key themes.

- How far did mass media and popular culture promote rather than reflect more liberal values in British society after 1945?
- How far did mass media and popular culture undermine authority in British society after 1945?
- To what extent did mass media and popular culture affect the lives of British women after 1945?
- To what extent did mass media and popular culture affect the lives of racial minorities after 1945?
- How significant to social change in Britain since 1945 was youth culture?
- How far has popular culture been influenced by 'elite culture' in Britain since 1945?
- Of the following aspects of mass media, which has had the greatest impact on popular culture and British society since 1945: technology or ownership?
- How far have changing patterns of ownership or control of mass media affected popular culture? Have these changes led to a 'dumbing down' of British culture?
- How far has British popular culture been affected by foreign, especially American, culture since 1945?
- During what decade did the British experience:
  - the greatest growth in materialism?
  - the greatest change in morality?

  Conservatives say the 1960s, liberals say the 1980s; what will you decide?
- How far have mass media contributed to changes in attitudes towards:
  - the family
  - class
  - consumerism?

Choose one of these thematic review questions that you plan to answer. Working through the next section will make much more sense if you have an actual question in mind.

Answering a thematic review question

There are two keys to answering a thematic review question: *select* and *deploy*.

Select You need to select appropriate source material and select appropriate knowledge.

Deploy You need to deploy what you have selected so that you answer the question in as direct a way as possible.

Unpacking 'select'

You will see that all the thematic review questions are asking for an evaluation. They ask 'How far . . .', 'To what extent . . .', 'How significant . . .', which means that you will have to weigh up the evidence given by the sources you have selected. You will, therefore, have to select sources that will give you a range of evidence. Six diary entries, for example, will not give you the range you want. You will also need to select sources that seem to provide evidence that pulls in different directions. Eight sources saying more or less the same thing but in different ways will not help you weigh up the significance of different sorts of evidence and reach a reasoned, supported conclusion.

So now go ahead

1 Look back through this book and select the sources, primary and secondary, that you think will give you the appropriate range, balance and evidence.

2 Make notes of the knowledge you will need to use to contextualise the sources and create an argument.

You can't, of course, simply use the sources in an answer and hope that whoever is reading what you have written can sort things out for themselves. You need to evaluate the sources you have selected and use that evaluation to create the argument you will be making when you answer the question. You will have practice of doing this in the Exam zone (see pages 184–90), but here is a reminder of some of the questions you will need to ask of a source before you can turn it into evidence.

- Is the *content* appropriate for the question I am answering?
- Can I supply the appropriate *context* for the source?
- How *reliable* is the source as evidence? Was the author or artist *in a position to know* what he or she was talking/painting about?
- What was the intended *audience* of the source? What was the *purpose* of the source?
- If the source is a photograph, did the photographer *pose* the people in the picture? Was the photographer *selective* in what he or she chose to photograph?
- How *useful* is this source in developing an answer to the question? Remember that a source that is unreliable can still be useful.

Now you have your selection of source material, you need to think about it as a package. Does it do the job you want it to do? Does it supply you with enough evidence to argue your case, while at the same time providing you with enough evidence of different points of view so that you can show you have considered what weight the evidence will bear in reaching a reasoned, supported conclusion? In other words, can you effectively *cross-reference* between the sources, showing where they support and where they challenge each other?

Unpacking 'deploy'

The key to successful deployment of evidence and knowledge in answering a question like the one you have selected is always to keep the question in the forefront of your mind. Keep focused! Don't be tempted to go off into interesting by-ways. Make every paragraph count as you build your argument.

You will have a lot of practice in essay planning and writing as you work through the Exam zone, but here is a reminder of the main things you need to bear in mind.

Plan

Plan carefully how you are going to construct your answer and make out your case.

Structure

Structure your answer. You could use the framework below as a guide.

Introduction

Here you 'set out your stall', briefly outlining your argument and approach.

Paragraphs

These should develop your argument, using the evidence you have created by questioning the sources. As you create the case you are making, remember to cross-reference between the sources you are using so as to weigh the evidence, showing on which you place the greater weight.

Conclusion

This should pull your case together to provide a supported summary of the arguments you have made in coming to a reasoned, supported judgement.

In other words, say what you are going to do, do it, and show that you have done it.

You do not, of course, have to respond to these thematic review questions by writing an essay all by yourself. You could work collaboratively in a small group, or you could use one or more of the questions to prepare for a class debate. In whatever way you are going to use these questions, the approach will be the same: select, deploy and keep to the point.

Good luck!

Exam zone

Relax and prepare

Hot tips: what other students have said

From GCSE to AS level

- I really enjoyed studying modern world History at GCSE but I am glad that I had the chance to look at some nineteenth- and twentieth-century English history at AS level. It has been challenging but enjoyable to study a different period.
- Many of the skills that I learned at GCSE were built upon at AS level, especially in Unit 2 where the skills of source evaluation and analysis are very important.
- AS-level History seems like a big step up at first with more demands made on independent reading and more complex source passages to cope with. However, by the end of the first term I felt as if my written work had improved considerably.
- The more practice source-based questions I attempted, the more confident I became and quite quickly I picked up the necessary style and technique required for success.
- I found it really helpful to look at the mark schemes in the textbook (see pages 187–89). It was reassuring to see what the examiners were looking for and how I could gain top marks.

What I wish I had known at the start of the year

- I used the textbook a lot during the revision period to learn the key facts and practise key skills. I really wished that I had used it from the beginning of the course in order to consolidate my class notes.
- I wished that I had taken more time reading and noting other material such as the photocopied handouts issued by my teacher. Reading around the subject and undertaking independent research would have made my understanding more complete and made the whole topic more interesting.
- AS History is not just about learning the relevant material but also developing the skills to use it effectively. I wish that I had spent more time throughout the year practising source-based questions to improve my style and technique.
- I wish I had paid more attention to the advice and comments made by my teacher on the written work I had done. This would have helped me to improve my scores throughout the year.

How to revise

- I started my revision by buying a new folder and some dividers. I put all my revision work into this folder and used the dividers to separate the different topics. I really took pride in my revision notes and made them as thorough and effective as I could manage.
- Before I started the revision process, I found it helpful to plan out my history revision. I used the Edexcel specification, given to me by my teacher, as a guideline of which topics to revise and I ticked off each one as I covered it.
- I found it useful to revise in short, sharp bursts. I would set myself a target of revising one particular topic in an hour and a half. I would spend one hour taking revision notes and then half an hour testing myself with a short practice question or a facts test.
- I found it useful to always include some practice work in my revision. If I could get that work to my teacher to mark all the better, but just

attempting questions to time helped me improve my technique.

- Sometimes I found it helpful to revise with a friend. We might spend 45 minutes revising by ourselves and then half an hour testing each other. Often we were able to sort out any problems between us and it was reassuring to see that someone else had the same worries and pressures at that time.

Refresh your memory

Revision checklist

- The role of newspapers, radio, cinema and television in society since 1945; the relationship between mass media and changes in attitudes and values in British society. Use the relevant pages on radio, cinema and television and on attitudes to women, racial minorities, class, authority, the family and consumerism from throughout the book.
- The impact of the mass media on British society: investigative journalism and its consequences; the impact of satire; privacy and individual rights; 'celebrity culture'; challenges to authority and authority figures. Primarily use Units 4 and 8.
- Popular and youth culture from the mid-1950s: its growing importance and its impact on society; significance of the US in changing leisure patterns; the relationship between 'elite' and 'popular' culture. Use the relevant pages on youth culture and Americanisation from throughout the book.
- Electronic technology and its impact: the Internet and the World Wide Web; information highways; implications for patterns of work and leisure; changing relationship between individuals and society. Use Unit 7.

Unit 1: Mass media: moulder or mirror of popular culture?

- Mass media as content and technology.
- Forms of ownership and control of mass media.
- Definitions of 'popular culture'.
- Ways in which mass media, popular culture and society are linked.

Unit 2: How austere was 'Austerity Britain' 1945–54?

- The key features of British society in the years 1945–54: quantifiable and intangible aspects.
- The 'austerity' of popular culture in Britain between 1945 and 1954.
- The effect of newspapers, radio and cinema on British society in the years 1945–54.

Unit 3: Did rock and roll change British society 1955–69?

- The 'invention of youth'.
- The impact of rock and roll on youth culture.
- Rock and roll and the extent of the Americanisation of British youth culture.
- The relationship between cinema, radio, television, newspapers and rock and roll.
- The impact of The Beatles on popular culture in Britain in the 1960s.

Unit 4: Did mass media undermine deference and promote the growth of a 'permissive society' in Britain 1954–69?

- The idea of a 'cultural revolution' in Britain in the 1960s.
- The context of greater wealth, new legislation, and the Pill.
- The impact of television, cinema and newspapers on the social hierarchy in Britain between 1954 and 1969.
- The impact of television, cinema and newspapers on attitudes to sex in the years 1954–69.

Unit 5: Anarchy in the UK? Media, popular culture and society in the 1970s

- The financial, political and economic context of social change in the 1970s.
- The impact of television, radio and popular music, cinema and newspapers on social relations in Britain in the 1970s.
- The impact of mass media and popular culture on British attitudes in the 1970s.

Unit 6: How far was mass media, popular culture and British society 'Thatcherised' after 1979?

- The context of Thatcherism: her social and economic views and policies.
- The impact of Thatcherism on television, radio, cinema and newspapers.
- The extent to which television, radio, cinema and newspapers promoted Thatcherism after 1979.
- The impact of investigative journalism on political figures of authority.

Unit 7: Britain 2.0? New media and its impact on popular culture and British society

- The impact of videos, satellite television, digital television and mobile phones on popular culture and British society.
- The impact of the Internet on television, radio, newspapers and news reporting in general.
- The impact of the Internet on popular culture, including leisure pursuits and popular music.
- Limits to the impact of the Internet on mass media, popular culture and British society.

Unit 8: How far have mass media undermined figures of authority in Britain?

- Mass media access to parliament and the private lives of politicians.
- Satire and its effects on the authority of politicians.
- The impact of mass media on respect for the royal family.
- The impact of mass media on respect for the police.
- The rise of 'celebrities' and the effect of this on respect for authority figures.
- The mass media's relationship with Diana, Princess of Wales.

Unit 9: How far have mass media moulded or mirrored British attitudes?

- The impact of mass media and popular culture on women as workers.
- The impact of mass media and popular culture on women's role in the family.
- The portrayal of women in the mass media.
- The impact of mass media and popular culture on attitudes to sexuality.
- The demographic, legal and political context of race relations since 1945.
- The impact of mass media and popular culture on attitudes to racial minorities since 1945.
- The impact of mass media and popular culture on faith and attitudes to religious minorities.

This revision checklist is very knowledge based. The examination, however, will test your source-based skills as well. So remember that when dealing with sources you must be able to:

- Comprehend a source and break it down into key points.
- Interpret a source, drawing inferences and deductions from it rather than treating it as a source of information. This may involve considering the language and tone used as well.
- Cross-reference points of evidence between sources to reinforce and challenge.
- Evaluate the evidence by assessing its quality and its reliability in terms of how much weight it will bear and how secure are the conclusions that can be drawn from it. This will include considering the provenance of the source.
- Deal with the sources as a set to build up a body of evidence.

Result

You have spent a lot of time working on plans and constructing answers to the (a) and (b) questions. So you now have a pretty good idea about how to plan an answer and write a response to the questions on the examination paper. But what are the examiners looking for? And what marks will you get?

What will the exam paper look like?

There will be three questions on the paper.

(a) Compulsory: everyone has to do this.

(b) (i) and (b) (ii) You will have a choice here and will only have to answer one (b) question.

Sources

There will be nine sources on the examination paper. But don't worry: you won't have to deal with them all! You'll only need to deal with a maximum of six sources – three for each of the questions you will be answering. And here is the good news. So far, you have worked with very long sources, some of which were complicated. In the examination, because you will only have 1 hour 20 minutes to answer the two questions, the sources will be much shorter. You'll probably be dealing with no more than around 550 words altogether.

Question (a)

What will you have to do and what marks will you get for doing it?

You will have to focus on reaching a judgement by analysis, cross-referencing and evaluation of source material. The maximum number of marks you can get is 20. You will be working at any one of four levels. Try to get as high up in the levels as you can. Remember that the only knowledge, outside of that which you can find in the sources, is what examiners call 'contextual' knowledge. This means you can write enough to enable you to interpret the source, but no more. For example, if one of the three sources is by Mary Whitehouse, you should show the examiners that you know she was head of the National Viewers' and Listeners' Association, but you should not describe the work of the NVLA unless this information helps the understanding of a particular source.

Level 1

1–5 marks

Have you shown that you understand the surface features of the sources, and have you shown that you have selected material relevant to the question? Does your response consist mainly of direct quotations from the sources?

Level 2

6–10 marks

Have you identified points of similarity and difference in the sources in relation to the question asked? Have you made at least one developed comparison or a range of undeveloped ones? Have you summarised the information you have found in the sources? Have you noted the provenance of at least one of the sources?

Level 3

11–15 marks

Have you cross-referenced between the sources, making detailed comparisons supported by evidence from the sources? Have you shown that you understand you have to weigh the evidence by looking at the nature, origins, purpose and audience of the sources? Have you shown you have thought about considering 'How far' by trying to use the sources as a set?

Level 4

16–20 marks

Have you reached a judgement in relation to the issue posed by the question? Is this judgement supported by careful examination of the evidence of the sources? Have you cross-referenced between the sources and analysed the points of similarity and disagreement? Have you taken account of the different qualities of the sources in order to establish what weight the evidence will bear? Have you used the sources as a set when addressing 'How far' in the question?

Now try this (a) question

(a) Study Sources A, B and C. How far do Sources A, B and C support the view that punk rock promoted 'rotten social attitudes' in the 1970s?

Source A

Punk gives the message that no one has to be a genius to do it him/herself. Instead of waiting for the next big thing in music to be excited about, anyone . . . can make it happen themselves by forming a band. Instead of depending on commercial media to tell them what to think, anyone can create a fanzine . . . . they can even publish and distribute it. Such personal empowerment leads to other possibilities in self-employment and activism.

From A.S. Van Dorston, *A History of Punk* published in January 1990

Source B

British punk rock became successful and notorious in the space of a few months. This is because British punk rock seemed to be designed to articulate young people's dissatisfaction with the post-war social democratic consensus.

From Stuart Borthwick, 'Punk Rock: Artifice or Authenticity' in *Popular Music Genres: An Introduction*, published in 2004. Borthwick is a lecturer in Popular Music Studies

Source C

There is a genuine social point to punk rock. In a society where there remain extremes of wealth and of poverty you are bound . . . to find a reaction among young people who do not have that wealth . . . But that does not excuse what punk rock is: it is anti-life, anti-human nature. It is rotten music and damn rotten social attitudes for most of the time. The people however who are most to blame in this are those people who inflate it. There is a quite deliberate commercial gimmick afloat at the moment to inflate punk rock into something and the people who are trying to do this should be ashamed of themselves.

From an interview in 1977 with Derek Jewell, pop critic of *The Sunday Times* in the 1970s

Now use the marking criteria to assess your response.

How did you do?

What could you have done to have achieved a better mark?

Question (b)

What will you have to do and what marks will you get for doing it?

You will have to analyse and evaluate an historical view or claim using two or three sources and your own knowledge. There are 40 marks for this question. You will get 24 marks for your own knowledge and 16 marks for your source evaluation. You can be working at any one of four levels. Try to get as high up in the levels as you can. The examiners will be marking your answer twice: once for knowledge and a second time for source evaluation.

This is what the examiners will be looking for as they mark the ways in which you have selected and used your knowledge to answer the question:

Level 1

1–6 marks

Have you written in simple sentences without making any links between them? Have you provided only limited support for the points you are making? Have you written what you know separately from the sources? Is what you have written mostly generalised and not really directed at the focus of the question? Have you made a lot of spelling mistakes and is your answer disorganised?

Level 2

7–12 marks

Have you produced a series of statements that are supported by mostly accurate and relevant factual material? Have you made some limited links between the statements you have written? Is your answer mainly 'telling the story' and not really analysing what happened? Have you kept your own knowledge and the sources separate? Have you made a judgement that isn't supported by facts? Is your answer a bit disorganised with some spelling and grammatical mistakes?

Level 3

13–18 marks

Is your answer focused on the question? Have you shown that you understand the key issues involved? Have you included a lot of descriptive material along with your analysis of the issues? Is your material factually accurate but a bit lacking in depth and/or relevance? Have you begun to integrate your own knowledge with the source material? Have you made a few spelling and grammatical mistakes? Is your work mostly well organised?

Level 4

19–24 marks

Does your answer relate well to the question focus? Have you shown that you understand the issues involved? Have you analysed the key issues? Is the material you have used relevant to the question and factually accurate? Have you begun to integrate what you know with the evidence you have gleaned from the source material? Is the material you have selected balanced? Is the way you have expressed your answer clear and coherent? Is your spelling and grammar mostly accurate?

This is what the examiners are looking for as they mark your source evaluation skills.

Level 1

1–4 marks

Have you shown that you understand the sources? Is the material you have selected from them relevant to the question? Is your answer mostly direct quotations from the sources or re-writes of them in your own words?

Level 2

5–8 marks

Have you shown that you understand the sources? Have you selected from them in order to support or challenge the view given in the question? Have you used the sources mainly as sources of information?

Level 3

9–12 marks

Have you analysed the sources, drawing from them points of challenge and/or support for the view contained in the question? Have you developed these points, using the source material? Have you shown that you realise you are dealing with just one viewpoint and that the sources point to other, perhaps equally valid ones? Have you reached a judgement? Have you supported that judgement with evidence from the sources?

Level 4

13–16 marks

Have you analysed the sources, raising issues from them? Have you discussed the viewpoint in the question by relating it to the issues raised by your analysis of the source material? Have you weighed the evidence in order to reach a judgement? Is your judgement fully explained and supported by carefully selected evidence?

Now try this (b) question

Read Sources D, E and F and use your own knowledge.

Do you agree with the view that mass media has had little positive impact on race relations in Britain since 1945?

Source D

It did a tremendous amount of good having an ordinary character in there who happened to be black. Enoch Powell caused a great deal of racial tension and I was worried people in the street would recognise me, and be hostile towards me. But when I went into Birmingham, fans of the show would stop me and ask about *Crossroads*. They loved the programme and obviously liked Melanie. I never had any trouble.

From an interview with Cleo Sylvestre, who played Melanie Harper in the ITV soap opera *Crossroads*, in Stephen Bourne, *Black in the British Frame*, published in 2005

Source E

One of the most offensive recurrent images of Blackness could be seen in the *Black and White Minstrel Show* (BBC 1958–78) . . . The 'Nigger Minstrel' debased Black people and pertained to a particularly racist tradition of popular entertainment. During the two decades in which the Saturday-night phenomenon was transmitted, there were very few alternative images of Black and Asian people on British television. Despite its widespread popularity, some such as the Campaign Against Racism in the Media petitioned (as early as 1967) for its removal from our screens and the BBC finally stopped producing the programme in the late 1970s.

From S. Malik, 'Race and Ethnicity', in A. Briggs and P. Colbey (eds) *The Media: An Introduction*, published in 1998

Source F

. . . The ideas of race on TV carry a resonance far beyond the medium of entertainment . . . Why then did the BBC (who I generally believe to have been true to their overall agenda of trying to produce better race relations) keep [*Till Death Do Us Part*] going, which they knew was certainly not having any kind of positive impact on what was a very volatile race relations situation. I myself think that it . . . was repeatedly the most popular show on TV . . .

From Gavin Schaffer, 'Till Death Do Us Part', a conference paper delivered at the University of Portsmouth in July 2008

Now use the marking criteria to assess your response.

How did you do?

What could you have done to have achieved higher marks?

The examiners will not be nit-picking their way through your answer, ticking things off as they go. Rather, they will be looking to see which levels best fit the response you have written to the question, and you should do the same when assessing your own responses.

How will I time my responses?

You have 1 hour 20 minutes to answer two questions. Remember that the (a) question is compulsory and that you will have a choice of one from two (b) questions. Take time, say, 5 minutes, to read through the paper and think about your choice of (b) question. The (a) question is worth half the marks of the (b) question, so you should aim to spend twice the time on the (b) question. This means that, including planning time, you should spend about 25 minutes on the (a) question and about 50 minutes (again, including planning) on the (b) question.

You have now had a lot of practice in planning, writing and assessing your responses to the sort of questions you can expect to find on the examination paper. You are well prepared and you should be able to tackle the examination with confidence.

References

Allen, S. and Zeizer, B. (2004) *Reporting War: Journalism in Wartime*, Routledge

Black, J. (2004) *Britain since the Seventies*, Reaktion

Blanning, T. (2008) *The Triumph of Music*, Allen Lane

Borthwick, S. and Moy, R. (2004) *Popular Music Genres: An Introduction*, Edinburgh University Press

Bourke, J. (2005) *Eyewitness: The 1950s, The 1960s, The 1970s, The 1980s, The 1990s*, BBC Audio books

Bourne, S. (2005) *Black in the British Frame: The Black Experience in British Film and Television*, Continuum

Briggs, A. (1979) *The History of Broadcasting in the UK, Vol IV: Sound and Vision*, Oxford University Press

Briggs, A. (1995) *The History of Broadcasting in the UK, Vol V: Competition*, Oxford University Press

Briggs, A. and Colbey P. (eds) (1998) *The Media: An Introduction*, Longman

Caughie, J. (2000) *Television Drama: Realism, Modernism and British Culture*, Oxford University Press

Cooke, L (2003) *Television Drama: A History*, BFI Publishing

Crisell, A. (1997) *An Introductory History of British Broadcasting*, Routledge

Curran, J. (2005) *Mass Media and Society*, Hodder Arnold

Curran, J. and Gurevitch, M. (2005) *Mass Media and Society*, Hodder Arnold

Curran, J. and Seaton, J. (2003) *Power Without Responsibility, The Press and Broadcasting in Britain*, Routleledge

Davies, N. (2008) *Flat Earth News: An Award-winning Reporter Exposes Falsehood, Distortion and Propaganda in the Global Media*, Chatto & Windus

Day, R. (1989) *Grand Inquisitor: Memoirs*, Pan Books

Donnelly, M. (2005) *Sixties Britain: Culture, Society and Politics*, Longman

Drazin, C. (2007) *The Finest Years: British Cinema of the 1940s*, I B Taurus and Co

Elsaesser, T. (2003) *European Cinema: Face to Face with Hollywood (Film Culture in Transition)*, Amsterdam University Press

Evans, E. J. (2004) *Thatcher and Thatcherism*, Second Edition, Routledge

Evans, H. (1983) *Good Times, Bad Times*, Weidenfeld & Nicolson

Friedman L. D. (ed.) (2006) *Fires Were Started: British Cinema and Thatcherism*, Wallflower Press

Gorer, G. (1955) *Exploring English Character*, Criterion

Gorman, L. and McLean, D. (2009) *Media and Society into the 21st Century*, Blackwell

Harper, S. and Porter, V. (2003) *British Cinema of the 1950s: The Decline of Deference*, Oxford University Press

Hoggart, R. (1957) *The Uses of Literacy*, Penguin

Hollowell, J. (ed.) (2003) *Britain Since 1945*, Blackwell

Jack, I. (1987) *Before the Oil Ran Out*, HarperCollins

Jenkins, R. (1959) *The Labour Case*, Penguin

Klein, V. and Myrdal, A. (1956) *Women's Two Roles: A Contemporary Dilemma*, Routledge

Kynaston, D. (2007) *Austerity Britain 1945–51*, Bloomsbury

Lambert, S. (1982) *Channel Four: Television With A Difference?*, BFI Publishing

Lessing, D. (1997) *Walking in the Shade: Volume Two of My Autobiography*, Flamingo

Livingstone, S. (1998) *Making Sense of Television: The Psychology of Audience Interpretation*, Routledge

MacDonald, I. (1994) *Revolution in the Head: The Beatles' Records and the Sixties*, Pimlico

Malcomson, P. and Malcomson, R. (2008) *Nella Last's Peace: The Post-war Diaries of Housewife, 49*, Profile Books

Marr, A. (2008) *A History of Modern Britain*, Pan Books

Marwick, A. (1998) *The Sixties: Cultural Transformation in Britain, France, Italy and the United States, c. 1958–c. 1974*, Oxford University Press

Marwick, A. (2003) *British Society Since 1945*, Penguin

Mass Observation project, 1937–, Mass Observation Archive, University of Sussex

McKibbin, R. (1998) *Classes and Cultures: England 1918–1951*, Oxford University Press

McQueen, D. (2008) '1970s Current Affairs: A Golden Age?' In: 41970s British Culture Conference, 2008, Portsmouth University

Miller, J. (1999) *Flowers in the Dustbin: The Rise of Rock and Roll, 1947–1977*, Simon and Schuster

Monk C. and Sargeant, A. (2002) *British Historical Cinema*, Routledge

Morgan, K. (1990) *British History Since 1945: The People's Peace*, Oxford University Press

Mullan, B. (1997) *Consuming Television: Television and its Audiences*, Blackwell

Murphy, D. (ed.) (2000) *Britain 1914–2000*, Collins Educational

Negrine, R. (1998) Television and the Press since 1945, Manchester University Press

Nie, N. et al (2000) *Internet and Society: A Preliminary Report*, Stanford

Panayi, P. (1998) *The Impact of Immigration*, Manchester University Press

Reith, J. (1949) *Into the Wind*, Hodder and Stoughton

Report of the Committee on Broadcasting, 1960 (1962), HMSO

Ringmar, E. (2007) *A Blogger's Manifesto*, Anthem Press

Rolston, B. and Miller, D. (eds) (1996) *War and Words*, Beyond the Pale Publications

Rosen, A. (2003) *The Transformation of British Life 1950–2000*, Manchester University Press

Sandbrook, D. (2005) *Never Had It So Good*, Abacus

Sandbrook, D. (2006) *White Heat: A History of Britain in the Swinging Sixties*, Abacus

Tiratsoo, N. (ed.) (1997) *From Blitz to Blair: a New History of Britain Since 1939*, Weidenfeld & Nicolson

Turner, A. (2008) *Turner Crisis? What Crisis? Britain in the 1970s*, Aurum

Wharfe, K. (2002) *Diana: Closely Guarded Secret*, Michael O'Mara Books

Williams Report on Obscenity and Film Censorship (1979) HMSO

Zweig, F. (1948) *Labour, Life and Poverty*, Gollancz

Websites

To access useful websites, go to www.pearsonhotlinks.co.uk and enter the express code 5063P.

Further reading

Overview

Black, J. (2004) *Britain since the Seventies*, Reaktion

Bourke, J (2005) *Eyewitness: The 1950s, The 1960s, The 1970s, The 1980s, The 1990s*, BBC Audio Books

Marwick, A. (1998) *British Society Since 1945*, Penguin

In depth

Harrison, B. (2009) *Seeking a Role: The United Kingdom 1951–1970*, Oxford University Press (especially Chapters 1, 4, 5, 7 and 9)

Harrison, B. (2009) *Finding a Role? The United Kingdom 1970–1990*, Oxford University Press (especially Chapters 3, 4 and 6)

Glossary

Albermarle Report A report into the workings of the Youth Service in England and Wales; it was commissioned by the government, partly in response to growing concerns about a 'youth problem'.

Allegory A symbolic representation.

Alpha and omega The first and last letters of the Greek alphabet; it means 'the be all and end all' of something.

Analogue Analogous means 'similar to'. Analogue information is sent by generating a wave similar to light or sound waves that a receiver can convert into usable information.

Anarchy Literally 'without government', it can more generally mean a state of social confusion.

Anthropologist Someone who studies how people behave and creates theories to explain this.

Austerity Strong self-discipline and moral strictness, with simple living and a lack of luxury.

Axiomatic Something that is self-evident, or indisputably true.

Baby boom A rapid increase in the rate of birth, common after the end of a war as husbands return home. The children born during this period are referred to as 'baby boomers'.

Bandwidth The size of a band of frequencies used to transmit signals. Frequency means the number of times a wave is repeated in a second. For example, many local radio stations transmit on 102 FM; this means your radio must be tuned to receive waves that oscillate 102 million times a second.

BBC Charter A series of rules by which the BBC must operate to justify its funding by license fee. Legally this is renewed every 10 years by the monarch, but some feel that governments have put ever greater pressure on the BBC to conform to its needs before the Charter is now renewed.

Bigotry Intolerant and narrow-minded views based on a range of prejudices.

Blockbuster This was originally American slang used to describe a successful play, possibly because of the numbers of people who would swamp the 'block' (a mass of buildings between two streets) where the theatre was. It was then taken to mean a very successful film. Nowadays it has come to mean a film with very high production and marketing costs geared towards huge audiences and merchandising.

Blog Short for weblog, an online diary of comments usually displayed in reverse chronological order. Blogs usually contain a mixture of text, images and video and have an area for people to post comments.

Bloody Sunday 27 protesters were shot and 14 of these killed by British troops in the Bogside area of Londonderry, Northern Ireland.

British Social Attitudes This is a survey conducted by the National Centre for Social Research. It has been carried out every year since 1983. It asks questions about social, political, economic and moral issues. It is an invaluable tool for modern social historians; see their website BritSocAt.

Broadcasting The term originally described the way farmers used to scatter their seeds. In 1909, an American radio technician coined the term to mean transmissions that were meant for many different radio receivers, as opposed to 'narrowcasting' for just one receiver, like a ship's radio.

Broadsheet A newspaper printed on large sheets of paper.

Butskellism A blend of R. **But**ler (Conservative Chancellor 1951-5) and H. Gait**skell** (Labour Chancellor 1950–1); economic policies acceptable to both parties.

Cable Cable had been laid since the 1920s to transmit radio signals in areas with poor reception. In 1951, Gloucester became the first town to receive television signals via cable. For many years both the BBC and ITV argued against allowing commercial cable operators to bring in signals from other regions or even abroad. Ironically, when this was finally allowed to happen in 1985, the expansion of cable television was small because of the rise of satellite television!

Camp Exaggerated, theatrical, effeminate behaviour.

Causalist Davies invented this term to mean a view of legislation based on its social consequences rather than a 'moralist' view based on a moral code.

Celebrity From the Latin for 'renowned', it means to be a widely known popular figure. Increasingly, celebrities appear in gossip magazines with revelations about their intimate private lives. Whereas in the past, people had to be exceptional in their field to be a celebrity, now the label applies to anyone who can attract media attention for long enough.

Civil partnership A legally joining contract like marriage but without the religious ceremony.

Commercialised Exploiting an activity or product by turning it into something from which a profit can be derived.

Consortium An association of organisations formed for commercial or financial purposes.

Consumerism Preoccupation with consumer goods and their acquisition.

Convergence To converge means to approach nearer together as if to meet or join at a point. Digital technology has allowed the convergence of previously separate tools such as computer applications and the Internet, cameras and camcorders, and telephones in a single mobile device. This has further allowed the convergence of mass media, such as radio, television and the press, all available via the Internet on these devices.

Cross-media ownership The result of a merger or take-over between companies in different areas of mass media.

De facto In fact, in reality, whether by right or not.

De jure According to the law.

Deference Respect for social superiors.

Democratise The removal of barriers of class or rank in society.

Demographic The study of human populations: births, deaths marriages, migration etc.

Digital 'Digit' originally meant finger or toe, but also came to mean a number from 0 to 9. Digital information is sent in a stream of 0s and 1s (a high voltage and a low voltage) that receivers can read and turn into information such as a sound wave or a pixel colour.

Digital native Someone who cannot remember a time before the Internet; people born after the mid-1990s in developed countries such as the UK are members of this group. They are also sometimes referred to as the 'iGeneration' or 'Millenials'.

Disposable income Money left to spend after all essential expenditure and savings have been deducted from earnings.

Dominant elites People who hold a great deal of power over society because of their wealth, their position in important organisations, or a combination of both.

Draconian Names after Draco, a law-maker in ancient Athens, it means severe, harsh or strict.

Eady levy The tax, which started in 1957, was named after Sir Wilfred Eady, a treasury official.

E-commerce Business that is conducted via the Internet rather than though high street shops or shopping centres. Goods are delivered by post or by a shop's own delivery service.

Economies of scale Larger firms tend to be more efficient and profitable than smaller ones for a range of reasons; for example, a television studio has fixed costs but a production company with more workers could make more programmes to sell than a smaller company with the same studio.

'Elite' music, art, literature Artistic works that are thought to require a good deal of education and sophistication to enjoy and appreciate.

Embellish To spice up a story with fictitious additions.

Empire Day From 1901 this was a celebration of the British Empire held on 24 May, Queen Victoria's birthday. In 1958 it was re-named Commonwealth Day; since 1973 it has been held on the second Monday in March.

Enabling factor A factor which allows later developments to occur; a necessary but not sufficient cause of something.

Entrepreneur A person who takes risks by investing money in new businesses.

E-petition A petition is a demand sent to a figure or body of authority with a number of signatures that indicate people's support. An e-petition is an Internet version of this.

Ethnic minority A group with physical or cultural differences from the majority of people in society.

Exacerbate To make things worse.

Falklands war A brief, undeclared war, fought between Argentina and Great Britain in 1982 over the control of the Falkland Islands. Also referred to as the Falklands conflict.

Family Planning Association A charity, founded in 1930, that provides contraceptives and advice (at first to married couples only).

Flying picket Workers on strike who move from place to place to stop other workers going to work.

Focus group A group of people, representative of particular parts of society, who are questioned about political issues so that their opinions can be studied and used to inform policy.

Formica The brand name of a heat-resistant plastic work surface common in many kitchens.

Fourth Estate The term was popularised by writer and MP Thomas Carlyle (1800-59) to mean the press as a balance to the other three powers: clergy and nobility in the House of Lords and the House of Commons.

Franchise The authorisation given by a company to sell its goods or services in a particular area.

Freeview A consortium of the BBC, Sky and Arqiva that has provided free-to-air digital television since 2002.

Generation gap Differences in opinions, tastes and behaviour between those of different generations.

Homogenous All of the same kind.

Immediacy The quality of something being immediate or direct.

Independent television and radio Broadcasting by private companies who aim to make profits by maximising advertising revenue. While their programmes aim to attract the largest possible audience, the content has been regulated by quangos.

Intangible Something that can't be touched or measured precisely.

Intrinsically In itself, as opposed to extrinsic, meaning in terms of its possible effects.

ITMA *It's That Man Again*, a popular comedy show.

Jukebox The word originally came from the 1930s black American slang word for dance- 'juke'.

Junta A political or military faction that has seized power following a revolution or coup.

Liberal Broad-minded, without prejudice. Respect for individual rights and freedoms.

Maverick Samuel Maverick (1803-70) was a Texan cattle-owner who did not brand his cattle. His unbranded cattle became known as mavericks; it now means an unorthodox or independent-minded person.

Media The plural of medium.

Mediation An attempt to reach an agreement through negotiation.

Monopolies Commission Now called the Competition Commission, it investigates any mergers or take-overs that would result in one firm having more than a quarter of a particular market and too much influence over that market.

Monopoly The position of having no competition in a given trade or market.

Nostalgia A longing for conditions or things from the recent past.

Nouveau riche From the French for 'new rich'; someone who has made a lot of money in their own lifetime rather than inherited their wealth. It is usually used as an insult to draw attention to a person's lack of taste or refinement.

Nugatory Worthless or trivial.

Op Art A style of painting pioneered in Britain by Bridget Riley that made use of black and white (later bold colours) and geometric shapes. This style was thought to be very modern and influenced not only fashion, but design more generally.

Paparazzi From the Italian for the irritating buzzing sound of mosquitoes, they are freelance photographers who pursue celebrities to take their pictures.

Permissive An attitude that allows something to be done; in particular tolerates sexual freedom.

Police Federation A staff association for police officers (they are not allowed to join a trade union).

Private members' bills Pieces of legislation that are not official government policy, or part of an election manifesto. The bills may be introduced by backbenchers from any side of the House.

Progressive Politicians or their policies that sought to advance the living and working conditions of the working classes.

Proprietor An owner of a business or shop.

Public service broadcaster A radio or television company run to serve the public interest rather than for profit.

Quango From quasi non-governmental organisation, an administrative body outside the government, but whose members are appointed by the government.

Quantifiable Things that can be counted or measured with a good degree of accuracy.

Quota The share of a total allocated to or allowed by an individual or group.

Radio From the Latin *radius*; just as a radius of a circle goes out from the centre, so radio waves are sent out in all directions from their point of origin. 'Radio' was the American name for the 'wireless'; its usage was popularised in Britain by the Second World War.

Rag and bone men Men who went around town in a horse-drawn cart asking for any unwanted items which they could sell on.

Regressive tax A tax which takes a higher percentage of a person's income the poorer they are.

Remit A set of instructions or an area or responsibility.

Satellite This can refer to any celestial body that orbits a larger object. The Moon is therefore the largest satellite of the Earth.

Satire Humour that makes fun of (usually famous) people; it often exposes their vices.

Secularisation The process whereby religious thinking, practices and institutions lose their social significance.

Shotgun wedding An enforced or hurried wedding.

Sit-com Short for situation comedy, a programme where the humour derives from putting together certain characters in certain places.

Skiffle A style of jazz or blues played on improvised instruments such as washboards and the tea-chest bass.

Social realist An artistic style that portrays ordinary people going about their everyday lives. It often focuses on the working classes, hardship and struggle.

Socialite A prominent person in fashionable society; a modern example is the 'it girl'.

Sound bite The phrase was coined by American author Mark Twain to mean 'a minimum of sound to a maximum of sense'. They are short, memorable quotes that sum things up neatly, clearly intended by politicians for use in news bulletins.

Spin A slant on information used to create a favourable impression when it is presented to the public.

Squidgygate James Gilbey referred to Princess Diana as 'Squidge' or 'Squidgy' 53 times during a taped telephone conversation. 'Gate' is frequently added to any scandal by the press after the scandal at the Watergate Hotel in 1972 where President Nixon ordered secret agents to steal information about political enemies.

Tabloid Tabloid originally referred to tablets made from compressed medicine powder. To begin with, the 'tabloid press' referred not to the shape of the newspaper, but to the compressed nature of the news. Most modern tabloids, such as the *Daily Mail* or *Daily Express*, were in fact printed in a broadsheet format until the 1970s.

Teddy Boy Teddy, short for Edward, from the Edwardian style (i.e. during the reign of Edward VII 1901-10) of their long coats and drainpipe trousers.

Teenpic Films about teenagers targeted at teenagers. Plots often revolve around problems with parents, school or relationships with the opposite sex.

Thalidomide A sedative that caused the malformation or absence of baby's limbs when taken during the mother's pregnancy.

The Sweeny From the Cockney rhyming slang 'Sweeny Todd' for Flying Squad, a branch of the Metropolitan Police who respond to and investigate serious armed crime.

Total Exclusion Zone (TEZ) An area of around 200 miles around the Falkland Islands within which the British, on 30 April, declared they would attack any Argentine vessel.

Traduce From the Latin for 'to lead', it means to misrepresent or speak ill of someone.

Transnational business A firm with production, distribution, marketing, management and sales operations in more than one country.

Vacuity Vacancy of mind, thought, from 'vacuous' meaning unintelligent.

Vinyl A type of plastic used to make records. Grooves were etched into the plastic, which caused a needle to move and, when amplified, produce the desired sound.

Welfare state A system where the government provides a range of services to promote the health and well-being of the people.

'Wet' This was Thatcher's term for more liberal members of her Cabinet who favoured less censorship and less extreme free market policies.

Wiki Comes from the Hawaiian language for fast. The idea of a wiki web page is that it is able to be edited quickly by its users.

Wildcat strike A strike without the authorisation of trade union officials.

Wire copy The 'wires' are items of news that are sent to journalists by press agencies such as the Press Association or Reuters. These agencies have their own reporters on the ground but also feed PR releases to the journalists. Wire copy is the direct use of this information in newspaper stories.

Wireless Just as today we talk of 'wireless broadband' when we refer to an Internet connection without a cable connection, so British people referred to radio as 'wireless', short for wireless telegraphy: the information was sent without a wire, unlike a telegram.

Women's lib A movement for the recognition and extension of women's rights.

Index

J

K

L

M

N

O

P